architecture

of the

everyday

STEVEN HARRIS AND DEBORAH BERKE

PRINCETON ARCHITECTURAL PRESS
YALE PUBLICATIONS ON ARCHITECTURE

PUBLISHED BY
PRINCETON ARCHITECTURAL PRESS
37 EAST 7TH STREET
NEW YORK, NEW YORK 10003
212.995.9620

CALL 1.800.722.6657 FOR A CATALOG OF BOOKS.
WWW.PAPRESS.COM

03 02 01 00 5 4 3 2 1
FIRST EDITION

PROJECT COORDINATOR: MARK LAMSTER
BOOK DESIGN: SARA E. STEMEN

SPECIAL THANKS TO: EUGENIA BELL,
CAROLINE GREEN, CLARE JACOBSON,
THERESE KELLY, AND ANNIE NITSCHKE
OF PRINCETON ARCHITECTURAL PRESS
          —KEVIN C. LIPPERT, PUBLISHER

LIBRARY OF CONGRESS
CATALOGING-IN-PUBLICATION DATA

ARCHITECTURE OF THE EVERYDAY / EDITED BY STEVEN
    HARRIS AND DEBORAH BERKE.
        P. CM.
        INCLUDES BIBLIOGRAPHICAL REFERENCES.
        ISBN 1-56898-114-7 (PBK. : ALK. PAPER)
        1. ARCHITECTURE AND SOCIETY. 2. ARCHITEC-
    TURE—PSYCHOLOGICAL ASPECTS. I. HARRIS, STEVEN,
    1950–   . II. BERKE, DEBORAH.
    NA2543.S6A633   1997
    720' . 1'03—DC21   97-20294
                                                  CIP

CREDITS

MARY MCLEOD | *HENRI LEFEBVRE'S
CRITIQUE OF EVERYDAY LIFE*
10: COURTESY JEAN DENIS ROBERT, ATELIER PASCAL
VERCKEN. 21: INTERNATIONAL SITUATIONISTE, NO. 4
(JUNE 1960): 25. THE MUSEUM OF MODERN ART
LIBRARY, NEW YORK. PHOTOGRAPH ©1997 THE
MUSEUM OF MODERN ART. 22: ARCHITECTURAL
DESIGN, VOL. 38 (JUNE 1968): 277. 23: INTERNA-
TIONAL SITUATIONISTE, NO. 6 (AUGUST 1961): 8.

HENRI LEFEBVRE | *THE EVERYDAY AND EVERYDAYNESS*
TRANSLATED BY CHRISTINE LEVICH WITH ALICE
KAPLAN AND KRISTIN ROSS, REPRINTED COURTESY
YALE FRENCH STUDIES 73 (1987): 7–11.

JAMES CASEBERE
ALL WORK APPEARS COURTESY THE ARTIST.

MARK BENNETT
ALL WORK APPEARS COURTESY THE ARTIST AND
MARK MOORE GALLERY.

GREGORY CREWDSON
ALL WORK APPEARS COURTESY THE ARTIST AND
LUHRING AUGUSTINE.

SHEILA LEVRANT DE BRETTEVILLE | *OMOIDE NO
SHOTOKYO*
68, 70 BOTTOM, ALL ON 71–73: JIM SIMMONS,
ANNETTE DEL ZOPPO STUDIO. 70 TOP: MARTHA RONK.

DEBORAH FAUSCH | *UGLY AND ORDINARY*
96 (PHOTOGRAPHS WITHIN ILLUSTRATION): TOP AND
BOTTOM LEFT BY JOHN BAEDER; BOTTOM RIGHT BY
STEVEN SHORE. 97 (PHOTOGRAPHS WITHIN ILLUS-
TRATION): LAS VEGAS STUDIO. 106 (PHOTOGRAPH
WITHIN ILLUSTRATION): STEVEN SHORE.

JOAN OCKMAN | *TOWARD A THEORY
OF NORMATIVE ARCHITECTURE*
128 LEFT: ©ESTATE OF HANS NAMUTH. 128 RIGHT,
140 LEFT, 143: EZRA STOLLER © ESTO, ALL RIGHTS
RESERVED. 132: HEDRICH-BLESSING (CHICAGO HIS-
TORICAL SOCIETY: HB-22362-A. 140 RIGHT: ROBERT
SCHERSCHEL–LIFE. 142: ©JULIUS SHULMAN. 149:
OPPOSITIONS 6 (FALL 1976).

cultural center.

CONTENTS

ACKNOWLEDGMENTS

We have been interested in the everyday and its relationship to architecture for almost ten years. This interest initially came from an attempt to locate the impetus behind our own built work—not as a dry theoretical exercise but as a way of thinking about how to make things in general and architecture in particular. The inquiry evolved through conversations with colleagues and friends, seminars and studios at Yale, organizing material for lectures and lecture series, and endless reading. Our own struggling attempts to put our thoughts into written words led us to gather the work of clear and diverse thinkers on the subject. As practicing architects we found the process of editing a book far more difficult than that of creating buildings. We are grateful to our contributors and our publisher, Kevin Lippert, for their faith in us.

We are singularly indebted to Henry Urbach for his tireless work in organizing the present publication, and for his intelligent insights in editorial matters and his wise suggestions of contributors. The book is a richer collection because of his efforts.

Our conversations with Maitland Jones and Robert Schultz were instrumental in determining the earliest vision of the project. We thank them and John Woell for his steadfast presence and persistence as the book developed.

All of the contributors have been generous with their time and work, and we appreciate their patience during the long editorial process. We would like to particularly thank Joan Ockman and Mary McLeod, not only for their essays, but for their inspiration and unflagging support.

The School of Architecture and the School of Art at Yale have also been instrumental in the creation of this book. We thank our students and colleagues for the supportive intellectual environment they provided. We particularly thank Peggy Deamer, Sheila Levrant de Bretteville, Gregory Crewdson, and Alan Plattus. We are indebted to Sandra Cloud and to Fred Koetter, the Dean of the School of Architecture, for the school's financial support of the project.

We also want to acknowledge Sara Stemen and Mark Lamster of Princeton Architectural Press for their efforts, assistance, and sympathetic understanding of the subject matter. Joan Bourne assisted in typing and correspondence, and we are indebted to her, too.

Ernest Pascucci died prior to the publication of this collection. In addition to contributing a wonderful article, he made valuable suggestions that improved the quality of this book. He had a keen vision and an irrepressible spirit. He will be missed.

Finally, for their good spirits and patient support throughout the process, we would like to thank Lucien Rees-Roberts and Peter McCann.

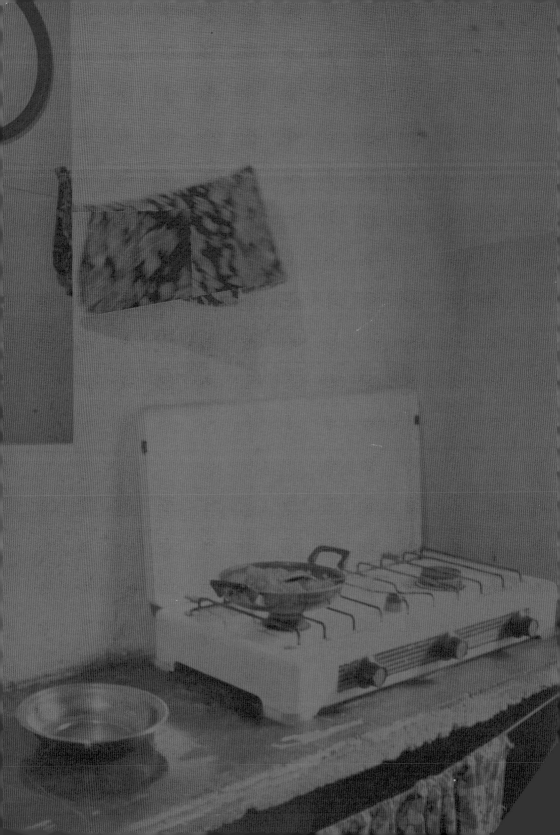

EVERYDAY ARCHITECTURE

STEVEN HARRIS

> Instead of the sublime and beautiful, the near, the low, the
> common, was explored and poeticized. That which had been
> negligently trodden under foot by those who were harness-
> ing and provisioning themselves for long journeys into far
> countries, is suddenly found to be richer than all foreign
> parts. The literature of the poor, the feelings of the child, the
> philosophy of the street, the meaning of household life, are
> the topics of the time. It is a great stride. It is a sign—is it
> not?—of new vigor when the extremities are made active,
> when currents of warm life run into the hands and the feet.
> —Ralph Waldo Emerson, "The American Scholar"

In the twenty years since Deborah Berke and I finished school, the
nature of architectural discourse has fundamentally changed. In the
mid-1970s there were those still discussing architecture from within
the discipline. Peter Eisenman was lecturing on the political implications latent in Le Corbusier's Maison Dom-ino, Anthony Vidler on the
redemptive geometry of the Cité de Refuge. In a series of lectures at the
Institute for Architecture and Urban Studies in 1976, Colin Rowe
inveighed against the failed political agenda of modernism.

At that time, the introduction into architectural discourse of theoretical models from other disciplines—mathematics, logic, linguistics,
literary criticism—had already been underway for a number of years.
Contemporary architectural theory began to differ significantly from

texts that had come before, particularly those preceding 1968. By the mid-'80s, French structuralism and its derivatives, particularly poststructuralism, had become institutionalized within the architectural academy, superseding theories derived from other fields. Why structuralism eclipsed other schools of theory is not difficult to grasp: as a pedagogically efficient technique of textual analysis, it could be deployed on a purely formal level, safely removed from the intense intellectual and political critique of consumer society inherent in theories derived from Marxist analysis.

The hegemony of structuralism and its derivatives coincided with the virtual abandonment of architecture's social and political ambitions and the estrangement of direct experience from architectural discourse. Textual "readings" of the architectural project and a tendency toward formal hermeticism exacerbated the alienation of architecture from lived experience. Meanwhile, competing schools of theory associated with Marxist analysis, at least in America, became affiliated with theorists such as Herbert Marcuse and Norman O. Brown, and with student activists and anarchists groups. To a large degree, the success of structuralism and its derivatives within the academy can be seen to correspond to the failures of the social movements of the '60s in America and France.

While this theoretical wrangling was underway, the production of architectural objects continued, albeit more slowly in New York's late-'70s recession. Neither neo-Marxist critiques of consumer culture nor poststructuralist analyses jeopardized the patron-dependent architectural commission. The focus on authorship and the obsession with the display of heroic formal dexterity in both the fabrication of the architectural object and the representation of the architectural project resulted in a series of architectural commodities marketed and consumed in ever-quickening cycles. Between the early '70s and the early '90s, for example, the same apartment on Central Park West was renovated three times. The original apartment by Emory Roth was first renovated by Robert Stern. About five years later, the apartment was redone by Michael Graves, only to be redesigned a few years later by Diana Agrest and Mario Gandelsonas. Each iteration was duly published in the architectural press and shelter magazines, and parts of the Graves version was even disassembled and tax-deductibly donated to the Brooklyn Museum.

The consideration of everyday life as a critical political construct represents an attempt to suggest an architecture resistant to this commodification/consumption paradigm, a paradigm that has come to dominate contemporary architectural practice. Neither sentimental nor nostalgic, this alternative to theories derived from structuralism and its descendants proposes reconsideration of another strain of French thought developed between the 1930s and '70s that is represented by the critique of everyday life advanced by Henri Lefebvre. Engaged intimately with the quotidian, with lived experience and political struggle, this line of thought did not find the broad American audience of structuralist discourse, but was known primarily among activist groups such as the Situationists.

What unites the articles and projects collected here is a distrust of the heroic and the formally fashionable, a deep suspicion of the architectural object as a marketable commodity. Consideration of the everyday in architecture is seen as potentially able to resist, in Lefebvre's words, "the bureaucracy of controlled consumption," that is, the forces of late capitalist economy and their complicit governmental authority. The resistance lies in the focus on the quotidian, the repetitive, and the relentlessly ordinary. The everyday is that which remains after one has eliminated all specialized activities. It is anonymous, its anonymity derived from its undated and apparently insignificant quality.

Lefebvre's aphoristic and episodic critique of everyday life can also be related to other theories that place emphasis on the role of the quotidian. The Annales school of historiography, sociological critiques of popular culture, theories of abjection, histories of the vernacular, issues of authorship, and contemporary feminist theory are among the discourses that underlie many of the projects and articles included in this volume.

This collection is neither a blueprint nor a recipe for an architecture of the everyday; no examples for the pages of the magazines, no projects to be marketed as the latest fashion. There is no Howard Roarke of the everyday. Instead these are tentative proposals and tangential provocations that describe a territory irregular and open, inexact and conceptually fragmented. Alliances are often unlikely, contradictions blunt. There is no perfect order, no grand scheme. It is in the dialectical relationships among and between these various contributions that the everyday resides: between Mary Tyler Moore and Franz Kafka, among Levittown and Old Little Tokyo and Las Vegas.

Potential sites for an architecture of the everyday begin with the body. Secretive and intimate, it is marked by the routine, the repetitive, and the cyclical; as the locus of desire, it is often home to the transgressive, the perverse, and the abject. Both Peggy Deamer's essay, "The Everyday and the Utopian," and Pat Morton's investigation of the *WomEnhouse* web site can be read in terms of—to use Deamer's phrase—the body/subject/individual. Deamer's article reconsiders the work of 1960s and '70s utopian architects in terms of the writings of Marshall McLuhan, Herbert Marcuse, and Fredric Jameson. Morton's presentation of the *WomEnhouse* web site, on the other hand, is probably best understood relative to contemporary feminist theory. Issues of the body are conflated with issues of domesticity—one moves from the home page through the *Throat* to the *Hymen*—in the virtual spaces of (the) *WomEnhouse*.

WomEnhouse represents one of the multiple and sometimes contradictory considerations of the domestic that underlie a number of these projects and essays. The quotidian nature of domesticity is foregrounded in Mark Robbins and Benjamin Gianni's "Family Values (Honey I'm Home!)." By documenting the private, ordinary realm of the everyday lives of purportedly extra-ordinary people—homosexuals—the project offers a view of marginalized domesticity and demonstrates the often banal character of the unauthorized.

Issues of domesticity are also central to several other projects included in this volume. Mabel Wilson and Peter Tolkin's photographic essay on John Outterbridge's residence/studio/gallery in South Central Los Angeles documents the insinuation of domestic life into the public space of the art gallery. Wilson's text and Tolkin's photographs provide specific tectonic readings of a building process formally and materially improvisational. Similarly, Mary Ann Ray's photographic analysis of *gecekondu*—houses taking advantage of a Turkish law allowing those who build in one night to remain—develops a taxonomy of formal strategies deployed by anonymous builders. While the Wilson/Tolkin project focuses on the juxtaposition of domestic routine with the authored work of art, the Ray essay suggests an authorless vernacular architecture whose legal status is a product of specific domestic routine.

While Ray's photographs of *gecekondu* record the tectonic result of a law that defines property ownership in terms of specific domestic activities, Robert Schultz's graphic analyses of various Levittown houses demonstrates the marketing of domestic accommodation through the manipulation of suburban imagery. As opposed to Ray's categories, which are primarily formal and material, Schultz's distinctions are economic and iconographic; he lists the appliances that come with the house, diagrams public spaces within the house, and develops a "pretension index" keyed to the front elevation. Schultz's gentle irony exploits the disjunction between simple democratic ideals—represented by the housing of returning World War II veterans—and the literal production and highly sophisticated marketing of the house as a commodity.

Discussion of the Levittown house recurs as one of the three domestic models in *Signs of Life*, Robert Venturi, Denise Scott Brown, and Steven Izenour's 1976 show at the Renwick Gallery in Washington. Deborah Fausch's essay about this exhibition, "Ugly and Ordinary: The Representation of the Everyday," traces the debate among often contradictory uses of the term *everyday* and its relationship to ideas of vernacular, populist, and nominally democratic architecture.

A less benign reading of the postwar American suburb occurs in the photographs of Gregory Crewdson. Constructing tableaux within his studio, he manipulates the familiar and ordinary to create a realistic unreality, made strange and alien. As A. M. Homes has noted, Crewdson's world includes the stiff-stocked dioramas of museums of natural history, train set suburbs spread out across ping-pong tables, and the high happy colors of Disney, all seen as though we were burglars come calling on our own lives. The suburban domestic environment is rendered simultaneously desirable and fearful.

Suburban desire and the class associations inherent in what Herbert Gans referred to as "taste-cultures" underlie Margie Ruddick's article on the garden of her neighbor Tom. Contrasted with the upper-middle-class conceit of discretion and restraint—ironically produced at great expense—Tom's garden is a matter-of-fact compilation of pragmatic accommodation. Straightforward and at times vulgar, it is seen to possess an authenticity reflecting a direct engagement with the natural world. Peter Halley's essay also examines issues of class and coded representation, distinguishing between one use of the everyday as a signifier of wealth and power, and another as the embodiment of common democratic culture. For Halley, the first use is elitist and perverse, while the second is firmly rooted in twentieth-century American art.

Issues of popular culture also inform Mark Bennett's floor plans of American television situation comedies. As Ernest Pascucci's essay "Intimate (Tele)visions" notes, television is the most everyday medium of architectural representation, broadcast directly into the home and participating—as Pat Morton points out in her *WomEnhouse* essay and Peggy Deamer describes in her comments on McLuhan—in the dissolution of the strict division between public and private. The adjacency of Bennett's drawings and Pascucci's text is intended to invite speculation about television's architectural representation of everyday life. Indeed Pascucci's essay specifically questions the tendency to associate television with the death of public life, exemplified by the writing of Richard Sennett and Kenneth Frampton in the 1970s.

Highly-mediated representations of everyday reality also occur in the work of James Casebere. Photographing a world entirely of his own making—whitewashed models of commonplace landscapes and interiors—his often Foucaultian subjects (courtroom, storefront, prison cell, pulpit) are rendered in an extraordinarily banal and matter of fact manner. In Casebere's work, architecture uncannily embodies social ideals at both the individual and collective level.

Casebere's photographs along with the essays by Fausch and Pascucci shift the discussion of the everyday from the domestic to the public realm and the more overtly political. Unlike the "Signs of Life" exhibition where Venturi, Scott Brown, and Izenour's analysis was insistently neutral, Sheila Levrant de Bretteville's "Remembering Old Little Tokyo" project is explicitly political. It is theoretically indebted to the Annales school of historiography and is entirely public in focus. Based on a kind of history from below, it uses text, images, and timelines imbedded in the sidewalk to tell the stories of a Japanese-American community. This narrative begins in the 1890s and extends through the 1940s, when many of the neighborhood's residents were forced out of their homes and into internment camps.

De Bretteville's project can also be understood relative to the notion of deterritorialization that informs Joan Ockman's essay on normative architecture. Tracing the transformation of revolutionary European modern architecture of the 1920s into American corporate architecture of the '50s and '60s—particularly that of Mies van der Rohe and Skidmore, Owings, & Merrill—Ockman chronicles the shifting relationships between minor and major architecture, between the glass utopias of the '20s and the fully embodied expressions of advanced capitalism of the '50s and '60s. Rejecting the approaches of both Tafuri and Venturi and Scott Brown, Ockman's proposal for a critical theory of normative architecture depends on strategies neither heroic nor nostalgic, but incremental, subtle, and persistent.

Finally, two essays serve as bookends to this volume. The first, Henri Lefebvre's "The Everyday and Everydayness," is accompanied by an introductory text by Mary McLeod. Her essay not only situates Lefebvre within twentieth-century French intellectual history, but also chronicles his involvement with the Surrealists, the Situationists, the Utopie group, and the events of 1968 in France.

The final essay is that of my co-editor, Deborah Berke. Aphoristic and anecdotal, modest and direct, her essay proposes eleven characteristics an architecture of the everyday might possess. Reading her essay, one begins to imagine, in physical and tectonic terms, an architecture that suppresses authorship, denies celebrity, and flirts with invisibility: an architecture of the everyday.

HENRI LEFEBVRE'S CRITIQUE OF

EVERYDAY LIFE: AN INTRODUCTION

MARY McLEOD

Man must be everyday, or he will not be at all.

What is the goal? It is the transformation of life in its smallest, most everyday detail.

—Henri Lefebvre, *Critique de la vie quotidienne*, 1947

Probably more than any other philosopher of the century, Henri Lefebvre
addressed themes intrinsically relevant to urbanism and architecture:
everyday life and the nature of space. Although Lefebvre's writings were
almost completely unknown to American architects and architectural
theorists until recently, his work played a critical role in French cultural
and architectural debates from the 1920s to his death in 1991: in the
1920s and '30s with the Surrealists, in the '50s and early '60s with the
Situationists, in the '60s with the Utopie group, and in the '70s with Anatole Kopp, Manuel Castells, and other contributors to the review *Espaces et
Sociétés*. Lefebvre's numerous writings on urban issues,
as well as his active association with architects and
planners, helped generate in France a widespread critique of modern planning methods and architectural
functionalism, a critique that sparked many in these
fields to participate in the events of 1968 and that contributed significantly to socialist planning policy in the
1980s.[1] After the *Production de l'espace* (*Production of Space*)
was translated into English in 1991, it was predictably

1] Michel Trebitsch claims that Lefebvre's notion of
everyday life had its greatest impact in Germany during
the 1970s, not among architects but among political
thinkers and activist groups, and parallels can readily be
drawn between Lefebvre's "everyday life" and Jürgen
Habermas's notion of *Lebenswelt*. Trebitsch, preface to
Henri Lefebvre, *Critique of Everyday Life*, vol. 1: *Introduction*, trans. John Moore (New York: Verso, 1991),
xxviii. Trebitsch's preface to the first volume of the *Critique of Everyday Life* is one of the best introductions to
Lefebvre's thought in English. The original French edition was titled *Critique de la vie quotidienne* (Paris:
Grasset, 1947).

HENRI LEFEBVRE, C. 1975.

only a matter of time before Lefebvre's rich thinking about space and daily life entered the broader American cultural debate. Today the growing interest in Lefebvre's ideas among American architects stems from a relatively modest aesthetic and political program: a rejection of avant-garde escapism, pretension, and heroicism in favor of a more sensitive engagement with people's everyday environments and lives.

Lefebvre was acutely conscious of the relationship between his philosophy and the historical moment from which it emerged. He insistently historicized his claims, frequently reminding the reader of the conflicts and conditions in France that generated his investigations. Thus, there is a certain paradox in republishing Lefebvre's essay "The Everyday and Everydayness" now, in another cultural context, twenty-five years after its original publication.[2] Certainly, he would see everyday life, and especially American everyday life, differently today. But while Lefebvre's analysis emerges from a particular French situation and can only be understood in that context, it offers a provocative critique of and challenge to present-day American architecture. To what extent do contemporary architectural movements perpetuate the cultural practices that Lefebvre criticizes? How might an awareness of everyday life inform American architectural debate and practice? What are the limitations and potentials of Lefebvre's theory today? Can it retain a transformative potential?

Lefebvre developed his concept of everyday life over the course of more than half a century. He proposed the notion as early as 1933 in an article, "La Mystification: Notes pour une critique de la vie quotidienne," published in the small leftist review *Avant-Poste*. One of the first French philosophers to consider seriously Hegel's and young Marx's writings on alienation, Lefebvre regarded everyday life as a means of countering the "mystified consciousness" that encoded alienation in all spheres of existence.[3] Like many French intellectuals of his generation, Lefebvre condemned the aridity and detachment of traditional philosophy and sought a

2] Henri Lefebvre, "Quotidien et Quotidienneté," in *Encyclopaedia Universalis*, vol. 13, ed. Claude Grégory (Paris: Encyclopaedia Universalis, 1972).

3] Henri Lefebvre and Norbert Guterman, "La Mystification: Notes pour une critique de la vie quotidienne," *Avant-Poste*, no. 2 (August 1933): 91–107, as cited by Trebitsch in his preface to Lefebvre, *Critique of Everyday Life*. Many of the themes of this essay are later developed in Guterman and Lefebvre's book *La Conscience mystifiée* (Paris: Gallimard, 1936). During the 1930s Lefebvre collaborated frequently with Norbert Guterman, who, like Lefebvre, had been a member of the revolutionary Philosophies circle in the 1920s. Guterman was expelled from the Communist Party, and *Avant-Poste* was published independently of its control.

mode of analysis that engaged daily life. He saw Marxism's materiality as an important foil to both Bergsonian irrationalism and contemporary neo-Kantianism, but he rejected orthodox Marxism's emphasis on economic determinants. In the 1930s, the financial crash, mass unemployment, the perpetual parliamentary crises, and the rise of Nazism and Fascism had led numerous young French thinkers in various factions—including fascists, Catholic reformers, existentialists, and nonconformist Marxists—to seek "the concrete" and the "real." Their goal was "total man" or "real man"—in Marx's phrase, the development of "human powers as an end in itself." Embracing all aspects of man's subjectivity, including biology, spirituality, creativity, and emotion, this vision of liberty as personal development countered economic models as well as abstract democratic (Enlightenment) ideals. Lefebvre, however, was quick to oppose the "spiritualism" of right-wing thinkers such as Denis de Rougemont, seeking instead a position that would unite thought and action. In 1928 he had already joined the French Communist Party and was actively committed to revolutionary transformation. During these same years he also read the early works of Martin Heidegger, and while deeply influenced by his notion of *Alltäglichkeit* (everydayness),[4] he disdained Heidegger's purely phenomenological view of consciousness, his archaicism, and his pessimism. By the 1950s Lefebvre's position had evolved full-fledged into a form of existential Marxism, though one closer to Nietzschean joy and Dionysian plenitude than to Jean-Paul Sartre's haunting specter of "nothingness." But as a witness to Nazism and an active member of the French resistance, Lefebvre was supremely conscious of the risks of nihilism and the dangers of the "superman" as model. His alternative postulation of "superhumanism," with its embrace of the humble and prosaic, rejected the elitism and heroism inherent in Nietzsche's rhetoric.

While his preoccupation with alienation would remain constant, Lefebvre's focus shifted gradually

4] Heidegger's notion of *Alltäglichkeit* has negative connotations, in that it characterizes the inauthentic aspects of *Dasein*, or human existence. In *Being and Time*, Heidegger associated *Alltäglichkeit* with disquiet and a lack of direction. According to Lucien Goldmann, Heidegger was deeply indebted to Georg Lukács, who first proposed the notion of *Alltäglichkeit* in his 1911 essay "The Metaphysics of Tragedy," in *Soul and Form*, trans. Anna Bostock (Cambridge, MA: MIT Press, 1978). Lukács contrasted *Alltäglichkeit*, "trivial life," which is dreary, mechanical, and repetitive, with "authentic life." Lefebvre's concept of everyday life contains both aspects, and in this respect is a rejection of Lukács's holistic dream. See Trebitsch, preface to Lefebvre, *Critique of Everyday Life*, xvii–xviii.

from reassessments of Marxist categories of production and class in the 1930s and '40s to examinations of mass culture, consumption, and urban space in the following three decades. Immediately after World War II, he was the French Communist Party's leading philosopher, but by 1958 he was expelled for his critiques of Soviet policy; while still a committed Marxist—if, as always, an unconventional one—his framework broadened, absorbing and responding to contemporary social and intellectual developments, most notably structural linguistics. In addition to his writings of the 1930s, he devoted four books specifically to everyday life: the three volumes of the *Critique de la vie quotidienne* (Critique of Everyday Life), published in 1947, 1961, and 1981, respectively, and *La Vie quotidienne dans le monde moderne* (Everyday Life in the Modern World) in 1968, probably his best-known book in America.[5] "The Everyday and Everydayness," first published in the *Encyclopaedia Universalis* in 1972, encapsulates many of the themes of that book, though in a necessarily synoptic form in which much of the richness and complexity of his argument, as well as the pleasures and irritations of his rhapsodic prose, are difficult to discern.

EVERYDAY LIFE

Lefebvre's concept of everyday life is elusive, due in part to his intensely dialectical approach and his refusal of any static categorization. At its most basic, it is simply "real life," the "here and now"; it is "sustenance, clothing, furniture, homes, neighborhoods, environment"—i.e., material life—but with a "dramatic attitude" and "lyrical tone."[6] Lefebvre stressed that contradiction is intrinsic to its very nature. While it is the object of philosophy, it is inherently nonphilosophical; while conveying an image of stability and immutability, it is transitory and uncertain; while governed by the repetitive march of linear time, it is redeemed by the renewal of nature's cyclical time; while unbearable in its monotony and routine, it is festive and playful; and while controlled by technocratic rationalism and capitalism, it stands

5] Henri Lefebvre, *Critique de la vie quotidienne*, vol. 1 (Paris: Grasset, 1947); vol. 2: *Fondement d'une sociologie de la quotidiennété* (Paris: L'Arche, 1961); vol. 3: *De la modernité au modernisme (Pour une métaphilosophie du quotidien)* (Paris: L'Arche, 1981). Only the first volume has been translated; see note 1. Henri Lefebvre, *La Vie quotidienne dans le monde moderne* (Paris: Gallimard, 1968); *Everyday Life in the Modern World*, trans. Sacha Rabinovitch (New York: Harper and Row, 1971); new ed. with introduction by Philip Wander (New Brunswick, NJ: Transaction, 1984). All quotations from the latter are from this last edition.

6] Lefebvre, *Everyday Life in the Modern World*, 21–22.

outside of them. Everyday life embodies at once the most dire experiences of oppression and the strongest potentialities for transformation. However inhuman, it reveals the human that still lies within us. "A revolution," Lefebvre claimed, "takes place when and only when...people can no longer lead their everyday lives."[7]

When Lefebvre wrote his first volume of *Critique of Everyday Life* in 1945, he proposed the notion of everyday life, as he had in the 1930s, as a means of broadening Marxist ideological critique beyond issues of production, class struggle, and economic determinants. He felt that a more encompassing philosophical category was needed to analyze the very pervasiveness of alienation, extending beyond labor and specialized functional spheres to include all that which eluded definition, "the residuum." In his first volume, he stressed the diminishing importance of class, the contraction of the work week, and the increase in leisure time; in his subsequent writings of the 1950s and '60s, he gave greater emphasis to the rise of advertising and the media, the expanding role of consumption in daily life, and the increasing systematization of urban life. In Marxist terms, his notion of everyday life can be seen as existing somewhere between the base (economic determinants) and the superstructure (ideas, concepts, values), or, more precisely, as challenging any hierarchical division between the two. Lefebvre considered everyday life more significant than work itself in determining experience and social transformation.

At first glance, Lefebvre's notion of everyday life seems pessimistic, especially in its post-1957 manifestations. In *Everyday Life in the Modern World* he contrasted contemporary everyday life with pre-industrial daily life, which he characterized as having been regionally diverse yet locally unified—i.e., it possessed an unconscious "style." Everyday life, which emerged in the nineteenth century, lacked this integrated style; increased rationalization brought increased fragmentation. Lefebvre argued that in the two decades following World War II, technocratic and bureaucratic organization had permeated nearly every sphere of existence, resulting in ever increasing functional specializa-

7] Ibid., 32.

tion, social separation, and cultural passivity; hardly a facet of domestic life, leisure time, or cultural activity escaped systematization. For Lefebvre, one of the most vivid embodiments of this relentless "rationalization" was the contemporary city. He was deeply affected by the construction of a new town, Lacq-Mourenx (1957–60), near his birthplace in southwestern France, and decried its desertlike spaces that killed any quality of public spontaneity or play. As did Jean-Luc Godard in his films *Alphaville* (1965) and *Two or Three Things I Know about Her* (1966), Lefebvre presented a bleak picture of urban and suburban homogenization—the anonymous *grands ensembles* dominating the urban peripheries; the sterile, repetitive office blocks; the antiseptic *supermarché*; and the endless proliferation of suburban pavilions across the hillsides like "hundreds of dead chickens in an immense shop window."[8] He equated this relentless homogenization with "Americanization" and, despite his intensely French perspective, by the late 1960s saw it as a potentially global phenomenon.[9] In this respect, his vision of everyday life is darker than that of Michel de Certeau, who was profoundly influenced by him. De Certeau largely ignored the monotonies and tyrannies of daily life, stressing the individual's capacity to manipulate situations and create realms of autonomous action—what he called a "network of antidiscipline."[10] However, Lefebvre's emphasis on the oppressions of daily existence is also countered by a transcendent belief that everyday life cannot be contained by bureaucratic regimentation, that it harbors the desire that generates transformation. Nature, love, simple domestic pleasures, celebrations, and holidays all erode any prospect of total, static systematization.

One of the most moving sections of Lefebvre's first volume of *Critique of Everyday Life* is his account of rural festivals, "Notes Written One Sunday." In this chapter, drafted at the height of post-Liberation euphoria, he presented the peasant festival as indicative of the joy, freedom, and sense of community that everyday life might come to provide in a more enduring and

8] Lefebvre, foreword to the Second Edition of *Critique of Everyday Life*, vol. 1, 43.

9] Lefebvre, *Everyday Life in the Modern World*, 67.

10] Michel de Certeau, *L'Invention du quotidien* (Paris: Union Générale d'Éditions, 1980); *The Practice of Everyday Life*, trans. Steven Rendall (Berkeley: University of California Press, 1984). In a footnote, De Certeau cited Lefebvre as a fundamental source for his notion of everyday life (xv).

11] The book was written between August and December 1945 and published in February 1947, just before the outbreak of the Cold War. Trebitsch, preface to *Critique of Everyday Life*, x.

12] This vision of festival as privileged moment was to haunt the Situationists' explorations in the 1950s; it also anticipates Foucault's inclusion of the festival in his list of heterotopias, out-of-the-ordinary spaces that invite acute perceptions of the social order. See Michel Foucault, "Of Other Spaces: Utopias and Heterotopias," 1967, in Joan Ockman with Edward Eigen, eds., *Architecture Culture, 1943–1968: A Documentary Anthology* (New York: Rizzoli, 1993), 420–26. While Foucault may well have derived his interest in festivals from other sources—for instance, Mikhail Bakhtin—his notion of heterotopia as "a sort of place that lies outside all places and yet is actually localizable" is strikingly similar to Lefebvre's conception of the festival as contrasting "violently with everyday life" but without being "separate from it." Lefebvre, *Critique of Everyday Life*, 207.

13] Henri Lefebvre, *Le Matérialism dialectique* (Paris: Alcan, 1939); *Dialectic Materialism*, trans. John Sturrock (London: Jonathan Cape, 1968), 87, 108. For a discussion of Lefebvre's idea of totality, see Martin Jay, *Marxism and Totality: The Adventures of a Concept from Lukàcs to Habermas* (Berkeley: University of California Press, 1984), 293–99.

14] Lefebvre, *Everyday Life in the Modern World*, 25.

15] In this respect Lefebvre was much closer to Ernst Bloch than Georg Lukács, despite similarities between Lukács's notion of reification and Lefebvre's concept of systematization. Numerous other parallels could be drawn between Lefebvre's concept of everyday life and contemporary Marxist thinking. Lefebvre's interest in art and mass culture, and his emphasis on culture as a social determinant, invite comparisons with the Frankfurt School. Walter Benjamin had some familiarity with Lefebvre's early writings, and quoted a passage of *La Conscience mystifiée* in his essay "Eduard Fuchs: Collector and Historian," *New German Critique*, no. 5 (Spring 1975): 50. See also Perry Anderson, *Considerations on Western Marxism* (London: New Left Books, 1976), 37. And as Trebitsch points out (preface, xviii), Lefebvre's *Critique of Everyday Life* prefigured Theodor Adorno's *Negative Dialectics* in its acknowledgment that negativity embodies another, less visible dimension of reality—a difference that allows us to distance ourselves from a situation in order to criticize it. [cont.]

meaningful way.[11] Lefebvre envisioned, as he would throughout his life, a future society of abundance, increased leisure, and personal liberty, grounded in everyday desires and needs. The limitless possibilities of this future were already present in everyday life, but only in "moments."[12]

While the subsequent two volumes of *Critique of Everyday Life* emphasize the growing domination of society by bureaucracy and "controlled consumption," Lefebvre's dialectical thinking continues to convey optimism. His method is less a positing of binary opposites leading to a new synthesis than a depiction of multiple tensions that will generate an unpredictable transformation. For Lefebvre, totality was not a product of a content "begetting itself," but a concrete reality open to the future.[13] As he confessed, he was more interested in subjective praxis than in objective determinism.[14] Utopia was an essential component of that praxis; only by proposing alternative possibilities, conducting endless experiments, and constructing new futures could individuals and groups actively initiate the process of social transformation. And like his concept of totality, his notion of utopia precluded any totalitarian synthesis or controlling a priori vision. Lefebvre insisted on the necessary incompleteness of Marxist thought.[15]

But while Marxism remained the primary springboard for Lefebvre's thinking, other intellectual developments in the interwar and post-World War II periods were central to the emergence of everyday life as an analytical category in his work. Besides existentialism, there was a tremendous growth of the social sciences in France—in sociology, anthropology, demography, and geography—and of history, owing largely to the emergence of the Annales School, which dispensed with diplomatic and political history (the history of great men and great events) to investigate general *mentalités* and structures of ordinary life. In his first volume of *Critique of Everyday Life* Lefebvre paid hommage to Annales historian Marc Bloch's ground-breaking work *Caractères originaux de l'histoire rurale française* (*French Rural History*) and to geographer Albert Demangeon's studies of rural life.[16] The Annales School and Demangeon, however, emphasized the stasis and persistence of everyday structures, whereas Lefebvre underscored their contradictions and tensions. Another, quite different parallel might be drawn between Roland Barthes's essays in the 1950s, compiled in *Mythologies* (1957), and Lefebvre's readings of humble, ordinary events. Lefebvre admired Barthes's "brilliant" investigations, closely followed his semiological research, and made frequent references to his writings.[17] Both thinkers contributed to the review *Arguments* (1956–1962), which attracted a group of intellectuals disillusioned with Communist Party doctrine. Yet by the 1960s the differences between Barthes and Lefebvre were more important than any superficial similarities. Some of Lefebvre's most stringent intellectual attacks were aimed at structuralism, which he viewed as an escape from politics and as an extension of technocratic rationality to the intellectual sphere. Evoking Marshall McLuhan, he characterized structuralism as "cool," lifeless, and lacking any passion or engagement. He was just as critical of Michel Foucault's rejection of dialectical history and subjectivity, and, later, of Jacques Derrida's elevation of writing over speech, a position he viewed as elitist. This does not mean Lefebvre was tied to traditional notions of humanism, which by the 1960s he regarded as a

15] [cont.] Herbert Marcuse's "one-dimensional society" and Lefebvre's portrayal of the "bureaucratic society of controlled consumption" also invite comparison, although Lefebvre believed that Marcuse underestimated the contradictions in capitalist society, and the "cracks" that these produce. Lefebvre devoted a chapter to Marcuse (who happened to be in Paris in May 1968) in Henri Lefebvre, *L'Irruption de Nanterre au sommet* (Paris: Anthropos, 1968); *The Explosion: Marxism and the French Upheaval*, trans. Alfred Ehrenfeld (New York: Modern Reader, Monthly Review Press, 1969), 24–33.

16] Marc Bloch, *Caractères originaux de l'histoire rurale française* (1931; reprint, Paris: Armand Colin, 1956); and Albert Demangeon, *Problèmes de géographie humaine* (Paris: Armand Colin, 1952). Demangeon's book, published posthumously in 1942, includes his famous study of rural habitation, which was first published in the *Annales de Géographie* in 1920. Lefebvre, who was born in the Pyrénées, had deep ties to rural life, which remained for him, somewhat nostalgically, an image of community that countered the fragmentation and isolation of urban life. As a result of his wartime exile in the Pyrénées, Lefebvre himself became immersed in sociological research of agrarian communities, gaining a doctorate in sociology in 1954. This research eventually resulted in his book *La Vallée de Campan* (Paris: Presses universitaires de France, 1963). One of the sociologists who influenced Lefebvre most was Georges Gurvitch, who brought him to the Centre National de la Recherche Scientifique in 1948.

17] Barthes and Lefebvre were close friends. They both had roots in the Pyrénées, and spent considerable time visiting each other's families there. See Rémi Hess, *Henri Lefebvre et l'aventure du siècle* (Paris: Métailié, 1988), 243, 321.

"sordid" product of bourgeois mystification; rather, his distrust stemmed from his refusal to abandon concepts of choice, political identity, and agency, which he considered essential to political action and social transformation.[18]

18] To trace Lefebvre's evolving notion of humanism is beyond the scope of this essay. Certainly, from the 1930s to the mid-1950s Lefebvre considered himself a humanist, though not one in the Enlightenment mode. In the 1950s it was common rhetoric among Marxists and existentialists alike to talk of a "new humanism." Lefebvre, whose thinking always responded to contemporary intellectual developments, understood all too well the challenge posed by structuralism and, subsequently, by poststructuralism. While he granted the unconsciousness of many historical processes, he believed that it was ideological mystification to conclude from that the necessity of the subject's absence. Like other existential Marxists, Lefebvre tried to construct a sociological and historical theory of the subject without making it an ontological entity. In his book *Position: contre les technocrates* (1967), he wrote: "Society cannot be defined as a subject but as an ensemble of social subjects (not without lacunae) and a network of sociological agents (not without lapses)." Quoted in Mark Poster, *Existential Marxism in Postwar France: From Sartre to Althusser* (Princeton, NJ: Princeton University Press, 1975), 254.

19] Lefebvre, *Everyday Life in the Modern World*, esp. 67.

20] One of Lefebvre's most blatantly sexist remarks appeared in *Everyday Life in the Modern World*, where he claimed that because of their ambiguous position in everyday life, women "are incapable of understanding it" (73). Such remarks appeared rarely in his writing after 1968, and, for the most part, Lefebvre conveyed a deep interest in and empathy for women. As early as the mid-1950s, he discussed the "women's press," which he saw as an important subject to analyze in terms of the needs and content of everyday life. He further developed this theme in the second volume of *Critique of Everyday Life*. In *Le Temps des méprises* ([Paris: Stock, 1975], p. 174), Lefebvre praised feminists' critiques of psychoanalysis and Lacan, specifically citing Luce Irigaray's work.

WOMEN AND EVERYDAY LIFE

For contemporary readers, one of the most interesting aspects of Lefebvre's thought, and one that is only hinted at in "The Everyday and Everydayness," is his acute analysis of the role of everyday life in women's experience. He asserted that everyday life "weighs heaviest on women" (as well as on children, the working class, and other marginal groups) and yet also provides women realms for fantasy and desire, for rebellion and assertion—arenas outside of bureaucratic systematization. Early on, Lefebvre recognized the impact of consumption on postwar French society and its particular role as both demon and liberator in women's lives. While oppressive and controlling—and degrading in its sexual objectification—consumption cannot be contained by rationalization as readily as production can; "desire" remains "irreducible," harboring hopes and needs, and "a spontaneous conscience."[19] Throughout his accounts of everyday life, Lefebvre referred to women's closer contact with cyclical time, the rhythms of nature, spontaneity, and tactility; and, despite moments of infuriating sexism and disturbingly essentialist rhetoric, these descriptions give credence to notions previously denigrated in French culture.[20] In his 1974 book The Production of Space, he traced the diminution of "feminine" qualities of space (for instance, the hidden, cryptlike spaces of the ancient world) with the emergence of perspective and absolutist control in the renaissance and baroque periods, and later with the dominance of technocratic rationality in the post-Enlightenment era. Lefebvre's appreciation of the feminine anticipated in different ways the writings of French feminists Hélène Cixous (her aesthetic of fluidity, multiplicity, and continual metamorphosis) and Julia Kristeva (the notion of women's time as simultaneously cyclical, monumental, and linear).[21] In the past decade, Lefebvre's writings have sparked investigations by a diverse group of feminist theorists exploring mass culture and women's occupation of public space, including Rosalyn Deutsche, Alice Kaplan, Doreen Massey, and Kristin Ross.

THE AVANT-GARDE AND UTOPIAN EXPERIMENTATION

Lefebvre's comments on modernism and avant-garde art also take on a particular relevance today, with the emergence of a neo-avant-garde. Lefebvre contrasted the modern and the quotidian as historically contemporaneous and interrelated categories, which counterbalance one another. The modern is novelty and brilliance, daring and transitory, proclamatory in its initiative; the everyday is enduring and solid, humble and "taken for granted"; "it is the ethics underlying routine and the aesthetics of familiar settings."[22] While Lefebvre appreciated the questioning and investigative qualities of modernity (a historical condition that he believed ended with Fascism and the failure of socialist revolution), he was deeply critical of the avant-garde's escapism, exoticism, and cult of the bizarre. In his view, its claims of generating social transformation were illusionary.

His critique of cultural practices emerged directly from his own experiences with avant-garde movements, and it is worth turning briefly to a few of these experiences to understand Lefebvre's view of

21] Although there are important differences between Kristeva and Lefebvre, their interest in understanding multiple experiences of time, especially for women, suggests interesting parallels. Both cited James Joyce as a source of inspiration for their meditations. See especially Julia Kristeva's essay "Le Temps des femmes," in *Cahiers de recherche de sciences des textes et documents* 5, no. 33/44 (winter 1979): 5–19.

22] Lefebvre, *Everyday Life in the Modern World*, 24–25. Lefebvre's opposition of the modern and the quotidian recalls Adolf Loos's distinction between art and architecture in his essay "Architecture" of 1910. In an earlier book, *Introduction to Modernity*, Lefebvre also distinguished between modernism and modernity. Modernism referred to "the consciousness which successive ages, periods and generations had of themselves" and thus included "triumphalist images and projections of self," providing little critical insight. In contrast, modernity represented "the beginnings of a reflective process, a more-or-less advanced attempt at critique and autocritique." See Henri Lefebvre, *Introduction à la modernité* (Paris: Minuit, 1962); *Introduction to Modernity: Twelve Preludes, September 1959–May 1961*, trans. John Moore (New York: Verso, 1995), 1.

art's role in social transformation. In the 1920s, as a member of the *Philosophies* circle, he became actively involved with the Surrealists, attracted to their radical critique of rationality, their indictment of bourgeois society, and their desire to transform life.[23] But Lefebvre soon broke with André Breton, attacking in his first postwar study of everyday life the Surrealists' "enormous pretension," "aesthetic individualism," "ersatz Romanticism," and "deep, lasting defeatism." Lefebvre felt that they failed to distinguish between the "abject reality" of the interwar years and "human reality" itself. He was one of the first to note the puerile aspect of their masculinist preoccupations and criticized their "adolescent" quest for the novel—exemplified by the "beautiful, unique, absolute, mysterious woman"—as an answer to life's ills. They promised a new world, but merely offered "spiritual charlatanism." For Lefebvre, the Surrealists' "far-left" critique, in its relentless rejection of life, resembled the reactionary critiques of capitalism that proliferated in the 1930s.[24]

During the 1950s Lefebvre again turned to art as a means of transforming everyday life; in the early 1950s, he had contacts with the CoBrA group, and, from 1957 to 1962, was in active dialog with the Situationists, who shared his disdain for avant-garde negation and were equally committed to a revolutionary transformation of everyday life.[25] Led by Guy Debord, the Situationists proposed concepts such as *dérive* (literally, "drift"), a semiprogrammed wandering intended to bring new urban connections and insights through displacement and dislocation; *psychogeography*, the study and manipulation of environments to create new ambiences and new psychic possibilities; and *situation*, a spatial/temporal event staged to catalyze liberatory transformation. Lefebvre and the Situationists were fairly close for a period of time. The Situationists borrowed heavily from ideas that Lefebvre

23] Lefebvre frequently spent whole nights wandering with the Surrealists through Paris—the same journeys that inspired Louis Aragon's *Le Paysan de Paris* (1926). "An Interview with Henri Lefebvre," *Environment and Planning D: Society and Space* 5, no. 1 (March 1987): 33.

24] However, in an "autocritique," he later conceded the importance of the Surrealists' hypothesis "that only the excessive image comes to grips with the profundity of the real world"—an idea, he asserted, that Pablo Picasso, Tristan Tzara, and Paul Éluard had also discovered. Lefebvre, foreword to *Critique of Everyday Life*, vol. 1, 261, (n. 49). In his autobiography, *La Somme et le reste*, written shortly after his expulsion from the Communist Party, Lefebvre admitted that he might have remained a Surrealist were it not for Breton's "insufferable personality." Lefebvre was also a close friend of Tzara, one of the founders of dadaism, whom he first met in 1924. Tzara helped Lefebvre get a job with Radio-Toulouse in 1945, after he lost his teaching position during the Vichy era.

25] CoBrA [Copenhagen, Brussels, Amsterdam] was founded in 1948 by a group of artists from Denmark, Belgium, and Holland, including Asger Jorn, Christian Dotrement, and Constant Nieuwenhuis. The group was actively committed to revolutionary transformation, but rejected the hardline position of the Communist parties, which saw all artistic activity as part of a greater political agenda. CoBrA sought a popular, libertarian art, emphasizing experimentation and play more than finished production. The group dissolved in 1951.

CONSTANT NIEUWENHUIS, VIEW OF
SECTORS G AND E, YELLOW ZONE, NEW
BABYLON, 1960. LEFEBVRE FREQUENTLY
PRAISED THE INTENTIONALLY LABYRIN-
THINE NEW BABYLON AS AN "EXPERI-
MENTAL UTOPIA" PROJECTING NEW
FORMS OF SOCIABILITY.

developed in his critique of everyday life, especially his depiction of encompassing alienation, his analysis of commodification as eroding symbolism and use value, and his idea of festival as a privileged moment. In turn, Lefebvre was inspired by their active engagement in spatial experimentation, their focus on urban transformation, and their global critique. He particularly admired Constant Nieuwenhuis's visionary project New Babylon, which in its collective and playful use of labyrinthine space "ridiculed" labor-based functionalism. Lefebvre appreciated the project's scale—something between an apartment complex and a city—which he saw as breaking down public/private dichotomies and promoting new social exchanges. Although he considered the project a bit obsessive and abstract, and premature in its proclamation of the disappearance of work,[26] Lefebvre did not criticize the scheme's potentially oppressive dimensions, such as its overtones of behavioral engineering or its obliteration of any sense of tradition, locale, and domesticity.

But by the early 1960s, Debord and Lefebvre had parted— acrimoniously. The break was prompted by personal matters (charges of plagiarism and relations with women), but there were important ideological differences as well. Lefebvre never accepted the Situationists' belief in the revolutionary potential of situations or short-term events. He believed that revolutionary change was a slower and more comprehensive process, less theatrical and individualistic, necessitating a more historically grounded engagement with everyday life. The

26] Lefebvre, *Le Temps des méprises* , 244, 246–47.

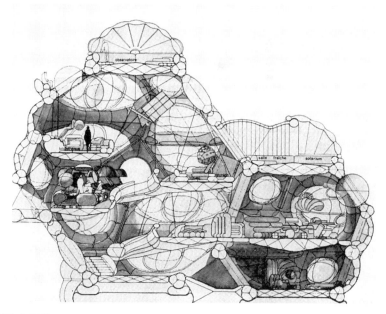

J. P. JUNGMANN, DYODON, C. 1968.
DESPITE UTOPIE'S OBSESSION WITH FLEXI-
BILITY, THIS PNEUMATIC COMPLEX, LIKE
MOST OF THE GROUP'S INFLATABLE PRO-
JECTS, APPEARS SOMEWHAT MONUMENTAL.

27] It is not entirely certain when the friendship
between Lefebvre and the Situationists dissolved. In a
1983 interview Lefebvre mentions 1961 or 1962. For
accounts of the relationship between the Situationists
and Lefebvre, see Hess, *Henri Lefebvre et l'aventure du
siècle*, 211–28; "Lefebvre on the Situationists: An Interview," with Kristin Ross, *October*, no. 79 (Winter 1997):
69–83; and Eleonore Kofman and Elizabeth Lebas, "Lost
in Transposition—Time, Space and the City," introduction to Henri Lefebvre, *Writings on Cities* (Oxford:
Blackwell, 1996), 11–13. While Lefebvre disdained Guy
Debord's dogmatism, which he compared to André Breton's, he liked Constant Nieuwenhuis, both personally
and programmatically. Constant's text of 1953 "Pour
une architecture de situation" was indebted to Lefebvre's first volume of *Critique of Everyday Life*. As late as
1975, Lefebvre cited Constant's New Babylon project as
a model of a "new unity." However, Lefebvre was also
interested in more practical and concrete experiments,
and praised Ricardo Bofill's project "City of Space" in
Madrid on similar grounds. See Lefebvre, *Le Temps des
méprises*, 246–47.

Situationists, in turn, criticized his theory of moments
as too passive and abstract: it implied waiting for
moments of revolutionary transformation rather than
initiating them; in addition, it lacked the spatial
dimension of situations. In hindsight, Lefebvre's critique seems closer to the mark, but the Situationists'
attacks contained an element of truth. As much as
Lefebvre wanted to engage everyday life, he remained
more successful as a critic and observer, inspiring others to action more than himself.[27]

However, Lefebvre's interest in experimental-
ism and utopianism, the postulation of the possible as
the real, persisted, and just prior to the events of 1968
he became actively involved with another avant-garde
faction committed to the transformation of everyday
life: the Utopie group. This marginal interdisciplinary
group, which published a review of the same title,
included urbanist Hubert Tonka, a former plasterer and

MOURENX, A NEW TOWN OF TWELVE THOUSAND RESIDENTS, 1958. LEFEBVRE DECRIED ITS STERILITY AND REGIMENTATION, ASSERTING THAT IT WOULD OBLITERATE SPONTANEOUS SOCIAL EXCHANGE. THE SITUATIONISTS, WHO PUBLISHED THIS IMAGE, DESCRIBED THE TOWN AS EMBODYING THE "CONCENTRATION CAMP ORGANIZATION OF LIFE."

protégé of Lefebvre; feminist and landscape architect Isabelle Auricoste; architects Jean Aubert, Jean-Paul Jungmann, and Antoine Stinco; and sociologist and critic Jean Baudrillard, who was Lefebvre's assistant at the University of Nanterre.[28] The magazine presented a revolutionary critique of the city and French cultural practices, publishing satirical drawings and excerpts of comic strips to make their acerbic points. By this time, Paris had become surrounded by the *grands ensembles*, and the office towers of La Défense were a testament to the triumph of technocratic modernity. Influenced by both the Situationists and the British group Archigram, the architects in the Utopie group promoted ephemeral architecture as a means of creating festive, playful milieux, which they regarded as phalansteries of a world to come. But any tenuous links between the visual and political programs quickly dissipated, with the review becoming a strictly critical and purely textual forum, in Lefebvre's view a "negative utopia."[29]

Lefebvre's attraction to these three avant-garde movements carried its own contradictions. He was

28] I am grateful to Marc Dessauce for providing information about the group and access to their publications.

29] Lefebvre, *Le Temps des méprises*, 245–46. I am indebted to Jean-Louis Violeau for alerting me to this passage in *Le Temps des méprises*. Lefebvre commented that Baudrillard's and Tonka's concept of the mode of production was so constraining that it permitted no means—short of war or catastrophe—for transformation. In contrast, he insisted on the capacity of critical thought and imagination to create a fissure or break in productive processes and "open a way for real rupture." Lefebvre also complained that he simply did not understand what the Utopie group wanted. Although individual Utopie architects made projects, these were never published in the journal, and all artwork was eliminated by the third issue. Lefebvre was not alone in expressing skepticism about Utopie's capacity to offer a constructive vision. The British magazine *Architectural Design*, which published some of their pneumatic structures, noted: "so stringent are their ideals for the new architecture . . . that it is something of a surprise that they are willing and able to design anything at all." See "La Pneumatique," *Architectural Design* (June 1968): 273.

seduced by their revolutionary claims, their desire to merge art and life, their iconoclasm, and their creative visions. But his own insistence on the humble and ordinary, on a vibrant accessible art (a populism nei-ther sentimental nor simplistic), and on an engagement with the "real" led to either mutual incomprehension or active disagreements. He was too much the philosopher and sociologist to accept mystical claims, but, more significant, he was too committed to improving ordinary lives to accept fantasy projects as sufficient. By the late 1960s his com-mitment to transforming everyday life turned from avant-garde aes-thetic experimentation to strategies for the planning of cities.

URBANISM AS THEORY AND PRACTICE

Lefebvre's emphasis on the city distinguishes his notion of the quotidian from many English and American discussions of daily life, which tend to focus on domesticity and the private realm.[30] For Lefebvre, as for many feminists today, the rigid divisions between public and private, work and leisure, and monotonous routine and escape were exactly the reductive categorizations that everyday life challenged. Lefebvre saw the city as the greatest hope for a vital, liberatory everyday life, and from 1968 to 1974 he published seven books exploring urbanization and the production of space. The city was the locus of the most intense contradictions of capi-talism: on the one hand, it revealed the relentless tyranny of rationalized processes instituted by the state and advanced capital-ism, of which government urban planning was one of its clearest manifestations; on the other hand, it demonstrated the intense fragmentation created by private property. Lefebvre considered the very inability of capitalism to contain contradiction as opportunity for a revitalized urban life. His manifesto Le Droit à la ville (The Right to the City), written just prior to the events of 1968, served as such a program for reform. In it, Lefebvre decried the anonymity and lack of com-munity of recent French new towns and peripheral

30] For instance, this is the case of the New Empiricists during the 1950s in Britain, and of Denise Scott Brown and Robert Venturi during the late 1960s and '70s in the United States, despite their interest in Las Vegas. Major exceptions are Lewis Mumford, Jane Jacobs, and the advocacy planners of the late 1960s and '70s. Jacobs, like Lefebvre, sought to blur traditional public/private distinctions.

31] Lefebvre considered Le Corbusier a "good archi-tect" but a "catastrophic" urbanist, condemning his abolition of spaces where people could gather collec-tively. Though Lefebvre publicized this assessment in an interview in 1986, it reflects his position of the 1960s and '70s. See Henri Lefebvre, "No Salvation from the Center," in Writings on Cities, 207.

development and called instead for greater urbanity, centrality, street life, residential participation, and opportunities for spontaneity.[31] It was necessary, he believed, to see the city as a collective oeuvre, an ongoing act of human creation, diverse but unified. Lefebvre appreciated the need for symbolic monuments and public spaces, but condemned false picturesqueness and nostalgia. In an article in *L'Architecture d'Aujourd'hui* he proposed new programs—"multifunctional" and "transfunctional" buildings and spaces—that would generate new forms of urban contact and sociability.[32]

Always committed to combining theory and practice, Lefebvre was simultaneously involved with practicing architects and students in efforts to achieve a new urbanism. During the 1960s and '70s he taught courses and gave lectures at the École Spéciale d'Architecture, where his books *Le Droit à la ville* (1968) and *La Révolution urbaine* (*The Urban Revolution*) (1970) served as manifestos for a generation of students eager to reject Beaux Arts academicism. In 1970 he founded another review, *Espaces et Sociétés*, with architectural historian Anatole Kopp, but soon left that publication due to its inflexible dogmatism and exclusion of visionary speculation.[33] Over the next two decades, Lefebvre's activities and writings had a significant impact on urban policy in France, leading to programs for the revitalization of urban cores, the creation of new urban monuments of a more democratic cast, the renovation of the *grands ensembles*, and the inclusion of collective spaces in new towns such as Créteil.[34] But Lefebvre was rarely pleased with the results, which he saw as inevitably compromised by government contingencies and limited imagination.[35] He remained committed to a more poetic, experimental vision of urban transformation.

32] Henri Lefebvre, "Propositions," *L'Architecture d'Aujourd'hui*, no. 132 (June–July 1967): 14–15. Not coincidentally, Lefebvre's program anticipates many of Bernard Tschumi's recent claims. Tschumi's interest in "crossprogramming" and "transprogramming," as well as his interest in spontaneous events, recalls Lefebvre's urban writings, which Tschumi cited in his essays of the 1970s. Lefebvre and Tschumi, however, take strikingly different stands toward the issue of signification: by the mid-1980s Tschumi had accepted, and indeed sought to create "empty form," an "architecture that *means nothing*," whereas Lefebvre decried the loss of symbolic content in the endless signifiers, the reduction of form to "indexes," and actively sought an architecture and urbanism that invited collective understanding.

33] "Why," he asked, "must Marxism evacuate the symbolic, the dream and the imaginary and systematically eliminate the 'poetic being,' the oeuvre?" Henri Lefebvre, *De l'état*, vol. 4 (Paris: Union Générale d'Éditions, 1978), 270, as quoted in Kofman and Lebas, "Lost in Transposition" (see n. 27), 23.

34] Probably, the most notable example of Lefebvre's influence was Banlieues '89, a large-scale initiative to "urbanize" working-class suburbs. Launched in 1983 by Michel Chantal-Dupart and Roland Castro under the auspices of the Socialist government, this program sponsored approximately two hundred projects in the 1980s. A major priority was the introduction of cultural activities and collective spaces into postwar housing developments. He also participated in architectural competitions, working with a team of designers on the Galieni renewal project in the east of Paris and, later, in the 1980s, on New Belgrade in Yugoslavia. As director of the Institut de Sociologie Urbaine at Nanterre, he supervised several studies for the Ministère de l'Équipement. See Kofman and Lebas, "Lost in Transposition," 36; and J. P. Garnier, "La Vision urbaine de Henri Lefebvre: des previsions aux révisions," *Espaces et Sociétés* 76, no. 1 (1994): 123–45.

35] "An Interview with Henri Lefebvre," *Society and Space*, 35-37. In this interview, Lefebvre criticized the final form of the French new town Créteil, which was initially inspired by his writings.

In France, the most important legacy of Lefebvre's concept of everyday life undoubtedly resides in the extraordinary events surrounding May 1968. His sociology lectures at the University of Nanterre, which were typically crammed with a thousand or so students, helped energize a young, dissatisfied generation to action. But more significant, his long-standing critique of the systematization of everyday life, and his vision of social transformation, gave the dissident groups a framework for their own proclamations. Lefebvre's emphasis on experience, on everyday life as festival, on liberation in all spheres of existence—in conjunction with his rejection of global economic forces as a precondition for revolutionary change—all were fundamental to the emergence of the euphoric moment, which seemed, at least briefly, to fulfill his vision of collectivity, community, spontaneity, and play. Today, it is common to speak of the failures of 1968, the rapid absorption of reforms into new systems and bureaucracies. But 1968 also marked a significant shift toward the democratization of French society, and this brought a new series of conflicts and potentials. In some respects, 1968 clarifies the limits and strengths of Lefebvre's notion of everyday life. On the positive side, it reveals the significant role of everyday life as a motivating force for social change; the necessity of engaging such elements of commodity culture as advertising, rock music, slogans, and the media in order to transform everyday life; and the potential of new forms of conviviality and sociability in breaking down class lines, functional divisions, and spatial ghettos. On the negative side, though, 1968 reveals the difficulty of an open model that resists systematization. Although participants pressed and succeeded in obtaining significant reforms (including the decentralization of the École des Beaux Arts) and contributed to a gradual political shift to the left culminating in the Socialists' victory in 1981, they could hardly sustain the "festival" of daily life, the shortened work day, and the endless experiments in personal development that affected a small number of people at best. This invites comparison to the American student-led protest movement of the 1960s. In both cases, the sense of euphoria was short-lived. Nonetheless, a vision of personal and social liberation entered mass consciousness, one that contributed to changes in social mores, sexual practices, family life, class distinctions, notions of gender and race, and to the emergence of identity politics in the decades to come. In the cultural sphere, 1968, like Lefebvre's notion of everyday life, blurred distinctions between high and low culture, between avant-garde transgression and popular pleasure.

CONTEMPORARY ARCHITECTURE AND EVERYDAY LIFE

What seems most relevant to architects today is the cultural dimension of Lefebvre's critique of everyday life. His rich, complex, and joyous vision of transformation serves to counter, on the one hand, the banality and mediocrity of most of the built environment—the product of technical rationalization and market forces—and, on the other hand, the escapism, heroicism, and machismo of so much contemporary architectural thought. From the perspective of everyday life, such neo-avant-garde strategies as "folding," "disjunction," and "bigness" deny the energy, humanity, and creativity embodied in the humble, prosaic details of daily existence. Architecture's "star system" validates novelty and arrogance (even as big-name architects have become standardized and repetitive commodities), at the expense of what Lefebvre saw as the initial value of modernity: its relentless questioning of social life. In this context, Lefebvre's desire to ground philosophy and culture in the everyday—in the ethics of ordinary choices—offers an important check to the deracinated rhetoric and mystical claims that continue to be propagated by the neo-avant-garde.

It is perhaps paradoxical, but not entirely coincidental, that the emergence of this neo-avant-garde parallels a cultural revival of surrealism and situationism, which has made them newly fashionable. These movements are heralded for providing alternatives to modernism's formal autonomy and to postmodernism's commodification and political passivity, and for heroically attempting to bridge art and everyday life. Yet, this revival has largely ignored the critique that Lefebvre proffered: the extent to which mysticism, escapism, transgression, and the short-term event serve as substitutes for more rigorous analysis and sustained transformation. Moreover, architects and critics recycling surrealist and situationist concepts (notably, chance, event, transgression, and displacement) have largely ignored the sexism and puerile tendencies so pervasive in these earlier movements.

However, the notion of everyday life carries its own risks of commodification. Except for a brief period in the late 1960s and early '70s, at the height of the advocacy planning movement, rarely have people associated it in an Anglo-American context with social transformation, as Lefebvre and (for all their shortcomings) the Situationists did. Instead, everyday life usually becomes a justification for the status quo or for a nostalgic return to humanist assumptions, such as those propagated by the New Empiricists in Britain in the 1950s. Although the radical aesthetic programs of the Independent Group in the 1950s and of Robert Venturi and Denise Scott Brown in the 1960s and '70s come closer to Lefebvre's vision of "the extraordinary in the ordinary," their critique rarely extended beyond the aesthetic sphere. Too often, as the evolution of postmodern architecture revealed, mass culture became either part of high art (as a formal source) or alternatively, and more frequently, a justification for the excesses of capitalism.

Admittedly, it is difficult today to sustain the optimism of Lefebvre's vision. However, his emphasis on the concrete and the real, the humble and the ordinary, as reservoirs of transformation would seem to carry more potential than a recycling of tired avant-gardism. Perhaps an even more compelling dimension of Lefebvre's work, one that is problematic but strategically important in this postmodern moment, is his simultaneous insistence on contradiction and totality. His critique of everyday life reveals a world of conflicts, tensions, cracks, and fissures— a shifting ground that continually opens to new potentials—and at the same time it presents a historical picture that posits distinctions, hierarchies, and causality in a commitment to political agency and action. Specifically, this critique is a rejection of bourgeois humanism, of universal rationality, and of the suppression of difference. It is also a refusal to accept the death of subjectivity, the endless proliferation of signs, and the celebration of commodity forces—the "anything goes" mentality. If these poles seem irreconcilable, it is, as Lefebvre suggests, because we need another, larger "reason"—and, more important, another practice.

I wish to thank Joan Ockman and Jean-Louis Cohen for their insightful criticism of an earlier version of this article.

THE EVERYDAY AND EVERYDAYNESS[1]

HENRI LEFEBVRE

TRANSLATED BY CHRISTINE LEVICH WITH
THE EDITORS OF YALE FRENCH STUDIES

Before the series of revolutions which ushered in what is called the modern era, housing, modes of dress, eating and drinking—in short, living—presented a prodigious diversity. Not subordinate to any one system, living varied according to region and country, levels and classes of the population, available natural resources, season, climate, profession, age, and sex. This diversity has never been well acknowledged or recognized as such; it has resisted a rational kind of interpretation which has only come about in our own time by interfering with and destroying that diversity. Today we see a worldwide tendency to uniformity. Rationality dominates, accompanied but not diversified by irrationality; signs, rational in their way, are attached to things in order to convey the prestige of their possessors and their place in the hierarchy.

FORMS, FUNCTIONS AND STRUCTURES

What has happened? There were, and there always have been forms, functions and structures. Things as well as institutions, "objects" as well as "subjects" offered up to the senses accessible and recognizable forms. People, whether individually or in groups, performed various functions, some of them physiological (eating, drinking, sleeping), others social (working, travelling). Structures, some of them natural and others constructed, allowed for the public or private performance of these functions, but with a radical—a root—difference: those forms, functions and structures were not known as such, not named. At once connected and distinct, they

1] This essay originally appeared as "Quotidien et Quotidienneté," in *Encyclopaedia Universalis*, vol. 13, ed. Claude Grégory (Paris: Encyclopaedia Universalis, 1972).

were part of an undifferentiated whole. Post-Cartesian analytic thought has often challenged these concrete "totalities": every analysis of objective or social reality has come up with some residue resisting analysis, and the sum of such realities as seemed irreducible by human thought became a matter for infinite analysis, a reserve of divine thought. Every complex "whole," from the smallest tool to the greatest works of art and learning, therefore possessed a symbolic value linking them to meaning at its most vast: to divinity and humanity, power and wisdom, good and evil, happiness and misery, the perennial and the ephemeral. These immense values were themselves mutable according to historical circumstance, to social classes, to rulers and mentors. Each object (an armchair just as much as a piece of clothing, a kitchen utensil as much as a house) was thus linked to some "style" and therefore, as a work, contained while masking the larger functions and structures which were integral parts of its form.

What happened to change the situation? The functional element was itself disengaged, rationalized, then industrially produced, and finally imposed by constraint and persuasion: that is to say, by means of advertising and by powerful economic and political lobbies. The relationship of form to function to structure has not disappeared. On the contrary, it has become a declared relationship, produced as such, more and more visible and readable, announced and displayed in a transparency of the three terms. A modern object clearly states what it is, its role and its place. This does not prevent its overstating or reproducing the signs of its meaningfulness: signs of satisfaction, of happiness, of quality, of wealth. From the modern armchair or coffee grinder to the automobile, the form-function-structure triumvirate is at once evident and legible.

Within these parameters, there come to be constructed multiple systems or subsystems, each establishing in its own way a more or less coherent set of more or less durable objects. For example, in the domain of architecture, a variety of local, regional, and national architectural styles has given way to "architectural urbanism," a universalizing system of structures and functions in supposedly rational geometric forms. The same thing is true of industrially produced food: a system groups products around various functionally specific household appliances such as the refrigerator, freezer, electric oven, etc. And of course the totalizing system that has been constructed around the automobile seems ready to sacrifice all of society to its dominion. It so happens that these systems and subsystems tend to deteriorate or blow out. Are even the days of car travel numbered?

Whatever the case may be, housing, fashion and food have tended and still tend to constitute autonomous subsystems, closed off from one another. Each of them appears to present as great a diversity as the old modes of living of the premodern era. This diversity is only apparent. It is only arranged. Once the dominant forces making it possible for these elements to combine with one another is understood, the artificial mechanism of their grouping is recognized and the fatuousness of their diversity becomes intolerable. The system breaks down.

All such systems have in common a general law of functionalism. The everyday can therefore be defined as a set of functions which connect and join together systems that might appear to be distinct. Thus defined, the everyday is a product, the most general of products in an era where production engenders consumption, and where consumption is manipulated by producers: not by "workers," but by the managers and owners of the means of production (intellectual, instrumental, scientific). The everyday is therefore the most universal and the most unique condition, the most social and the most individuated, the most obvious and the best hidden. A condition stipulated for the legibility of forms, ordained by means of functions, inscribed within structures, the everyday constitutes the platform upon which the bureaucratic society of controlled consumerism is erected.

A COMMON DENOMINATOR

The everyday is therefore a concept. In order for it to have ever been engaged as a concept, the reality it designated had to have become dominant, and the old obsessions about shortages—"Give us this day our daily bread..."—had to disappear. Until recently, things, furniture and buildings were built one by one, and each existed in relation to accepted moral and social references, to symbols. From the twentieth century onward, all these references collapse, including the greatest and oldest figure of them all, that of the Father (eternal or temporal, divine or human). How can we grasp this extraordinary and still so poorly understood configuration of facts? The collapse of the referent in morality, history, nature, religion, cities, space, the collapse even of perspective in its classical spatial sense or the collapse of tonality in music.... Abundance— a rational, programmed abundance and planned obsolescence—replacing shortage in the first world, destructive colonization of the third world and finally of nature itself.... The prevalence of signs, omnipresent war and violence, revolutions which follow one after another only to be cut short or to turn back against themselves....

The everyday, established and consolidated, remains a sole surviving common sense referent and point of reference. "Intellectuals," on the other hand, seek their systems of reference elsewhere: in language and discourse, or sometimes in a political party. The proposition here is to decode the modern world, that bloody riddle, according to the everyday.

The concept of everydayness does not therefore designate a system, but rather a denominator common to existing systems including judicial, contractual, pedagogical, fiscal, and police systems. Banality? Why should the study of the banal itself be banal? Are not the surreal, the extraordinary, the surprising, even the magical, also part of the real? Why wouldn't the concept of everydayness reveal the extraordinary in the ordinary?

REPETITION AND CHANGE

Thus formulated, the concept of the everyday illuminates the past. Everyday life has always existed, even if in ways vastly different from our own. The character of the everyday has always been repetitive and veiled by obsession and fear. In the study of the everyday we discover the great problem of repetition, one of the most difficult problems facing us. The everyday is situated at the intersection of two modes of repetition: the cyclical, which dominates in nature, and the linear, which dominates in processes known as "rational." The everyday implies on the one hand cycles, nights and days, seasons and harvests, activity and rest, hunger and satisfaction, desire and its fulfillment, life and death, and it implies on the other hand the repetitive gestures of work and consumption.

In modern life, the repetitive gestures tend to mask and to crush the cycles. The everyday imposes its monotony. It is the invariable constant of the variations it envelops. The days follow one after another and resemble one another, and yet—here lies the contradiction at the heart of everydayness—everything changes. But the change is programmed: obsolescence is planned. Production anticipates reproduction, production produces change in such a way as to superimpose the impression of speed onto that of monotony. Some people cry out against the acceleration of time, others cry out against stagnation. They're both right.

GENERAL AND DIVERSIFIED PASSIVITY

Common denominator of activities, locus and milieu of human functions, the everyday can also be analysed as the uniform aspect of the major sectors of social life: work, family, private life, leisure. These sectors, though distinct as forms, are imposed upon in their practice by a structure allowing us to discover what they share: organized passivity. This means, in leisure activities, the passivity of the spectator faced with images and landscapes; in the workplace, it means passivity when faced with decisions in which the worker takes no part; in private life, it means the imposition of consumption, since the available choices are directed and the needs of the consumer created by advertising and market studies. This generalized passivity is moreover distributed unequally. It weighs more heavily on women, who are sentenced to everyday life, on the working class, on employees who are not technocrats, on youth—in short on the majority of people—yet never in the same way, at the same time, never all at once.

MODERNITY

The everyday is covered by a surface: that of modernity. News stories and the turbulent affectations of art, fashion, and event veil without ever eradicating the everyday blahs. Images, the cinema and television divert the everyday by at times offering up to it its own spectacle, or sometimes the spectacle of the distinctly noneveryday; violence, death, catastrophe, the lives of kings and stars—those who we are led to believe defy everydayness. Modernity and everydayness constitute a deep structure that a critical analysis can work to uncover.

Such a critical analysis of the everyday has itself been articulated in several conflicting ways. Some treat the everyday with impatience; they want to "change life" and do it quickly; they want it all and they want it now! Others believe that lived experience is neither important nor interesting, and that instead of trying to understand it, it should be minimized, bracketed, to make way for science, technology, economic growth, etc.

To the former, we might reply that transforming the everyday requires certain conditions. A break with the everyday by means of festival—violent or peaceful—cannot endure. In order to change life, society, space, architecture, even the city must change. To the latter, we might reply that it is monstrous to reduce "lived experience," that a recognition of the inadequacy of pious humanism does not authorize the assimilation of people to insects. Given the colossal technical means at our disposal and the terrifying dangers which lie in wait for us, we would risk, in that case, abandoning humanism only to enter into "superhumanism."

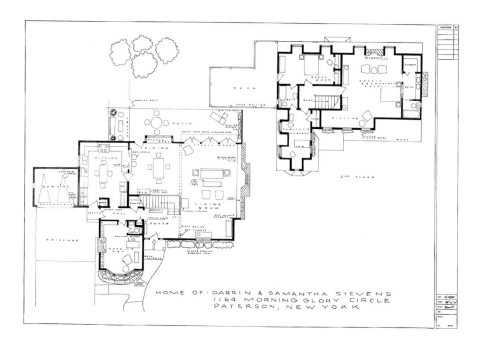

HOME OF: DARRIN & SAMANTHA STEVENS
1164 MORNING GLORY CIRCLE
PATERSON, NEW YORK

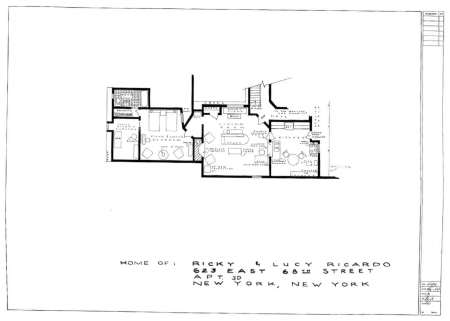

HOME OF: RICKY & LUCY RICARDO
623 EAST 68ᵀᴴ STREET
APT. 3D
NEW YORK, NEW YORK

MARK BENNETT

TOP: **HOME OF DARRIN & SAMANTHA STEVENS**, 1989-96. INK/PENCIL ON GRAPH VELLUM, 24" x 36".

BOTTOM: **HOME OF LUCY & RICKY RICARDO**, 1995. INK/PENCIL ON GRAPH VELLUM, 24" x 36".

INTIMATE (TELE)VISIONS

ERNEST PASCUCCI

Over the past thirty years or so, television has staged a number of unlikely everyday encounters between stars of situation comedies and buildings by star architects. Shortly after the completion of New York's Metropolitan Opera House at Lincoln Center in 1966, the building made its network television debut on the opening credits of *That Girl*. Wallace Harrison's building was upstaged by *That Girl*'s leading lady, who danced between the placards in front of the Opera House in the climactic scene of this fifty-second vignette. In September 1973, as *The Mary Tyler Moore Show* began its fourth season, the opening credits announced the malling of Minneapolis, replacing the outdoor location shots that lead up to Mary's famous toss of her blue hat with a thoroughly majestic image of Mary reaching the top of the escalator in Philip Johnson's IDS Center. Once again, television upstaged architecture. A full two months before Philip Johnson proudly presented his recently completed project as Minneapolis's new indoor downtown in *Architectural Forum*,[1] *The Mary Tyler Moore Show* enacted the transformation of downtown in front of a much larger audience than *Architectural Forum* could ever hope to attract.

From Archie Bunker's paranoid responses to the erosion of the once-solid white working-class enclave of Corona, Queens, to Rhoda's subway journey to the Bronx in her wedding dress, to David Letterman's nightly Times Square shenanigans that prefigured Disney redevelopment, television has assembled an immense and largely overlooked archive of architectural and urban representations. *That Girl*'s closing credits depict Marlo Thomas running along a

1] See Philip Johnson, "A There, There," *Architectural Forum* 140, no. 4 (November 1973): 38.

Hudson River pier launching a pink kite emblazoned with a trademark That Girl logo. As the aerial camera pulls away, it provides spectacular documentation of pre-Battery Park City lower Manhattan, thus unconsciously engaging in urban preservation.[2] Television's archive presents a markedly different history of architecture's so-called late modern and postmodern periods than is likely to be found in any published survey. Not only does television present architecture at its most everyday (city streets, apartment interiors, suburban homes, bars, diners, and offices), but television itself is arguably the most everyday medium of architectural representation, for its archive is broadcast directly into the home. The same spaces appear again and again, week after week, for the second time in summer reruns, ad infinitum in syndication, making it possible to grow up in someone else's home as easily as one's own.

While the television camera has frequently directed its gaze at architecture, architecture as a discipline has generally proven itself to be incapable of even looking at television. When architecture permits itself a glance, it tends to interpret television watching as escapist behavior that is symptomatic of a lost public deprived of face-to-face interpersonal encounters. For scholars armed with Frankfurt School theory seeking to recover a public realm they feel has been seriously eroded in the postwar era, television can only prevent people from engaging one another in conversation. In their parables of loss, the rise of television accompanies the decline of our metropolitan centers, effectively atomizing the public in isolated suburban homes.

This essay takes a critical look at the tendency to associate television with the death of public life as formulated in the influential writings of Richard Sennett and Kenneth Frampton in the '70s. From Sennett's diagnosis of "intimate vision" that impedes contemporary interpersonal relations to Frampton's more explicit denunciation of television as an "illusory public substitute," this strain of urban theory developed a televisual phobia that lingers in present-day architectural scholar-

2] Arguably, *That Girl*'s credits comprise one of the two great 1960s panoramas of New York City, the other being the *Panorama of the City of New York*, a 10,000 square-foot model of the five boroughs commissioned by Robert Moses for the New York City pavilion of the 1964 World's Fair. A few years ago, the *Panorama* was updated for its thirtieth anniversary. Thousands of piers, warehouses, and brownstones were lost. *That Girl*, by contrast, remains intact, and thirty years later its selective panorama of the city reveals itself to be an invaluable historical document.

ship. Earlier this year, in the introduction to *Architecture of Fear*, Nan Ellin dismissed the rebroadcasting of 1960s and '70s sitcoms on the Nickelodeon network's Nick at Nite as evidence of "the desire for familiarity—recalling one's own childhood or even someone else's—and the exhaustion of creative energies."[3] As a discipline, architecture needs to get over its pronounced fear of television. For one thing, such a phobia literally prevents scholars from looking at television's invaluable archive. But more trenchantly, this condescending refusal of television serves to reassure the discipline of one of its most cherished received ideas: that space is the absolute precondition for authentic public life, thus rendering those lives mediated by television somehow less authentic and somehow less than public. As someone whose suburban childhood coincided almost too well with the historic period that produced this blind spot regarding television, I find myself in the ideal position to refute each and every disparaging claim through my own personal relationship to television. Consider this flashback a polemical attempt to take back the '70s from architecture, to prevent architectural discourse from forcing us to live through any more public demises. We've suffered enough.

> Intimate vision is induced in proportion as the public domain is abandoned as empty.
> —Richard Sennett, *The Fall of Public Man*[4]

In 1974, *The Fall of Public Man* announced the decline of urban public life. With an archive of ideal public spheres spanning from Republican Rome to eighteenth-century Paris, the book directs its critique at contemporary New York, the city where public man has fallen. "Confusion has arisen between public and intimate life," Richard Sennett writes. "People are working out in terms of personal feelings public matters which properly can be dealt with only through codes of impersonal meaning" (5). In the absence of the logic

3] Nan Ellin, "Shelter from the Storm, or Form Follows Fear, and Vice-Versa," in *Architecture of Fear*, ed. Nan Ellin (New York: Princeton Architectural Press, 1997): 27.

4] Richard Sennett, *The Fall of Public Man* (1974; reprint New York: Vintage, 1978), 12. Numerals placed in parentheses in the text of this essay refer to page numbers in *The Fall of Public Man*.

of self-abstraction that formerly governed the public sphere, "the actor"—the public subject—finds himself "deprived of his art." Interpersonal relations thus succumb to "the tyrannies of intimacy"[5]—that is, "we have come to care about institutions and events only when we can discern personalities at work in them or embodying them"(338).

What has led to this compromised cultural condition? According to Sennett, modern psychology, psychoanalysis in particular. Ideally, it was supposed to enable people "to participate more fully and rationally in a life outside the boundaries of their own desires"—that is, to create good citizens. Instead, "masses of people are concerned with their single life-histories and particular emotions as never before; this concern has proved to be a trap rather than a liberation" (5).

This fallen psychological state is related to that mythic site that sociologists so often draw upon to sustain their pronouncements: "the city." The equation is direct for Sennett: "the forums for…public life, like the city, are in a state of decay" (4). A subsection of the introductory chapter, "Dead Public Space," locates the architectural analog to this hermetic psychological state among the postwar "International School skyscrapers" that rose up along New York's Park Avenue after the Second World War:

> Walls almost entirely of glass, framed with thin steel supports, allow the inside and the outside of a building to be dissolved to the least point of differentiation; this technology permits the achievement of what [Sigfried] Giedion calls the ideal of the permeable wall, the ultimate in visibility. But these walls are also hermetic barriers. Lever House was the forerunner of a design concept in which the wall, though permeable, also isolates the activities within the building from the life of the street. In this design concept, the aesthetics of visibility and social isolation merge (13).

5] The penultimate chapter of *The Fall of Public Man* is titled "The Actor Deprived of His Art," followed by the conclusion, "The Tyrannies of Intimacy."

The glass skyscraper becomes a metaphor for the hermetic individual, simultaneously transparent

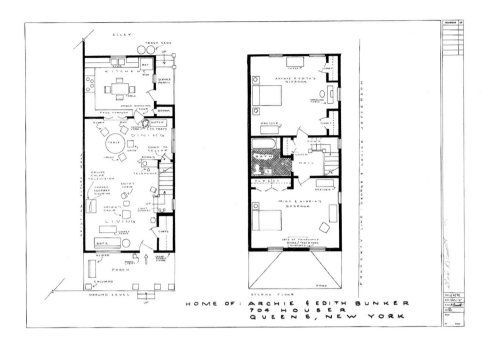

HOME OF: ARCHIE & EDITH BUNKER
704 HOUSER
QUEENS, NEW YORK

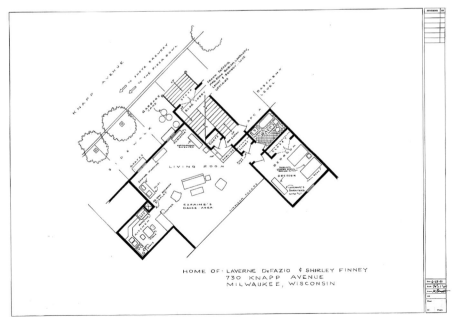

HOME OF: LAVERNE DeFAZIO & SHIRLEY FINNEY
730 KNAPP AVENUE
MILWAUKEE, WISCONSIN

MARK BENNETT

TOP: **HOME OF ARCHIE & EDITH BUNKER**, 1992–96. INK/PENCIL ON GRAPH VELLUM, 24" x 36".

BOTTOM: **HOME OF LAVERNE & SHIRLEY**, 1990–96. INK/PENCIL ON GRAPH VELLUM, 24" x 36".

and withdrawn—if it deigns to communicate with you, it confesses everything, forging an instant intimate relationship, telling you far more than you ever wanted to know. Private life threatens to erupt—inappropriately—into public life.

On a broader environmental level, modernism's systematic elimination of mixed-use streets, initiated by Haussmann in Second Empire Paris (297), has achieved its atomized apotheosis a century later in post-urban renewal New York. Sennett's dystopian historical present is a city of Lever Houses surrounded by physically and psychologically barricaded suburbs whose paranoid inhabitants vainly devote their energies toward a forced ideal of community that has already been destroyed. This new "uncivilized" society is marked by withdrawal from the city, fear of the city. Sennett concludes *The Fall of Public Man* with barbed irony: "In their nice, neat gardens, people speak of the horrors of London or New York; here in Highgate or Scarsdale one knows one's neighbors; true, not much happens, but life is safe. It is retribalization" (339).

Twenty-three years after Sennett isolated the problem of intimate vision, the anxieties that underwrite his diagnosis leap off the page. The title alone mourns the passing of the masculine urban subject, and despite the book's stated commitment to social diversity among urban populations, it privileges anonymous social relations among abstract public subjects. As Michael Warner has written, "the ability to abstract oneself in public has always been an unequally available resource," which provides the unmarked subject (the white, the male, the middle-class, the normal) with an unfair advantage.[6] What are we to make of a book announcing the decline of urban public life in 1974 that makes no mention of civil rights, the migration of rural southern blacks to large northern cities, women's liberation, and gay liberation? Twenty-three years after *The Fall of Public Man* retreated to a liberal bourgeois model of urban civility, its blind spots with regard to contemporary transformations in urban public life are painfully apparent.

6] See Michael Warner, "The Mass Public and the Mass Subject," in *The Phantom Public Sphere*, ed. Bruce Robbins (Minneapolis: University of Minnesota, 1993), 234–56.

On a more personal level, *The Fall of Public Man* reads a bit strangely precisely for the way that it situates me as a historical subject. For I am a product of retribalization. And I am a victim of intimate vision, induced in an abandoned public domain known as New Jersey. Life was safe for me there, a mere twenty miles from the city where Sennett formulated his analysis. Not much happened. I knew my neighbors, but not very well. My father sold ad space for *TV Guide*, and I grew up thinking it was natural and normal to have four copies of *TV Guide* in a household, or one *TV Guide* per family member. I still recall the shock of entering a friend's home to discover only one or, worse, no *TV Guide*. How could people live like this?

On occasion my sister Chris and I would be driven into Manhattan to see *The Wiz* or *Annie* or visit the dinosaurs at the Museum of Natural History. From the vantage point of a giant glass window on the twenty-eighth floor of 1290 Avenue of the Americas, where our father worked, we would lean over the metal vents and gaze across the glass and steel boxes of midtown, then down upon the Radio City Hall marquee. The view was much better on television.

My distinctly suburban childhood happened to coincide with a distinctly urban television program developed by the Children's Television Workshop for the Public Broadcast System that taught me how to count in Spanish. *Sesame Street* premiered on PBS in 1969 with a cast of adults, children, and pastel-colored muppets—that is, simultaneously racially mixed and racially abstract—who populated an inner-city neighborhood that revolved around Susan and Gordon's tenement stoop, Mr. Hooper's newsstand, Roosevelt Franklin's elementary school, Oscar the Grouch's garbage can, and Bert and Ernie's apartment (the program's only domestic interior). Patterned on pedagogical experiments that sought to incorporate the urban landscape into inner-city education, *Sesame Street* aired across the country (except where PBS affiliates refused to carry the controversial program), providing suburban children like myself with their first glimpse of the city.[7] The program emphasized the

7] See David Serlin, "The Commutative Black Property of Soul: Urban Education and Black Popular Culture in the 1970s," in *Soul: Black Power, Pleasure & Politics* (New York: New York University Press, 1997).

everyday bonds of community life with songs like "The People in Your Neighborhood":

> Who are the people in your neighborhood,
> in your neighborhood, in your neighborhood?
> Who are the people in your neighborhood?
> They're the people that you meet each day!

In the absence of such a recognizable neighborhood, television filled the void with spaces, characters, and contexts. Intimate relations were formed with people that I would meet each day—not on my street, but on my screen. My street was a nearly evacuated cul-de-sac in Franklin Lakes, New Jersey, my screen alive with possibilities. *Fabulous* possibilities.

My first knowledge of modern architecture and "the city" came through television. More specifically, through *Sesame Street* nearly every day, through Mary and Bob (on *The Mary Tyler Moore Show* and *The Bob Newhart Show*) every Saturday night, and through *That Girl*, which played in reruns on Channel 5. Every weekday morning throughout the summer I would await the train ride that brings That Girl into Manhattan, superimposes her face on its skyline, and delivers her to the glass and steel architecture and neon Broadway lights that are taken in through her wide eyes and gaping mouth. This was my introduction to New York as much as hers. It was inconceivable without her, without that relationship. An intimate relationship, a visual relationship, moreover a televisual relationship. A relationship that refutes Sennett's disparaging account of an evacuated public realm reduced to intimate vision.

Contrary to Sennett's diagnosis, these intimate (tele)visions were not inhibiting of proper interpersonal relations, but *enabling* of a subjectivity that I could barely recognize, a subjectivity that had no recognizable place in the "spaces of appearance" available to me. These intimate visions enacted a process of identification—queer in many senses of the term—that located its objects of desire on the television screen, among other places that are less easy for me to pin down. Spaces of appearance should remain elusive, despite architecture's tendency to assign distinct places to them.

Upon its publication, *The Fall of Public Man* struck a cultural nerve, exercising extraordinary influence across the intellectual left in the mid-'70s, eventually settling in the architectural academy. Aside from attaining canonic status as a classic of urban theory, *The Fall of Public Man* played a significant role in introducing Frankfurt School theory to architectural scholars in an easily assimilated form, given that the links to architecture's objects of study were already made. Sennett credits postwar Frankfurt School studies by Jürgen Habermas and Helmut Plessner for isolating "the problems of intimate vision" only to critique their relative lack of psychological depth (as compared to the work of Theodor Adorno and Max Horkheimer) that resulted in crude accounts of modern society's ills "couched in all the familiar catastrophic clichés of alienation, depersonalization, and the like."[8] Other Frankfurt School classics, namely Hannah Arendt's *The Human Condition* (1958) and Herbert Marcuse's *One-Dimensional Man* (1964), though never explicitly mentioned, clearly informed Sennett's analysis.

    The Fall of Public Man thus coincided with a moment in architectural thinking that drew inspiration from Arendt's notion of "the space of appearance."[9] In *The Human Condition*, Arendt derived the space of appearance as an always shifting site contingent upon situations and speech acts:

> Action and speech create a space between the participants which can find its proper location almost any time and anywhere. It is the space of appearance in the widest sense of the word, namely, the space

8] Sennet, *Public Man*, 31–32.

9] According to George Baird's schematic account of Arendt's reception, her reputation languished in the decade following her death in 1975, partially because her positions could not be easily assimilated into Marxist orthodoxy or the more dominant Frankfurt School theorists, even though her work is closely associated with the latter. Within architecture, Baird names himself and Frampton as the heirs of her ideas. See George Baird, *The Space of Appearance* (Cambridge, MA: MIT Press, 1995), 17–18 (esp. n. 25), 355–58. Baird notes of Sennett's work: "Insofar as the group of persons making up Sennett's public comprises strangers, it emphasizes 'heterogeneity' and 'anonymity' more explicitly than Arendt's does." (306).

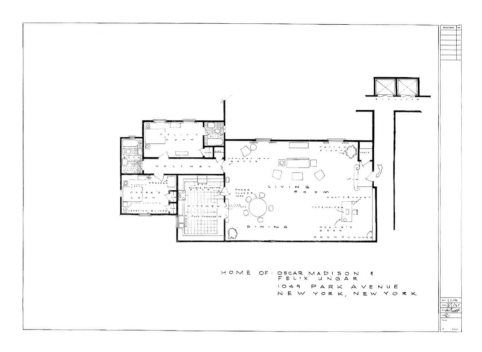

HOME OF: OSCAR MADISON &
FELIX UNGAR
1049 PARK AVENUE
NEW YORK, NEW YORK

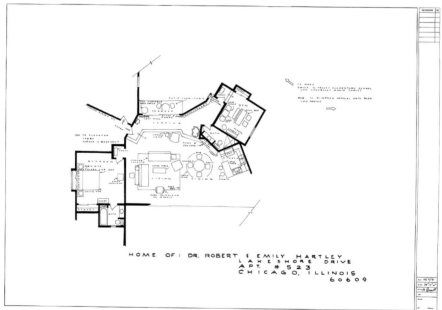

HOME OF: DR. ROBERT & EMILY HARTLEY
LAKESHORE DRIVE
APT. #523
CHICAGO, ILLINOIS
60609

MARK BENNETT

TOP: **HOME OF OSCAR MADISON & FELIX UNGER**, 1992–95. INK/PENCIL ON GRAPH VELLUM, 24" x 36".

BOTTOM: **HOME OF EMILY & BOB HARTLEY**, 1991–96. INK/PENCIL ON GRAPH VELLUM, 24" x 36".

where I appear to others as others appear to me, where men exist not merely like other living or inanimate things but make their appearance explicitly.[10]

Two years prior the publication to *The Fall of Public Man*, Kenneth Frampton delivered an essay, "The Status of Man and the Status of His Objects: A Reading of *The Human Condition*," in Arendt's presence that located specific typological reference points for the space of appearance.[11] In the talk, Frampton establishes that the *Oxford English Dictionary*'s two definitions of architecture—the first being "the art or science of constructing edifices for human use" and the second "the action and process of building"—parallel Arendt's distinction between "work" ("by definition *static, public*, and *permanent*") and "labor" ("inherently *processal, private, and impermanent*"). He then turns to the root of the word "edifice":

> The fact that the dictionary asserts that the word "edifice" may be used to refer to "a large and stately building such as a church, a palace, or a fortress" serves to support the work connotations of the first definition, since these building types, as the "representation" of spiritual and temporal power, have always been, at least until recent times, both public and permanent. Furthermore, the word "edifice" relates directly to the verb "to edify," which not only carries within itself the meaning "to build" but also "to educate," "to strengthen," and "to instruct"—connotations that allude directly to the political restraint of the public realm. Again the Latin root of this verb—*aedificare*, from *aedes*, a "building," or, even more originally, a "hearth," and *ficare*, "to make," has latent within it the public connotation of the hearth as the aboriginal "public" space of appearance.[12]

10] Hannah Arendt, *The Human Condition* (Chicago: University of Chicago Press, 1958), 198–99.

11] Baird, *The Space of Appearance*, 356, n. 25; The essay was published in 1979 as "The Status of Man and the Status of His Objects: A Reading of *The Human Condition*" in *Hannah Arendt and the Recovery of the Public Realm*, ed. Melvyn A. Hill (New York: St. Martin's Press, 1979), 101–30, and then republished in a compilation of Frampton's writings, *Modern Architecture and the Critical Present* (London: Architecture Design and Academy Editions, 1982), 6–19.

12] Frampton, "The Status of Man," in Hill, *Hannah Arendt*, 102–3.

What did it mean, in 1972 (and 1979 and 1982, when Frampton published and republished the talk), to recall the latent public meaning of the hearth and posit it as the foundational *public* space of appearance? It would seem that Frampton seeks here to trouble a facile distinction between public and private by locating the site of public discourse within the home, but his argument acquires a moralizing dimension as it zooms from aboriginal public space to the present:

> This aspect persists even today in the domestic realm, where surely no place is more a forum in the contemporary home than the hearth or its surrogate, the television set, which as an illusory public substitute tends to inhibit or usurp the spontaneous emergence of "public" discourse within the private domain.[13]

Just as Sennett would argue in the final pages of *The Fall of Public Man* that our cities possess a dormant potential to deliver us from our present uncivilized state, Frampton sees the contemporary home as a potential site for the spontaneous regeneration of public discourse—only that site has been robbed of its latent power by television, the "illusory public substitute," the bad object.

The architecture critic then turns his attention from the lost hearth to the lost agora, his target temporarily shifting from television to the automobile and its devastating effect of social atomization. Once again in this activist reading of *The Human Condition*, Frampton pushes Arendt's analysis toward contemporary referents in the American landscape to demonstrate how far our urban forms have strayed from this sanctioned ideal. "Arendt emphasizes, in contrast to our present proliferation of urban sprawl, the spontaneous 'cantonal' attributes of concentration."[14] Citing her assertion that "the living together of people" in the city is the most important material prerequisite for political organization,[15]

13] Ibid., 103.

14] Ibid., 102.

15] "The only indispensible material factor in the generation of power is the living together of people. Only where men live close together that the potentialities for action are always present will power remain with them and the foundation of cities, which as city states have remained paradigmatic for all Western political organization, is therefore indeed the most important material prerequisite for power." Arendt, *The Human Condition*, 201; quoted in Frampton, "The Status of Man," 103.

Frampton claims that "Nothing could be further from this than our present generation of motopia and our evident incapacity to create new cities that are physically and politically identifiable as such."[16] Continuing, Frampton targets sloganeering planners like Melvin Webber and Robert Venturi. Webber had propagated such aphorisms as "community without propinquity" and the "nonplace urban realm" that, according to Frampton, "devised to rationalize the absence of any adequate realm of public appearance within modern suburbia."[17] For his part, Venturi willingly espoused "apolitical" ideologies that dismissed efforts to create new public squares as so much "piazza compulsion." "Americans feel uncomfortable sitting in a square," Venturi wrote six years earlier in Complexity and Contradiction in Architecture. "They should be working at the office or home with the family looking at television."[18] For Frampton, "These and similar reactionary modes of beholding seem to emphasize the impotence of an urbanized populace who have paradoxically lost the object of their urbanization."[19]

Frampton's statement is but one of many declarations of loss—loss of the city, loss of a sense of place, loss of a critical role for architects to play in the contemporary American city—operative in Frankfurt School-inflected architectural criticism of the mid-'70s.[20] Frampton would repeat the phrase nearly verbatim—"the impotence of an urbanized populace which has paradoxically lost the object of its urbanization"—as late as 1983 in a version of "Towards a Critical Regionalism."[21] Like Sennett's critique of intimate vision,

16] Frampton, "The Status of Man," 103.

17] Ibid.

18] Robert Venturi, Complexity and Contradiction in Architecture (New York: Museum of Modern Art, 1966), 133.

19] Frampton, "The Status of Man," 103.

20] Two additional examples will suffice. Reacting to a wave of urban redevelopment schemes destined "to enrich only the archives of public agencies," Manfredo Tafuri cynically pronounced New York (or at least the New York architecture world) a "new Venice" wherein "the loss of identity is made an institution" and "the maximum formalism of its structures gives rise to a code of behavior dominated by 'vanity' and 'comedy.'" See Manfredo Tafuri, "The Ashes of Jefferson," [1976/ 1980] The Sphere and the Labyrinth (Cambridge, MA: MIT Press, 1990), 291. Throughout the 1970s, Tafuri repeatedly advanced criticisms of the New York Five for their collective lapse into a self-referential formalism that could only produce a "cardboard" architecture of "private" intellectual pleasures, but not an architecture of any "social value." See "L'architecture dans le boudoir," Oppositions 3 (fall 1974); "European Graffiti: Five x Five = Twenty-five," Oppositions 5 (summer 1976): 35-74; and "The Ashes of Jefferson," in The Sphere and the Labyrinth, 291–303.

From an entirely different (phenomenological) perspective but at the same moment, Christian Norberg-Schulz decried the "loss of place" in urban development following the second world war. In Genius Loci: Towards a Phenomenology of Architecture (1980), two of his three illustrated examples of the contemporary condition of placelessness come from the United States: "Visual chaos, USA," a roadside gas station dominated by billboards; and Mies van der Rohe's Federal Center in Chicago. His rhetoric, meanwhile, comes straight out of Kevin Lynch's The Image of the City (Cambridge, MA: MIT Press, 1960): "Nodes, paths, and districts lose their identity," Norberg-Schulz wrote of the detrimental effects of postwar urbanism, "and the town as a whole loses its imageability." See Christian Norberg-Schulz, Genius Loci: Towards a Phenomenology of Architecture (New York: Rizzoli, 1980), 189–90.

21] Kenneth Frampton, "Towards a Critical Regionalism: Six Points for an Architecture of Resistance," in The Anti-Aesthetic: Essays in Postmodern Culture, ed. Hal Foster (Port Townsend, WA: Bay Press, 1983), 25.

Frampton's pronouncement hits a little too close to home for me. For I count myself among those impotent, urbanized subjects who have lost the object of their urbanization. Yet—paradoxically—my object of urbanization was never lost, though I would never claim to have "had" it in the first place. It was always present on my television screen *as urban experience,* and it provided hours of active fantasizing.

My suburban childhood—that is, the time in life when I watched the most television—coincided almost too well with television's belated golden age, an era when single women traversed the avenues of great American cities week after week on the opening credits to television sitcoms like *That Girl* and *The Mary Tyler Moore Show.*[22] I used to consider these exercises in cross-identification—these overwhelming urges to *be* That Girl, the woman who has Lincoln Center all to herself almost the day after it is built—as my own private little fetishes. Nobody else heard the theme song to *The Mary Tyler Moore Show* playing in their mind's soundtrack when they wandered aimlessly in public. It was just my fantasy. And although the influential writings of Jean Baudrillard and Theodor Adorno and the Situationist critiques of everyday life that I read in college in the late '80s convinced me that my behavior was escapist, they couldn't quite deprive me of escapism's pleasures.

No, it was not until Sunday, June 28, 1992, the day of New York City's annual Gay Pride Parade that I realized that this fantasy of inhabiting the city as That Girl (or Mary, or even Rhoda on my less fabulous days) was hardly private, but always latently public. Running to the head of the parade with my childhood best friend, we happened upon the grand marshalls, Phil Donahue and Marlo Thomas, stars of *Donahue* and *That Girl,* respectively. The pioneering daytime talk show host and the pioneering single urban woman on television, husband and wife walking hand in hand, represented two distinct and pervasive models of gay subjectivity. In the '70s, Phil Donahue prodded a generation of misfits to articulate its symptoms on national television. A decade earlier, in front of the Metropolitan Opera with a parasol in one hand and a placard for a dance partner,

22] For an analysis of the single woman on television from the years 1966 to 1976, see my essay, "This City Belongs to That Girl," *ANY* 12 (1995): 50–59.

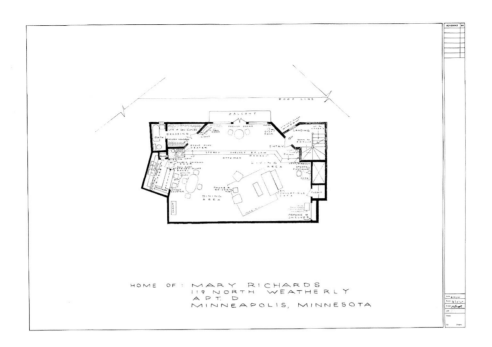

HOME OF: MARY RICHARDS
119 NORTH WEATHERLY
APT. D
MINNEAPOLIS, MINNESOTA

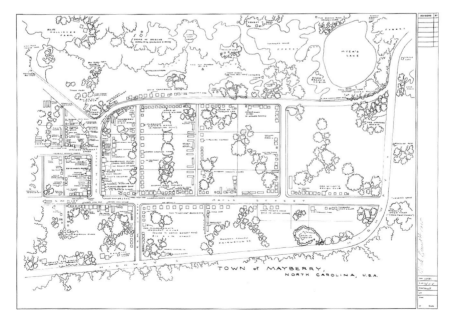

TOWN OF MAYBERRY,
NORTH CAROLINA, U.S.A.

MARK BENNETT

TOP: **HOME OF MARY RICHARDS,** 1995. INK/PENCIL ON GRAPH VELLUM, 24" x 36".

BOTTOM: **TOWN OF MAYBERRY,** 1989–95. INK/PENCIL ON GRAPH VELLUM.

Marlo Thomas taught a generation how to enjoy its symptom. Everyone along the parade route called out to her. Her right arm waved a big, continuous, fabulous wave.

An atomized, mass-mediated public raised on intimate (tele)-visions—the "me" generation that took in the city through television, watching That Girl traverse the same streets week after week in the '60s, day after day in reruns in the '70s, night after night on Nick at Nite in the '80s and '90s—fused into one temporary, beautiful collective of happy, self-proclaimed fags and dykes calling out to the star of That Girl along Washington Square North. A very real place. A very real experience. But the fact that these fantasies found their expression in a public place is not what made them real. For me, this collective coming out, occasioned by Marlo Thomas of all people, proved far more satisfying than my somewhat tortured coming out as a gay man a few years earlier. It really wasn't just about being queer, or being fabulous, or fabulously queer—though the two often go hand in hand—or even about taking the city back, but all of these things simultaneously. And something more. This eruption of a collective queer unconscious focused many different fantasies upon one well-broadcast object, one that suggested so many more. It wasn't just my closet door bursting open that day, but everyone's: a whole televised archive of streets we walked and houses we haunted in our own searches for ways to be queer that were unavailable to us on the streets we walked and in the houses where we lived. A temporary, though hardly impotent social formation paradoxically found the object of its urbanization—or, better, its space of appearance, which, as Arendt reminds us, "can find its proper location almost any time and anywhere"—on television, the last place that architectural theory would ever think to look.

CATFISH AND COLTRANE:

A CONVERSATION ABOUT

MAKING A HOMESITE

PETER TOLKIN AND MABEL O. WILSON

JOHN OUTTERBRIDGE

HOMESITE

In the South, people often call home, the place where one grows up, the origin of family roots, the homesite. At reunions, the homesite is the place for family gatherings, fish fries in the yard, and late night "do you remember when" sessions on the front porch.

Homesites can travel like people and packages. Any place where objects of remembrance are collected—model ships, family photographs—or rituals of everyday life are practiced—cooking fried catfish from old recipes, making lye soap—can provide spiritual entrée back to one's homesite.

UNCLE JOHN

John Outterbridge—artist, photographer, poet, blues flutist, and builder—grew up in the racially segregated American South of the 1930s and '40s. In spite of an absence of material wealth, his parents passed on to him and his seven siblings other precious gifts like a vital yearning for self-expression, and nurtured in each a rich poetic imagination. It was through his parents that he learned the art of improvisation—makin' do by makin' things. His mother Olivia made a living as a laundress. As an adept seamstress, she sewed clothes for her family and others, fashioned dolls out of old rags, and crafted quilts from leftover scraps of fabric. A multifaceted talent, Olivia could weave magic out of words as a poet and poeticize song as an accomplished pianist. His father, John Ivory, hauled goods and debris around town in his Model-T truck. From discarded

TOP LEFT: **MAIN GALLERY SPACE, VIEW TOWARD ENTRY HALL AND KITCHEN, SLEEPING LOFT ABOVE**

TOP RIGHT: **JOHN OUTTERBRIDGE'S STUDIO, EXTERIOR VIEW, LOS ANGELES, CALIFORNIA**

MIDDLE LEFT: **MAIN GALLERY SPACE OPPOSITE VIEW**

MIDDLE RIGHT: **BACK ("DEN") ROOM TOWARD MAIN GALLERY SPACE**

BOTTOM LEFT: **KITCHEN ENTRY FROM MAIN GALLERY**

BOTTOM RIGHT: **BATHROOM**

objects—vacuum tubes, motors, encasements, switches, relays, knobs, belts, and such—he refurbished and reassembled washing machines, engines, and radios. Always tinkering, John Ivory invented toys and gadgets from found parts, and these would dazzle and beguile neighborhood children. Their home was always alive with activity. Constantly buzzing in and around the house were aunties, uncles, teachers, and friends whose various talents in craft, music, art, and song, added mirth and optimism to a laborious existence in an impoverished, racist South. This culturally rich community in coastal North Carolina fostered the artistic talents of John Outterbridge, whose work echoes the sensibility common to folk art throughout the South, with found objects gathered and reformed into artful works.

At the American Academy of Art in Chicago in the 1950s, John Outterbridge fused the artistic sensibility of his youth with his formal training as an artist. Leaving Chicago, he and his wife moved to Los Angeles, where he would become a highly respected community activist and director of the Watts Tower Arts Center. In 1991 he resigned his municipal position to focus on his art. Since then he has lived in a refurbished warehouse in South Central Los Angeles.

VESSEL

Just off of a main avenue in South Central Los Angeles, behind a public medical clinic, surrounded by industrial buildings, two doors down from a row of single family houses, sits a small gray "light industrial" building. Is this neighborhood a mixed-use zone, or an unplanned, residual territory resulting from postwar attempts to put everybody and everything in its place?

Tacked to the light-aqua door, a primary-colored, diamond-shaped sign emblazoned with the letter *A* stands for something official: Artist. To the uninformed, the *A* could also stand for Architect, Architecture, African, American, Anything. The rather mundane gray exterior tells very little about the richness of life inside. This is the home/workspace of John Outterbridge.

CATFISH AND COLTRANE

As we sat dining with Mabel's Uncle John in the rear of his studio, luscious riffs of John Coltrane, emanating from the front gallery, mingled with the pungent flavors of our fried catfish (a sort of aural and gastronomic improvisation). Our conversation meandered from fishing in Los Angeles to hunting for materials in scrap yards, from the ethics of making to early morning walks, from junk shops and old stoves to family and love.

Much of what we discussed focused on Uncle John's ongoing project of transforming the warehouse into a residence/studio/gallery to accommodate his life as a public artist. At the front of the building, purchased a few years ago, is a hall that serves as a small gallery, an adjoining bathroom, and a bedroom loft above. The next section contains a vast, triple-height space subdivided into a large gallery that is sandwiched between the kitchen and garage. At the rear of the building is a workshop and den-like room for eating. By constructing new walls, infilling existing walls with corrugated aluminum and steel panels, and renovating the bathroom and kitchen with old appliances and thrift store cabinetry, he has fashioned a live/work space that serves as a place to make and display his art as well as the works of others.

> To build the rationale of a space is like building a piece of art...it's like putting together your life, it's an ongoing situation.
> John Outterbridge

MAKIN' THINGS

Uncle John's works are created from discarded objects, improvisations in form and feeling. This logic can be seen to extend to the larger environment of the interior of his live/work space, where the interventions made into what is perhaps a fairly common wood-trussed warehouse structure are made with the same sensibilities as reflected in the works on its walls. From this activity emerges a shaky, "unstable" theory of architecture based on what is available, what is at hand, what you can, salvage,

scavenge, dig up, find. Inexpensive materials, but ones that are nevertheless rich with deeply rooted meaning. Accretions of rust, oxidation,
scratches, indentations, discolorations, and frayed edges divulge the rich
histories of these found treasures.

In many ways, the space evokes the improvisatory structures of
jazz; actively in process, in performance. A contingent space—progra-
matically and formally—the studio has a complex mix of uses, some private, others public. A tension between these two realms, public and
private, emerges as signs of everyday life envelope the art on the walls of
the main gallery. Above the space, where a rectangular aluminum wall
relief hangs, a vent stack snakes from the hot water heater enclosure. On
all sides of the main gallery, openings—a sliding barn door, metal window, and open-web trusses—puncture the walls, allowing domestic life
to seep into the public space of the art gallery. In turn, art is found within
those spaces of everyday life, and relationships are created between that
space and objects of daily use. In the bathroom, for example, an abstract
painting and a figurative wall relief hang between bathrobes and towels.
In front of the bathroom entrance, an altar-like sculpture made of an old
kettle that holds chunks of lye soap echoes a ceramic vessel containing a
mound of blue soaps placed on a bathroom bureau. As totems, both
evoke memories of home brewed soaps, remedies, and cleansers.

> In the tradition of materials, there are certain ones that qual-
> ify themselves in particular ways. Material "stuff " has lan-
> guage: it's historical, and says a lot about our society and the
> waste we create. I often go into thrift stores looking for old
> rags. I can smell the spirit of a rag, where it has been, who
> forgot it, who discarded it. I think about how it will help me
> "spin" my own language of making. I also reflect upon how
> it, as material, is a remembrance thing. Old rags make me
> think about the boxes of clothes my Aunt Clementine who
> lived in and around Harlem and was a missionary of the
> streets, used to send us from New York.

JOINTS

Uncle John fashions joints that are somewhat akin to a transitional jazz riff between bassist and horn, an improvised bridge between two sounds, two materials. On the torso of a tall figural sculpture, In Search of The Missing Mule, bolts straddling a seam become buttons rhythmically stitching together rusted, patchwork panels. Below the water heater cabinet in his kitchen is a stainless steel sink and countertop, a "combine," constructed of inexpensive retail stock items. What separates this assemblage of items from an ordinary "do it yourself" home project are the self-conscious traces of the maker. The sink surround is comprised of two different counter tops of the same plastic laminate laid over particle board. A formica sill knits together the composition. A joint formed between the simulated wood grain and the faux marble is embellished by an irregular arrangement of five large screws: three on the right, only two on the left. Why? A message about symmetry and number, or perhaps a pragmatic response to something unseen under the counter?

Near the kitchen doorway, a turquoise, half-moon shaped rug forms another sort of joint. In this instance, the joint is a threshold that seams together two surfaces, the kitchen's navy floor and the main gallery's bare concrete. The rug infuses a domestic scale into the public realm of the gallery. Upstairs, in a bedroom corner, the intersection of a truss, a beam, and a corrugated metal wall patch creates a kind of a spatial joint-cum altar. Nested within this composition of rusted steel and bolts, surrounded by a pile of magazines and books, is a family photo in a soft red satin frame—a joint between architecture and memory.

WALLS

Aside from the exterior walls, which work to contain life inside, the mutable interior walls transcend the normative use of walls as traditional separators of space. The studio, however, is not configured in an open plan. Paradoxically, interior walls define and enclose distinct spaces, while allowing for a spatial porosity—space passes over, around, on top of, and through walls. Behind the 8-foot-tall north gallery wall, for exam-

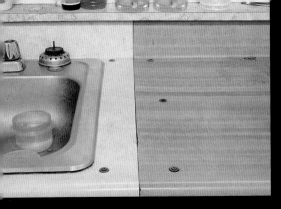

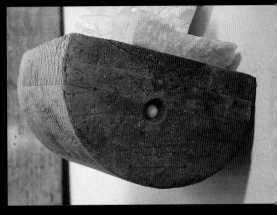

TOP LEFT: **KITCHEN SINK**

TOP RIGHT: **VIEW THROUGH ROOF TRUSS BETWEEN SLEEPING LOFT AND GALLERY**

MIDDLE LEFT: **CORNER DETAIL SLEEPING LOFT**

MIDDLE RIGHT: **WOODEN MALLET HEAD WITH SOAP**

BOTTOM LEFT: **DETAIL OF TORSO, "IN SEARCH OF THE MISSING MULE"**

BOTTOM RIGHT: **WORK-SHOP AREA**

ple, is the kitchen, which contains the sink, a water heater strapped to the corner in a wooden box, a stove, a washing machine, and a dryer, (the refrigerator is in a den-like room at the very rear of the building.) This wall has a double function: on the gallery side of the wall, with its rough coat of plaster (rougher than found in most commercial galleries where walls are supposed to be neutral backdrops on which to display art.) there hangs or leans finished work and work-in-progress. On the other side of this gallery wall, the exposed wood studs, painted white, literally become the shelves of a large, if thin, open pantry where spices and other kitchen condiments are stored. At this juncture, a $^5/8$ inch section of dry-wall separates the trappings of daily life from art—a jar of burnt-orange chili powder sits back-to-back with a rusted-steel wall relief; a tall spirit-conjuring scarecrow adorned with a rag and hollow gourds peeks over the gallery wall near the washing machine and dryer. In a similar gesture of juxtaposition, blackened steel panels skin the upper portion of the west wall of the gallery and frame the upper bedroom's casement window. In this play of architectural elements, the banal window, white wall, and bow truss metamorphosize. Perhaps the question of whether this fusing is art or architecture is immaterial. It is simply about the process of becoming rather than the thing itself—improvisation.

I've been in this building for such a short period of time. I'm still confronting how it will function and support itself, beyond facilitating my own particular needs as an artist. The creative process might be viewed as art or rather an art making process. If you practice art or other disciplines in the arts, you discover that what we often say that art is, is absolutely untrue. Art is a process, it has the audacity to be anything that it needs to be at any time. It is never elitist. If we subtract art from our social arrangement there is not very much left at all—architecture, the environment, becomes bereft. The essence of spirit is sacrificed, and all things meaningful diminish. Creative expression is the pulse of our lives. This is how I feel about art.

SOAP

Throughout Uncle John's home various constructions invoke the ritual of bathing and recall those processes around, conversations about, and recipes on the brewing of soaps, home remedies, and cleansers. The front gallery has a small, waist-high stand upon which sits a black iron pot with offerings, bits of lye soap, an altar to the ancestors—those "root" women who fashioned home brews. Broken chunks of homemade soap enwrap the head of a long, lithe mallet hanging in the main gallery near the sliding door to the workshop. Atop the bathroom bureau sits a green ceramic vessel holds an inviting mound of blue soaps. This offering gestures you to pick up a rubbed down bar and slowly, soothingly massage your hands under a cool stream of water. Another altar of remembrance?

The walls, joints, windows, and totems speak to one another across the space of the studio and connect to your own memories of things, peoples, and past homesites.

> I don't create art so much from an academic posture, I do art as a source of recall, as a source of my, shall I invent a word, "tributary." I build altars celebrating the remembrance of the things that have been kind to our sensibilities. . . . I build things because of the way I feel about living. I collect materials because of how they have been associated or identified over time. I used to go into old junkyards on Alameda Street. In these places the things almost speak out to you: telling how they have been used, who they meant something to. . . . I use found materials because it's a way of saying something about our social texture and political tonality. I bring these materials into my own personal arena, so I can share them with other people. So that when children and elderly visitors come through here there's something of a "remembrance nature" present, something that stimulates conversation. Some of the elders that come see an old pot with soap exclaim, "Where'd you get that old pot Mr. Outterbridge?! It reminds me of..."

GREGORY CREWDSON

UNTITLED, 1993

GREGORY CREWDSON

UNTITLED, 1991

OMOIDE NO SHOTOKYO:

REMEMBERING OLD LITTLE TOKYO

SHEILA LEVRANT DE BRETTEVILLE

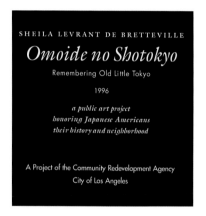

PLAQUE AT ENTRY TO PROJECT.

In 1990, the Community Redevelopment Agency of Los Angeles released a request for proposals to improve East First Street in the downtown area known as Little Tokyo. I saw an opportunity for a project that would transform 1,500 linear feet of sidewalk to show something of both the lives of the people who live there and the history of their community. I hoped that an acknowledgment of the past and present life of Little Tokyo would give public presence and permanence to its everyday gestures. I also hoped that public recognition of the greed and racism that almost destroyed Little Tokyo could make these kinds of acts more extraordinary, in the sense of rare. Seeing this common concrete sidewalk become extraordinary could enable people to "listen" to the rich and complex history of this seemingly ordinary street.

Although the east side of East First Street was designated a historic district in the late 1980s, its "history from below" remained unarticulated. I imagined that passers–by would be drawn onto the east side of the street, attracted by a multicolored concrete sidewalk glistening with inlaid brass, and texts and images in stainless steel. Once there, pedestrians could construct for themselves an understanding of this center of Los Angeles's large and dispersed Japanese-American community.

The texts and images imbedded into the concrete pavement were oriented to be read while facing the buildings, inviting viewers to encounter the old buildings and the stories they contain. Durable stainless steel was used to represent events enacted against people of Japanese descent in order to indicate the perseverance of nativistic racism. Brass was chosen for the outlines of images and for all other texts (including neighborhood history and quoted memories); when a local resident pointed out to me that the brass was likely to tarnish, I explained that it would remain bright so long as people walked on the sidewalk, buffing it inadvertently.

A timeline runs along the building edge to signify the continuity of the Japanese-American experience of this street, and is divided into six bands describing the individual decades from the 1890s through the 1940s. In front of each doorway, information is given about the building's history and changing uses. Inscribed between the doorways are some of the facts, events, and laws that shaped the lives of the people in this neighborhood. The northern and southern endpoints of the project—Union Church and the Nishi Hongwanji Buddhist Temple—are marked with Japanese kanji characters reading "Omoide no Shotokyo," or "Remembering Old Little Tokyo."

In developing this project, I arranged meetings and talked with issei, nissei, and sansei (first, second, and third generation Japanese-Americans) and asked them about their memories of everyday life on this street and what they would like future generations to remember of it. Certain subjects recurred through the interviews: the importance of community associations; music and other cultural activities; new and traditional foods; the need for communicating with others who speak the same language; child care; and the relation between family and commercial life. By selecting a range of quotations from the people interviewed, I tried to show something of the differences between the generations and the contradictory, multiple identities that make up this community.

LEFT: **THE AUTHOR WITH STEVE ORTIZ WHO, WITH EIGHT COWORKERS, POURED CONCRETE IN THE BLAZING HOT LOS ANGELES SUN.**

BELOW: **NISEI ARCHIE MIYATAKE STATED: "IMMIGRANTS WANTED TO HAVE A COMMU- NITY WHERE THEY COULD FEEL COMFORTABLE WITH THEIR NATIVE TONGUE."**

FACING PAGE: **THIS YOUNG FAMILY PASSES A GROUP OF TEXTS DESCRIBING THE STORY OF YASUJIRO KAWASAKI. IMMEDIATELY BEHIND THE TIMELINE IS THE BUILDING KAWASAKI PUR- CHASED IN HIS DAUGHTERS' NAMES IN 1913. INSCRIBED IN THE SIDEWALK IS INFORMATION ABOUT THE LAW OF THAT SAME YEAR THAT PREVENTED KAWASAKI FROM OWNING THE PROPERTY.**

I learned—as I hope pedestrians on the streets of Little Tokyo will learn—a great deal about the Japanese-American experience. Never-theless, one might ask, as I did when I was first interviewed by the community committee overseeing the project, if it is appropriate for a person not of Japanese descent to interpret the history of East First Street. The answer I received was that the community did not want to ghettoize knowledge of its place, its history, and the lives of its people.

913 California uses Alien Land Act to keep Japanese nationals from owning land

1922 Union Church is built as a religious and cultural center.

1942 Families awaiting detention gather here.

BUILDINGS' HISTORIES ARE PLACED IN FRONT OF THEIR DOORS. FACTS AND LAWS ARE WRITTEN BETWEEN
DOORWAYS. QUOTATIONS ARE IN ITALIC. MARKS INDICATING THE SPEAKERS' GENERATION AS A JAPANESE-
AMERICAN FOLLOW THEIR NAMES IN KANJI CHARACTERS. POSITIVE EVENTS ARE INSCRIBED IN BRASS
LETTERING; DISCRIMINATORY ACTS, SUCH AS THE 1942 DEPORTATIONS OF JAPANESE-AMERICANS TO INTERN-
MENT CAMPS, ARE IN STAINLESS STEEL.

FACING PAGE, TOP LEFT: BELOW THE CONTINUOUS TIME BAND ARE BRASS-OUTLINED IMAGES FILLED WITH
COLORED CONCRETE. I WAS TOLD BY FORMER RESIDENTS OF THE STREET THAT TRUNKS USED BY THE FIRST
GENERATION OF IMMIGRANTS WERE USED AGAIN WHEN RESIDENTS WERE FORCED TO MOVE TO THE
DETENTION CAMPS.

1905 Manaka Restaurant

1913 Yasujiro Kawasaki buys this property in his Nisei daughters' names.

1937 Kawasaki opens Matsu-no Sushi

1942 U.S. Executive Order 9066 forces all Nikkei out of their homes and into internment camps at Amache, CA, Acom, Heart Mountain, Manzanar...

JAMES CASEBERE

DESERT HOUSE WITH CACTUS, 1980

UGLY AND ORDINARY:

THE REPRESENTATION OF THE EVERYDAY

DEBORAH FAUSCH

Objectivism constitutes the social world as a spectacle presented to an observer who takes up a "point of view" on the action, who stands back so as to observe it and, transferring into the object the principles of his relation to the object, conceives of it as a totality intended for cognition alone, in which all interactions are reduced to symbolic exchanges. This point of view is the one afforded by high positions in the social structure, from which the social world appears as a representation (in the sense of idealist philosophy but also as used in painting or in the theatre) and practices are no more than "executions," stage parts, performances of scores, or the implementing of plans.

—Pierre Bourdieu, *Outline of a Theory of Practice*[1]

"Ugly and ordinary," thus Gordon Bunshaft and Philip Johnson labeled Robert Venturi and Denise Scott Brown's 1967 Brighton Beach Housing Competition entry, a project whose contextual massing and conventional facades surprised and offended those on the competition jury expecting to review revolutionary modern megastructures. Taking the insult for a compliment, Venturi and Scott Brown adapted "ugly and ordinary" as a code phrase for their attempts to incorporate the forms, data, and communication structures of postwar America into their architectural theory and practice.[2]

1] Pierre Bourdieu, *Outline of a Theory of Practice* (1972; reprint, Cambridge: Cambridge University Press, 1977), 96.

2] Philip Johnson, "Jury Report," in *Record of Submissions and Awards, Competition for Middle Income Housing at Brighton Beach* (New York: Housing and Development Agency, 1968). The phrase was perhaps also an echo of the title of Alison and Peter Smithson's book *Ordinariness and Light* (Cambridge, MA: MIT Press, 1970).

The idea of "ugly and ordinary" was put to multiple use in their written and designed work of the 1960s and '70s. In *Learning from Las Vegas*, Venturi, Scott Brown and Steven Izenour commented: "Architecture may be ordinary—or rather, conventional—in two ways: in how it is constructed or in how it is seen, that is, in its process or in its symbolism. To construct conventionally is to use ordinary materials and engineering, accepting the present and usual organization of the building industry and financial structure and hoping to ensure fast, sound, and economical construction."[3] Venturi and Scott Brown imitated the forms they found along the roadside commercial strip and in the night lights of Las Vegas, borrowing from these nonarchitectural sources of imagery and spatial organization in the MERBISC Mart in California City (1970), the Best Products Catalog Showroom (1977), the ISI Corporation Headquarters (1978), and the BASCO Showroom (1979). Guild House (1961) and the Brighton Beach Housing Competition adapted conventional or vernacular housing types to suit their urban contexts. From the Vanna Venturi House (1961) and the Guild House emerged the idea of the ordinary window as a conveyor of conventional messages of domestic scale. The Trubek and Wislocki Houses (1970) improvised on the traditional New England house in a sophisticated play on vernacular facades and the balloon frame, treating frame construction as a kind of vernacular for modern architecture.[4]

In parallel with this examination of the forms of the ordinary, Venturi and Scott Brown concerned themselves with ordinary activities—the "average person" going about daily life. Planning projects such as the Philadelphia Crosstown Community Study (1968) and the plan for Alameda, California (1972), they based their proposals on the needs of these places' inhabitants. The public spaces of Venturi and Scott Brown's academic and museum buildings, such as Gordon Wu Hall at Princeton University (1980), reconfigured, at public scale, Alison and Peter Smithson's residential street-in-the-air (an idea with a two-fold source in Le Corbusier's *rue intérieure* and soci-

3] Robert Venturi, Denise Scott Brown, and Steven Izenour, *Learning from Las Vegas: The Forgotten Symbolism of Architectural Form* (Cambridge, MA: MIT Press, 1972; rev. ed. Cambridge, MA: MIT Press, 1977), 85.

4] George Hersey, interview with the author, Guilford, CT, 19 August 1996.

ologists' perceptions of the street as the locus for unplanned, everyday activities). Finally, their insistence that architecture's meanings be understood by ordinary persons led them to focus on association—the idea that buildings communicate to their users within an everyday universe of commonly-held ideas—as the basis both for the creation and the perception of architecture.

The everyday resists theorizing. Venturi and Scott Brown's wide-ranging but incompletely systematized search for a means both to represent and to act within the everyday world of postwar America frustrated their contemporaries with its mixing of theoretical proposition and formal composition. Manfredo Tafuri complained about *Complexity and Contradiction*:

> Venturi does, of course, make many perceptive observations on the structures of complex architectural organisms, uncovering their less evident cultural matrices. What we criticize is: on one side, the failed historicisation of architectural ambiguity, that becomes, therefore, an *a priori* category with only generic meanings; on the other, the conclusions of his research that, through historiographical flattening and confusion between analyses and planning methods, manages to justify personal figurative choices.... Venturi's book employs "fashionable" analytical methods, turning them, without any mediation, into "compositive" methods. In this way the values of *ambiguity* and of *contradiction* lose their historical consistency and are reproposed as "principles" of a poetic.[5]

Why this mixture of theory and practice? Were Venturi and Scott Brown's insights too fresh to be encapsulated in well-formed concepts? Did the press of practice deny them the necessary distance from their material? Or was it something in the nature of the subject that made it difficult to formulate theoretically?

5] Manfredo Tafuri, *Theories and History of Architecture* (New York: Harper and Row, 1976), 213. Italics in original. In "Sign and Substance: Reflections on Complexity, Las Vegas, and Oberlin," Alan Colquhoun made a similar point. See Colquhoun, "Sign and Substance: Reflections on Complexity, Las Vegas, and Oberlin," in *Essays in Architectural Criticism* (Cambridge, MA: MIT Press, 1981), 139.

This question is itself difficult to bring into clear focus. Cultural theorist Gayatri Spivak has emphasized the "unconceptualized" nature of the quotidian. She has claimed that the very act of labeling a part of experience as "everyday" alters its fluid character and its immersion in an ongoing stream of events, substituting a hypostasized mental object formed according to the rules governing theoretical operations.[6] The same point was made twenty years earlier by Pierre Bourdieu in an Outline of a Theory of Practice. Using the example of the everyday life of the Algerian Kabyle, Bourdieu contrasted the thought structures of "practice," or unconceptualized action, with those of "theory":

> Automatic and impersonal, significant without intending to signify, ordinary practices lend themselves to an understanding no less automatic and impersonal...[but] in taking up a point of view on the action, withdrawing from it in order to observe it from above and from a distance, [the observer] constitutes practical activity as an *object of observation and analysis, a representation.*[7]

In fact, if Venturi and Scott Brown's diverse responses to the problem of an "architecture of the everyday" lacked a formal conceptual apparatus, they did possess a loose coherency. Yet the most direct presentation of their ideas about the everyday—*Signs of Life*, a 1976 exhibition of everyday American building forms at the Smithsonian Institution—was, of all their work, perhaps the least well understood. Why did this exploration of the forms of the everyday urban landscape meet with such a difficult reception? Why, despite the underlying consistency of their approach, did much of their work meet with bafflement and, often, dislike? Exploring the reasons for architects' negative reaction to the show will shed light on these questions as well as on some of the difficulties intrinsic to the creation of an architecture of the everyday.

6] Gayatri Spivak, lecture, Princeton University, April 1991.

7] Bourdieu, *Theory of Practice*, 80, 109. Italics in original.

SIGNS OF LIFE

Signs of Life, Symbols in the American City was exhibited at the Smithsonian Institution's Renwick Gallery in Washington from February 26 through September 30, 1976 as part of the national commemoration of the American Bicentennial. The exhibition presented the ordinary urban landscapes of mid-twentieth-century America—the traditional city street, the highway and its commercial strip, and the suburb—to architects as well as the "average Americans" who inhabited them. A linear sequence of three major parts was shoehorned into a portion of the Renwick Gallery's neoclassical layout. An entry hall with introductory material led into the Home section, which featured dioramas of three common housing types: the Levittowner, a lower-middle-class tract house, the Williamsburg, an upper-middle-class suburban home, and the urban working-class Row House. The furniture and decorative elements of the homes "spoke" in cartoon thought bubbles that gave the symbolic referents of each item, a technique reminiscent of the collages of Independent Group members Nigel Henderson and Richard Hamilton. Supporting material documented the variety within each of the three house types. The Strip section was an extravagant collection of neon signs and billboards compressed into a single room that evoked the experience of Las Vegas after dark. Corporate signage dominated the space; a "Tanya" billboard weighing several tons was mounted along one entire wall. Small McDonald's "in" and "out" signs stood dwarflike in the doorways, indicating the visitor's direction through the exhibition. The Street section, mostly small photographs assembled within loose categories and accompanied by descriptive text, was the most traditional in its format, a congeries of didactic material and interesting objects—such as a gigantic spigot—furnished with a few potted palms and benches.[8]

8] The material for the exhibition had been gathered over a period of almost a decade. Following Venturi and Scott Brown's initial explorations in their architecture studios at Yale on the subjects of Las Vegas and Levittown in 1968 and 1970, and the publication of *Learning from Las Vegas* in 1972, Scott Brown, Izenour, and other members of Venturi and Rauch had photographed dozens of suburban communities and strip commercial areas, accumulated thousands of photographs and large files of ads from popular magazines and mail-order catalogs, interviewed billboard companies, attended signage conventions, and combed through postcard files. For every image on display, there were dozens of unused examples on file. (Steven Izenour, interview with the author, Manayunk, PA, 2 January 1995). See Robert Venturi, Denise Scott Brown, and Steven Izenour, *Learning from Las Vegas, or, Form Analysis as Design Research, Studio Handouts* (New Haven: Yale University, Department of Architecture, Third Year Studio, fall 1968); Venturi, Scott Brown, and Izenour, *Learning from Levittown, or Remedial Housing for Architects, Studio Handouts* (New Haven: Yale University, Department of Architecture, Studio RHA, spring 1970).

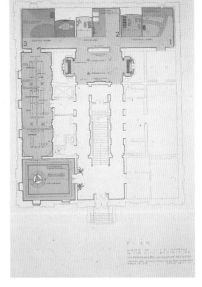

SIGNS OF LIFE EXHIBITION, SMITHSONIAN INSTI-
TUTION, WASHINGTON, DC, 1976. *CLOCKWISE FROM
TOP LEFT:* HOME SECTION, LEVITTOWNER EXTERIOR;
STRIP SECTION; ENTRY TO STREET SECTION; FINAL
EXHIBITION PLAN; HOME SECTION, LEVITTOWNER
INTERIOR; HOME SECTION, WILLIAMSBURG EXTE-
RIOR.

An assemblage of particulars with minimal analysis, composed more of pictures than words, the exhibition presented a largely implicit argument. The approximately seven thousand photographic images constituted a visual anthropology of American "settlement forms," documenting in detail the individual variations within common patterns.[9] Within each section of the exhibition, the multiplication of examples fairly inundated the visitor. The Home exhibit, for instance, contained some sixty photographs of row houses and another sixty of bungalows. The title of the exhibition, suggested by Joshua Taylor, the head of the National Gallery, echoed that of an editorial by John Brinckerhoff Jackson in the winter 1964–65 issue of his journal *Landscape*, and also resembled the title of the Smithsons' 1972 article "Signs of Occupancy." It indicated Venturi and Scott Brown's estimation of the vitality and coherence of the phenomenon they offered for the public's consideration.[10]

The exhibition's materials were also assembled into a manuscript bearing the title "Signs of Life," the organization of which intensified rather than eluci-dated the descriptive and aggregative structure of the

9] Suzanne Stephens, "Signs and Symbols as Show Stoppers," *Progressive Architecture* LVII, no. 5 (May 1976): 38.

10] Alison and Peter Smithson, "Signs of Occupancy," *Architectural Design* (February 1972).

exhibition. The extensive scholarly and field research that had gone into its preparation was carefully concealed behind a simple and direct writing style, easily understood by the "intelligent layman."[11] Even more pointedly than the exhibition, the manuscript took the form of an "argument from examples." Although the introduction stated its goals—to "survey the pluralist aesthetic of the American city and its suburbs, and to understand what the urban landscape means to people, through an analysis of its symbols, their sources and their antecedents"—there was in fact little interpretation of the data, which was instead laid out in a string of examples as if the facts spoke for themselves. Terms were used for classification rather than analysis. The eclectic ornament on the suburban house was labeled a "visual booster."[12] Signs were categorized as commercial signs, building signs, street signs, or civic signs.[13] "Duck" and "decorated shed," introduced in *Learning from Las Vegas*, made cameo appearances as headings. Planner David Crane's categorization of urban communication into three kinds of message systems—heraldic, physiognomic, and locational—previously applied to the modern city by Scott Brown in her 1965 article "The Meaningful City," was imported to serve as section headings, but with little of the explanation that accompanied the schema in the earlier article.[14]

The list of topics constituted a loose taxonomy rather than an algorithm for the creation of a similar set of forms or an analytic of their principles. The categories did not seem comprehensive. Instead, they seemed to reveal the record of a process of induction partially underway. Within each subsection, pages of small photos were accompanied by written litanies that took the form of description, additional data, or quotations from popular venues, assembled in series of declarative statements:

A house is the largest single purchase most families make in their lifetime.

11] Steven Izenour, interview with the author, Manayunk, PA, 2 January 1995. In fact, Venturi and Scott Brown considered the first draft, prepared by Virginia Carroll, a student in their studio, to be too dry and scholarly, not accessible to the average reader.

12] Robert Venturi and Denise Scott Brown, "From the Curb," in "Signs of Life" (1976), Venturi, Scott Brown and Associates [VSBA] Archive, 6.

13] Venturi and Scott Brown, "Signs in the Street," in "Signs of Life."

14] Denise Scott Brown, "The Meaningful City," *AIA Journal* XLIII, no. 1 (January 1965): 27-32. See also David A. Crane, "The City Symbolic," *Journal of the American Institute of Planners* XXVI, no. 4 (November 1960): 280-292. The terms were cited in Venturi and Scott Brown, introduction to "Signs of Life."

"Owning a house means being settled as opposed to being nomadic tribes of city flat dwellers." (*The American Home*, 1929)

"Nomads are seldom patriots."
(*The American Home*, 1929)

"Pride of home, reverence for home, affection for home, loyalty to home, lie at the very foundation of true patriotism."
(*The American Home*, 1929)[15]

The alphabetized catalog of names used by developers for new suburban subdivisions—"Bay, Bridge, Brook, Close, Copse, Corner, Court, Cove…"—was some twenty items long.[16] An illustrated list of "What Americans want in 1946"—from a convertible station wagon at $2,890 to a set of stainless steel kitchen pans at $33—occupied an entire page.[17] Fifty-four postage-stamp-sized images of gas stations accompanied a full-page photograph by Steven Shore.

The propensity to list intensified the additive

ILLUSTRATIONS FROM "SIGNS OF LIFE," 1976. *TOP AND BOTTOM:* **PHOTOGRAPHS FROM THE "STRIP BUILDINGS, GAS STATIONS" SECTION.**

construction of the text. However, this paratactic mode of exposition, which built up examples without explicitly disclosing the principle connecting them, was not without its own inductive logic: the first reports of a fascination for this visual material in the earliest drafts of the manuscript yielded, in the final draft, to an organization by subheadings broken up into text and illustration captions. In the course of the editing, topic sentences were consistently removed. Instead, there was a preference for clipped, punchy phrases without generalizations, whose offhand, slightly provocative tone forced the implicit connections to be made by the reader. Thus it is clear that the stylistic predilection for

15] Venturi and Scott Brown, "Personal and Social Identity," in "Signs of Life," 2.

16] Ibid., "In the Community," 7.

17] Ibid., "The Good Life—Technology," 2.

the assemblage of particulars revealed more than merely an aesthetic; it also entailed a form of logical construction in which the example was adduced as proof.

Venturi and Scott Brown's inductive approach to a theory of the everyday, accumulating examples toward a generalization, baffled architectural critics. Lacking an explicitly articulated theoretical description, this approach caused architects to focus on its particulars, reading them as an aesthetic instead of a theoretical position. The critics' difficulties raise certain questions: Was the exhibition's implicit argumentative form inherent in an attempt to show the internal logic of the practices of the everyday as well as its forms? Were Venturi and Scott Brown struggling to arrive at an intellectual structure for thinking about the everyday, one which could comprehend this internal structure "on the hither side of explicit statement"? Bourdieu describes the "practical thought" of the Kabyle as follows:

> Practice always implies a cognitive operation, a practical operation of construction which sets to work, by reference to practical functions, systems of classification (taxonomies) which organize perception and structure practice. Produced by the practice of successive generations, in conditions of existence of a determinate type, these schemes of perception, appreciation, and action, which are acquired through practice and applied in their practical state without acceding to explicit representation, function as practical operators through which the objective structures of which they are the product tend to reproduce themselves in practices.[18]

Was it these "practical schemes," the building practices outside architectural conceptualization, that Venturi and Scott Brown were interested in studying? How did their architectural training aid or interfere with this understanding?

18] Bourdieu, *Theory of Practice*, 97.

The exhibition also raised certain issues general to any search for an "architecture of the everyday": What effect could the mere display of the forms of everyday life have on the architectural profession? How ought these forms be employed? What was the proper role of architects, by training and class background devoted to the aims of high art, in the creation of an "art of the people"?

Although it was reviewed extensively by the media at large, coverage by the architectural press was slight and not uniformly favorable. English and European critics gave it thoughtful consideration. In an issue on housing, *Architectural Design* presented excerpts from the exhibition material with little commentary. *Architectural Design*'s editor, Haig Beck, expressed appreciation of Venturi and Scott Brown's intention to reveal the mechanisms of reading common to all experience of buildings, but he considered this revolutionary proposal inescapably compromised by the elite social position of architects.[19] Understanding the organization of the exhibition to mimic that of its subject, *Domus* called the urban environment presented by the exhibition a "continuous collage of quotations which seems to form the fabric of our civilisation, mind and memory."[20] Stanislaus von Moos contrasted the show's self-defined "realism" with that of Europeans like Aldo Rossi and Giorgio Grassi (whose versions of the real were, in his estimation, actually forms of idealism), and like Beck, questioned whether Venturi and Scott Brown's dedicated architectural populism could be truly popular.[21]

American reaction was less sympathetic, a difference that probably had something to do with home pride. The British and Europeans were titillated by still relatively unavailable American consumer culture, an attitude not shared by an American architectural profession anxious to reform its own environment with "high art." Of the American architectural journals, only *Progressive Architecture* reviewed the exhibition, in an article by Suzanne Stephens, who discussed it along with Venturi and Scott Brown's exhibition *200 Years of American Sculpture*, showing concurrently at the

19] "Signs of Life—Venturi and Rauch," *Architectural Design* XLVI (August 1976): 496–98; Haig Beck, "'Elitist!'," *Architectural Design* XLVI (November 1976): 662–66.

20] "America: An Exhibition by Venturi and Rauch, Formes et Symboles," *Domus* 565 (December 1976): 46–47.

21] Stanislaus von Moos, "Zweierlei Realismus," *Werk-Archithese* 7–8 (July–August 1977): 58–62.

Whitney Museum of American Art in New York and itself generating considerable outrage with its contextual settings.[22] Paul Goldberger, writing for *Artnews*, called *Signs of Life* "something of a disappointment":

> the exhibition's absolute refusal to be judgmental is one of its most serious problems....There are so many things in this show that...work better than other things, that look better, that serve their users better....we need Venturi and Rauch's expertise to help us make judgments about the broader set of architectural sources that is now commonly used.[23]

Although Goldberger himself was not charmed by the "row house with asbestos shingles," he disliked the mocking tone he thought he detected in the Home dioramas. He complained about the density of the material in the Street and Strip sections but at the same time charged that the show did not increase architects' knowledge of the everyday environment. That there was "something worth looking at out there" he considered beyond dispute, indeed old news, but he wanted a guide to it. Stephens, less burdened by distaste for American mass culture than Goldberger, more accurately characterized the message of the show: "people long for a symbolic environment laden with associations, connotations, and content to express their self-images, fantasies, and life styles. And they don't give a damn about the degree of sham they go to to get it."[24] The question unanswered by the show, she noted, was what this desire might mean for the practice of architecture.

Reaction to the manuscript was even more mixed, and eventually Venturi and Scott Brown decided not to publish it. Oxford University Press was willing to print the book but would not satisfy Venturi's request for $20,000 for its completion.[25] Indeed, it was rejected by at least eight publishers, including Viking Press,

22] Stephens, "Signs and Symbols," 37-38. *200 Years of American Sculpture* angered many critics by setting the pieces in what now seem to be fairly inoffensive backgrounds of pale, grayed-out colors with abstracted images of architectural forms appropriate to the historic period of each piece. Reviews of *Signs of Life* were also carried by *Interiors* ["Pop, Strip, and Sprawl," *Interiors* CXXXV, no. 11 (June 1976): 8], *Interior Design* ["At the Renwick Gallery—Signs, Symbols, and the American Way of Life," *Interior Design* 47, no. 5 (May 1976): 64–65], and *House and Garden* ["Real Life: It's Beautiful," *House and Garden* (August 1976): 79 ff].

23] Paul Goldberger, "How to Love the Strip: 'Symbols in the American City'," *Artnews* 75, no. 7 (September 1976): 50, 54.

24] Stephens, "Signs and Symbols," 37.

Architectural Record, McGraw-Hill, University Associates, Inc., Johns Hopkins University Press, Praeger, and the New York Graphic Society. The evaluation of the reader for architecture and planning at George Braziller was very favorable, praising it for precisely the nonjudgmental stance Goldberger had found problematic about the exhibition:

> [*Signs of Life*] is a serious, professional and thorough analysis of a large piece of American architectural reality. It is bound to make a lot of people angry, but it is a strong job and definitely not frivolous.
>
> The book's best point is its lack of editorial judgment.... There is a refreshing lack of elitist dogma and heavy theory in the book....
>
> The book seems to me a definitely new vision accurately seen and tightly presented. Very good and very disturbing.[26]

But Braziller himself thought it needed polishing and commented that it read "a bit too much like a term paper or survey." In addition, the company was unwilling to provide the funds to publish the book in color.[27] Like Goldberger, Viking Press suggested that the book needed a more definite point of view than that provided by the "rather cool tongue-in-cheek tone we seem to discern here."[28] The rejection letter sent by Walter F. Wagner, Jr., the editor of the Architectural Record, summed up the problem as far as the architectural mainstream was concerned:

> The data and information is intensely interesting, but I keep missing some conclusions or recommendations. I think there is much to be learned from Levittown by architects and builders alike, but if I were you I wouldn't continue to leave

25] James Raimes to Robert Venturi, 2 May 1974, VSBA Archive, Venturi Files, Learning from Levittown Financing.

26] Victoria de Ramel, letter of evaluation, 30 March 1973, VSBA Archive, Learning from Levittown Files, General Correspondence, Meeting Notes Publishers File.

27] Venturi, Scott Brown, and Associates, notes for meeting with George Braziller, 4 April 1973, VSBA Archive, Learning from Levittown Files, General Correspondence, Meeting Notes Publishers File.

28] Alan D. Williams to Steve Izenour, 14 May 1973, Learning from Levittown Files, General Correspondence, Meeting Notes Publishers File. Williams was Viking's editorial director.

it up to the reader to decide what they are. I would, at least, help them.[29]

Thus the majority of the architectural press expressed its bafflement and incomprehension with the inductive, anthropological aggregation of examples in "Signs of Life." Failing to understand the multiplication of examples as a deliberate strategy, it wanted either a guide to the use of this imagery or a hint as to what aesthetic and ethical position to take with respect to it. Mere observation seemed out, and appreciation untenable. In the end, only a small pamphlet, containing a few photographs, a list of lenders and photographers, and a few articles was published by the museum.[30]

But Venturi and Scott Brown's serious consideration of the products of consumer culture also angered others better able to comprehend their intellectual references and methods. Although written five years before, Kenneth Frampton's 1971 essay "America 1960–1970: Notes on Urban Images and Theory" provided perhaps the most trenchant critique of their attitude toward the everyday landscape, precisely because Frampton was one of the few critics who took the trouble to understand the full range of their intellectual sources.[31] He questioned not just their taste or their refusal to judge contemporary urban forms, but their very conception of the everyday and their relation to the materials of everyday life. In disagreement with other critics, Frampton pointed out that although Venturi and Scott Brown claimed the pop artists as their forebears, their attitude toward the popular was not the same as that of the pop artists: they seemed neither ironic nor detached. His major difficulty, however, was with what he saw as their confusion of the "mass administration of the visual forms of American culture" with a truly popular culture. His critique raised several important issues about Venturi and Scott Brown's approach to the everyday: Was the traditional view of a culture split

29] Walter F. Wagner to Steve Izenour, 1 May 1973, VSBA Archive, Learning from Levittown Files General Correspondence, Meeting Notes Publishers File.

30] *Signs of Life: Symbols in the American City*, (Washington, DC: The Smithsonian Institution, 1976).

31] Kenneth Frampton, "America 1960–1970: Notes on Urban Images and Theory," *Casabella* 35, nos. 359–60 (December 1971): 24–38, in response to "Learning from Pop," *Casabella* 35, nos. 359–60 (December 1971): 15–24. The issue was devoted to a discussion of the American city by the Institute for Architecture and Urban Studies. A similar critique was also aimed at *Learning from Las Vegas* by Fred Koetter in *Oppositions* 3: "On Robert Venturi, Denise Scott Brown and Steven Izenour's *Learning from Las Vegas*," *Oppositions* 3 (May 1974): 98–104.

into two equally vital halves, popular and elite, still a valid conception in postwar, postindustrial America? Could an "architecture of the everyday" be constructed on the basis of building forms created by large corporations for consumption by a mass market? Were the products of mass culture truly reflective of the desires and perceptions of the people? And in any case, who were "the people"?

Finally, rather than celebrating its forms, should architects not provide an alternative? Here Frampton was reinforcing the modernist conviction that the forms of industrial technology would bring about a revolution in the lives of ordinary persons (defined as the working class) through the establishment of new building forms. The standardized forms of industrial production would replace the customary practices of "folk" building. These new forms would benefit everyone though low cost, efficient production, and by facilitating life patterns suited to modern culture and technology. The dilemma for architects in the postwar period was that the forms that industrial society had arrived at on its own did not correspond to architects' views of how the new society ought to look and function. Frampton thought architects had an obligation to propose something better.

In "Pop Off" (1971), Scott Brown replied to Frampton and summarized the positions underlying *Signs of Life*. A vital popular culture was still active within the dynamics of consumer capitalism. Anticipating Michel de Certeau, Venturi and Scott Brown saw this vitality in terms of an active consumption, composed of several activities: choosing among alternatives in the market place, customizing those choices through often cosmetic but highly symbolic and readable alterations, and reading the landscape in this symbolic fashion. In view of this vitality, the appropriate attitude of the architect toward the building forms produced by consumer culture was to respect them and study them, rather than to dictate new forms. Predicting current multicultural theory, Venturi and Scott Brown believed modernism's reform of the popular "for its own good" to be patronizing and in any case ineffective.[32]

32] Denise Scott Brown, "Pop Off: Reply to Kenneth Frampton," *Casabella* 35, nos. 359–60 (December 1971): 41–45.

VERNACULAR, POP REALISM, THE ARCHITECTURE
OF DEMOCRACY, AND "THE PEOPLE"

This disagreement between Scott Brown and Frampton took place within several important contemporary debates on the nature of architecture and its relation to its users. Thus, to be understood, Venturi and Scott Brown's ideas must be juxtaposed to contemporary architectural conceptions of the vernacular, the architecture of democracy, and "the people." A preoccupation with the vernacular—usually conceived of as buildings not designed by architects, but rather created by ordinary people out of a common set of understandings to facilitate a common set of social practices—was part of early modernism's enthusiasm for a larger complex of exotic "others" including Western medieval society, non-industrialized peoples, and Japanese culture. Modern architects saw these cultures as alternatives to modern industry, their primary source of forms for an architecture true to its own structural and functional nature. After World War II, articles on vernacular architecture appeared in most journals. Le Corbusier's references to grain elevators and anonymous Mediterranean construction were amplified in a 1957 issue of *The Architectural Review* devoted to anonymous building and echoed in 1960 in James Stirling's "The 'Functional Tradition' and Expression." Stirling saw vernacular buildings as examples of the direct expression of the "actual accommodation volumes" of architecture, a salutary model for a profession given to structural exhibitionism or "styling."[33]

This investigation of the vernacular was metonymic of modernism's quest to secure a foundation for form in an architecture "representative of our times." In *Bath—Walks within the Walls*, Peter and Alison Smithson described their search for a "new aesthetic" that would, "in an altogether natural way...establish a unity between the built form and the men using it,"[34] something that would have the "certainty, of knowing what to do, what is correct...beyond intellect, and like

33] "The Functional Tradition," *Architectural Review* (July 1957); James Stirling, "The 'Functional Tradition' and Expression," *Perspecta* 6 (1960). In the postwar period, articles on vernacular architecture appeared in many journals, including *Perspecta, Zodiac, L'Architecture d'Aujourd'hui, Architectural Design, The Architectural Review,* and John Entenza's West Coast journal *Arts and Architecture.*

34] Alison and Peter Smithson, "Urban Reidentification," *The Architectural Review* (June 1955); republished as "The Built World: Urban Re-Identification," in *Ordinariness and Light* (Cambridge, MA: MIT Press, 1970), 104–13; Peter Smithson, *Bath—Walks within the Walls* (London: Adams and Dart, 1971), cited in Alison and Peter Smithson, *Without Rhetoric: An Architectural Aesthetic 1955–1972* (Cambridge, MA: MIT Press, 1974), 86.

the tides or the seasons what we should do is let it flood into us." Venturi had, like the modernists, treated the vernacular primarily as a source of architectural form in *Complexity and Contradiction*—but not as a paradigm of a pure, natural, and undesigned order. Rather, he hoped the Italian farmhouse's dynamic jostling of local symmetries and its "vivid play of order and the circumstantial" could inject new life into a moribund artistic practice along the lines of Beethoven incorporating folk tunes into his symphonies.[35] Like Beethoven, Venturi wanted to employ importations from "low" culture to move beyond the classical conventions of current practice. Unlike the modernists, however, his interest in the "endless adjustments" of the vernacular was founded in a desire to relay, through the forms of architecture, the true complexity of the experience of contemporary life.[36] Venturi quoted Wordsworth, who wrote that he had described "incidents and situations from common life [so that] ordinary things should be presented to the mind in an unusual aspect," to support his contention that using conventional elements in an unconventional way would address the complications of postwar architectural programs.[37]

Venturi had conceived of the vernacular as one half of a high/low dichotomy, an unequal opposition in which the high could appropriate from the low but not the other way around. Sprinkled throughout *Complexity and Contradiction*, however, were images that hinted at a version of vernacular closer to home than the Italian countryside. The equality implied in his juxtaposition of Piazza San Marco with Times Square seemed to validate the latter as a source of architectural forms. The final view of Main Street, inspired by Peter Blake's *God's Own Junkyard*, sitting in jangled contrast opposite the serene image of the University of Virginia campus mall, illustrated the book's elegiac evocation of "the everyday landscape, vulgar and disdained" as a source of "the complex and contradictory order that is vital and valid for our architecture as an urbanistic whole." It also placed the entire

35] Robert Venturi, *Complexity and Contradiction in Architecture*, 2nd. ed. (New York: Museum of Modern Art, 1977), 46.

36] In the introduction to *Complexity and Contradiction*, Vincent Scully contrasted the pure forms of the Greek temple with Venturi's inspiration in the "urban facades of Italy, with their endless adjustments to the counter-requirements of inside and outside and their inflection with all the business of everyday life." Vincent Scully, introduction to Venturi, *Complexity and Contradiction*, 9.

37] William Wordsworth, *Lyrical Ballads*, quoted in Venturi, *Complexity and Contradiction*, 43.

enterprise within the province of the contemporary American city.[38] Other postwar architects also applied vernacular forms to urban issues rather than to individual buildings—the life of the streets, the structural integrity of public life, the need for a perceptual urban order. As a review of Myron Goldfinger's popular photographic essay *Villages in the Sun* (1969) noted, these designers viewed vernacular settlements as sources of mainly aesthetic guidelines for solving increasingly pressing contemporary problems, especially the "absence of community expression in our urban environments."[39]

Thus the continued search by modern architects for "the architecture representative of our times" occasioned a ransacking of the forms of preindustrial settlements for motifs that could be made expressive of the life patterns of technological society. Like their contemporaries, Venturi and Scott Brown's search for architectural forms adequate to everyday life was framed in terms of the vernacular. But by placing a positive valuation on contemporary forms of urbanism and suburbanism, Venturi and Scott Brown challenged their colleagues' well-intentioned but, they believed, somewhat nostalgic enterprise. In an argument similar to one rehearsed by Alison and Peter Smithson a decade or so earlier, in *Learning from Las Vegas* they situated this investigation by means of a short genealogy of the idea of the vernacular. The Smithsons had written:

> Traditionally the fine arts depend on the popular arts for their vitality, and the popular arts on the fine arts for their respectability. It has been said that things hardly "exist" before the fine artist has made use of them; they are simply part of the unclassified background material against which we pass our lives. The transformation from everyday object to fine art manifestation happens in many ways: the object can be discovered—*ôbjet trouvé* or *l'art brut*—the object itself remaining the same; a literary or folk myth can arise; or the object can be used as a jumping-off point and is itself transformed.... Why certain folk art objects, historical

38] Venturi, *Complexity and Contradiction*, 54, 104–5.

39] Myron Goldfinger, *Villages in the Sun: Mediterranean Community Architecture* (New York: Praeger, 1969); reviewed by Donald Watson in *Architecture Forum* 123, no. 5 (June 1970): 76.

styles or industrial artifacts and methods become important at a particular moment cannot easily be explained. *Gropius wrote a book on grain silos, / le Corbusier a book on aeroplanes, / and Charlotte Perriand—it was said—brought a new object to / the office every morning; / but in the 'fifties, we collected 'ads'.*[40]

Unlikely partners consorted, however, in Venturi and Scott Brown's conception of the vernacular—artistic realism and artistic borrowing; Venturi's high/low dichotomy with the notion of the life to be found in the (European) street; an interpretation of modern architecture as an updating of vernacular construction with the idea that commercial buildings were the buildings of the people; and the forms of the American highway strip as the representative of this putative new commercial/urban vernacular:

> We believe that a careful documentation and analysis of [Las Vegas'] physical form is as important to architects and urbanists today as were the studies of medieval Europe and ancient Rome and Greece to earlier generations. Such a study will help to define a new type of urban form emerging in America and Europe, radically different from that we have known.... Learning from the existing landscape is a way of being revolutionary for an architect....
>
> To gain insight from the commonplace is nothing new: Fine art often follows folk art. Romantic architects of the eighteenth century discovered an existing and conventional rustic architecture. Early Modern architects appropriated an existing and conventional industrial vocabulary without much adaptation. Le Corbusier loved grain elevators and steamships; the Bauhaus looked like a factory; Mies refined the details of American steel factories for concrete buildings.... Modern architecture has not so much excluded the commercial

40] Allison and Peter Smithson, *Without Rhetoric*, 10–11.

vernacular as it has tried to make it over by inventing and enforcing a vernacular of its own, improved and universal. It has rejected the combination of fine art and crude art. The Italian landscape has always harmonized the vulgar and the Vitruvian: the *contorni* around the *duomo*, the *portiere's* laundry across the *padrone's portone*, *Supercorte-maggiore* against the Romanesque apse. Naked children have never played in our fountains, and I. M. Pei will never be happy on Route 66.[41]

Venturi and Scott Brown characterized their investigation of the new urban vernacular as a form of realism; and indeed, the tradition of nineteenth-century realistic French literature and painting, whose very depiction of the facts of bourgeois and lower-class life was felt to be so revolutionary as to be excluded from the salons, lay behind their interest in the existing landscape. Nineteenth-century realism viewed "the empirical investigation of reality" as a tool to "confront reality afresh." Its struggle against the "schemata or conventions of academic art" employed a technique of aesthetic shock as social critique.[42] This revolutionary strain was part of the intellectual ancestry of modernism, a characteristic combination of aesthetics and politics that Venturi and Scott Brown carried forward in their own work. "Concrete, direct observation and notation of ordinary, everyday experience" played an important part in Venturi and Scott Brown's program of investigation.[43] Reiterating Le Corbusier's diatribe against "eyes which do not see" the beauties of vernacular and standardized industrial construction, *Learning from Las Vegas* emphasized the need to "question how we look at things" in an "open-minded and nonjudgmental investigation," and to use both old and new techniques for documenting the details of the new urban forms.[44] The research leading to *Signs of Life* represented the culmination of *Learning from Las Vegas*'s program of careful documentation.

Their separate backgrounds led Venturi and Scott Brown to see realism as the most appropriate stance to take toward the forms of the everyday world

41] Venturi, Scott Brown, and Izenour, *Learning from Las Vegas*, viii, xviii, 1.

42] Ernst Gombrich, cited in Linda Nochlin, *Realism* (Harmondsworth, England: Penguin Books, 1971), 20.

43] Nochlin, *Realism*, 19.

44] Venturi, Scott Brown, and Izenour, *Learning from Las Vegas*, viii, xviii.

of postwar America. But their revolutionary realism existed in uneasy combination with a sensibility of bemused detachment inherited from Andy Warhol, Jasper Johns, Robert Rauschenberg, and the Smithsons. In fact, it was with the Smithsons, at the Architectural Association in the mid-'50s, that Scott Brown had learned to appreciate the imagery of consumer culture. The Smithsons had extrapolated Le Corbusier's dictum to include a focus on ads for American consumer goods and an interest in working class use of public places in the East End of London.[45] From her planning professors at the University of Pennsylvania, Scott Brown had also learned to see the "undesigned" urban environments of the West Coast as prototypes for the future. Venturi's reaction to the postwar environment tended on the whole toward what he called "irony," a position with multiple referents including the New Critics' discussions of the English metaphysical poets of the seventeenth century; August Heckscher's exhortations of American citizens to accept the complexity of their environment in The Public Happiness; the pop artists' fascination with urban visual culture; and Marshall McLuhan's celebration of the effects of the media on modern life.[46]

Venturi and Scott Brown were also inspired by a diverse group of contemporaries who might be termed twentieth-century American realists—theorists and observers of popular culture who sought to bring to the public's attention the emergence of new forms of life in postwar America. These writers and artists included Tom Wolfe, whose essays in Esquire and other popular magazines provided a trenchant commentary on American culture. Wolfe's article "Las Vegas, (What?)…" was an uproarious account of the various types of people and signs to be found in Las Vegas in the early '60s. He analyzed the impetus behind the building of Las Vegas in the most succinct terms: "style equals form plus money."[47] Also important to Venturi

45] The connections between Venturi and Scott Brown's theoretical work during this period and that of the Smithsons have often been noted. Along with the Smithsons, Independent Group members Nigel and Judith Henderson's sociological and photographic observations questioned the premises of (upper-middle-class) socialist architecture after World War II. Reyner Banham's discussions of popular culture and especially Los Angeles also arose out of this milieu. Although Peter Smithson was not yet teaching at the Architectural Association when Scott Brown was a student there, she has described her relationships with student groups who held points of view similar to those being propounded by the Independent Group in its exhibits Parallel of Life and Art and This is Tomorrow. Scott Brown also used Peter Smithson as an informal critic for her thesis (Denise Scott Brown, interview with the author, Manayunk, PA, 4 February 1995). See also Denise Scott Brown, "Between Three Stools," Urban Concepts (London: Academy Editions, 1990); and David Robbins, ed., The Independent Group: Postwar Britain and the Aesthetics of Plenty (Cambridge, MA: MIT Press, 1990).

46] August Heckscher, The Public Happiness (New York: Atheneum, 1962); Marshall McLuhan, Understanding Media: The Extensions of Man (New York: Signet, 1964).

47] Tom Wolfe, "Las Vegas (What?)…," and introduction to The Kandy-Kolored Tangerine-Flake Streamline Baby (New York: Farrar, Strauss, and Giroux, 1965).

**"ANATOMY OF SIGNS," ILLUSTRATION
FROM "SIGNS OF LIFE," 1976.**

48] *Landscape's* philosophy owed a great deal to Marc
Bloch's and the French Annales school's ideas about
human geography and the importance of the quotidian
to the study of history. According to Marc Treib, Jackson
was the first critic to take the American strip seriously.
Jackson taught at Berkeley from 1962 to around 1977,
and Scott Brown, who taught at Berkeley in 1965,
would have met him there. Marc Treib, "The Measure
of Wisdom: John Brinckerhoff Jackson (1909–1996),"
Journal of the Society of Architectural Historians 55,
no. 4 (December 1996): 381.

49] Charles Hagen, *American Photographers of the
Depression: Farm Security Administration Photographs
1935–1942* (New York: Pantheon Books, 1985) n. p. By
the '60s a younger group of artists, interested in new
subjects and in a more ironic or deadpan stance toward
their material, was being fostered by the Museum of
Modern Art. See Christopher Phillips, "The Judgment
Seat of Photography," *October* 22 (1982): 27–63.

50] Venturi, Scott Brown, and Izenour, *Learning from
Las Vegas*, 26–29, 126–27. The photographs of Las
Vegas parking lots on pages 11, 32, and 48 also resem-
ble strongly Edward Ruscha's parking lot photographs in
Thirty-four Parking Lots in Los Angeles (Los Angeles:
Edward Ruscha, 1967). A friend of Venturi and Scott
Brown's, Ruscha had given presentations to their Las
Vegas studio. Izenour, interview with the author, Man-
ayunk, PA, 2 January 1995.

and Scott Brown were the essayists who contributed to
the journal *Landscape*. Begun in spring 1951 by John
Brinckerhoff Jackson and under his editorship until
1968, this "journal of human geography" was dedicated to providing an unprejudiced view of the current
American social and visual environment. Scott Brown,
Charles Moore, Donlyn Lyndon, and others contributed articles documenting and analyzing these emerging cultural forms.[48]

Photographers Edward Ruscha and Steven
Shore also formed part of this disposition toward realism. Ruscha and Shore were heirs to a long tradition
of documentary art photography in America that included Farm Security Administration photographers
such as Berenice Abbott, Walker Evans, and others,
work that had presented images of ordinary small-
town environments as well as the plight of poor share-
croppers.[49] Steven Shore's laconic images of gas stations, main streets, building signs, and tract houses
figured prominently in "Signs of Life." That Ruscha
was a strong influence on Venturi and Scott Brown's
work is evident not only from his presence at the final
critique of the Las Vegas studio, and from the program
of the Levittown studio, in which he was quoted, but
also from the style of the images in *Learning from Las
Vegas*. There, his photographs of the Sunset Strip were
reproduced in company with Venturi and Scott
Brown's images of the Las Vegas strip and South Street
Philadelphia—where the firm was doing advocacy
planning—in the same format.[50] The technique
of "multiplication of examples" explored in "Signs
of Life" owed much to Ruscha's photographic
work, done between 1963 and 1978—collections of

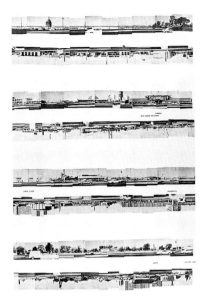

Los Angeles artifacts from parking lots to "real-estate opportunities" to nearly-identical photographs of Los Angeles cacti.[51] These photographs were almost anthropological in their spare and non-committal depiction of heretofore unremarked elements of the urban experience of Los Angeles. Ruscha's art has been called documentary, pop, conceptual, and even minimalist. Interviews reveal his connection to the project of the avant-garde, his self-confessed debt to dada, futurism, and pop, his love of the odd, and his interest in providing an experience of shock. For Ruscha, as for Venturi and Scott Brown, the object itself was more interesting than any theory about it, and it was undoubtedly this combination of shock and display that attracted them to his work.[52] The attitude shared by all of these authors and artists is clearly stated in this quotation from the Levittown studio program:

"AN 'EDWARD RUSCHA' ELEVATION OF THE STRIP," LAYOUT FROM LEARNING FROM LAS VEGAS, 1972.

> What new techniques are required to document new forms? We should aim to dead-pan the material so it speaks for itself. Ruscha has pioneered this treatment in his monographs....It is a way to avoid being upstaged by our own subject matter. It can lead too toward the methodical rigor which will be required of architectural form analysis once it is recognized as a legitimate activity.[53]

Venturi and Scott Brown's belief in the efficacy of the technique of "deadpanning," or realistic display, helps to explain their use of a structure of "display as argument" in (both the exhibition and manuscript forms of) *Signs of Life*. The realistic approach was explicitly non-judgmental, and the intent was to substitute, for theories about what ought to be,

51] See also Edward Ruscha's other books, *Every Building on the Sunset Strip* (Los Angeles: Edward Ruscha, 1966); *Nine Swimming Pools and a Broken Glass* (Los Angeles: Edward Ruscha, 1968); *Real Estate Opportunities* (Los Angeles: Edward Ruscha, 1970); *Some Los Angeles Apartments* (Los Angeles: Edward Ruscha, 1965).

52] Elbrig de Groot, *Edward Ruscha: Paintings* (Rotterdam: Museum Boymans-van Beuningen, 1989), 132–36.

53] Venturi, Scott Brown, and Izenour, *Learning from Levittown*, II, 11.

description of what existed. This stance does not, however, completely explain why the architectural community, whose avant-garde training had schooled them similarly in the techniques of aesthetic shock, did not sympathize with Venturi and Scott Brown's intellectual method. Part of the problem, of course, was that the avant-garde method was being used to attack its own promulgators. But to understand architects' distaste for the exhibition more completely requires an examination of another contemporary preoccupation, the "architecture of democracy."

Consideration of realism and the vernacular during the postwar period orbited within wide-ranging deliberations about architecture's role in a democracy. Much discussed by modernists debating the "new monumentality" in the late '40s, and considered even earlier by the Regional Plan Association of America in its development of the "neighborhood unit," the "architecture of democracy" remained an important topic through the '60s, when it was given renewed impetus by the civil rights movement, urban riots, and student revolts. Although coined by European architects attempting to adapt modernism's socialist philosophies to the political situation in their new American home, by the '60s the term encompassed architects' and planners' attempts to bring the way of life of the "other"—whether a person of another class or of a different race, ethnic group, or gender—to bear on the formation of the urban environment. This effort was seen as beneficial not only to the disadvantaged; in a 1968 article in *Architectural Design*, John Turner and others who had studied squatter settlements concluded that despite the poverty of their inhabitants, the flexibility, adaptability, and self-determination of these settlements—the ability they provided for their inhabitants to express themselves in building—made them better in some ways than American standardized housing, where the high level of technological development prevented individual involvement in the creation of dwellings.[54]

Critics like Turner believed that "aesthetic judgments are and must be penetrated by human meanings and relevances," that the built environment ought to be the "vehicle and

54] Rolf Goetze et. al., "Architecture of Democracy," *Architectural Design* 38, no. 8 (August 1968): 354.

expression of our human life." Here the term "expression" did not signify, as architects usually interpreted it, architecture as a representation by
the designer of the values of a larger group or of qualities inherent in the
building itself. Rather, it meant architecture as a vehicle through which
each individual could act to articulate his or her own values and atti-
tudes.[55] Turner's stance was similar to that of Nicholas J. Habraken, who
criticized the failure of mass housing to allow human beings to "dwell,"
a word which he defined in Heideggerian terms meaning to "actively
create one's own environment."[56] Habraken's solution to the problem of
mass housing was to provide what he called "supports"—infrastructure
developed on a large scale—while leaving the design and construction of
individual units to their inhabitants. In practice this meant presenting
prospective occupants with a set of optional plans and elevations from
which they could assemble their own designs.

The Smithsons' interest in "the life of the street" led them to similar conclusions about the effects of "mass housing." Their preoccupation
with an active public street culture grew out of their own childhoods in
Glasgow as well as their friendship with Nigel and Judith Henderson—
the latter a sociologist who studied the daily lives of London's working-
class East Enders. This concern took form in the Smithsons' proposal to
replace the four functions of urban life developed by CIAM (Congrès
Internationaux d'Architecture Moderne)—living, working, recreating,
and circulating—with "patterns of association" at four levels—the house,
the street, the district, and the city. Human association was the key, they
felt, to the development of a new city form. Their major focus was on
activity at the street level—the public life immediately
outside the door. Golden Lane, their project of 1952
for a bombed-out section of London, proposed as the
pattern for cities a framework similar to Habraken's
infrastructures—a street deck system that they likened
to the lines of the main sewers. The project's order was
intended to be based on the living patterns of the
inhabitants rather than on architectural geometries—

55] Goetze, et. al., 354.

56] Nicholas J. Habraken, *Supports* (1961; reprint, London: The Architectural Press, 1972). Habraken explained his ideas of dwelling in the same issue of *Lotus* in which excerpts from "Signs of Life" appeared in 1975: Virginia Carroll, Denise Scott Brown, and Robert Venturi, "Styling, ovvero 'Queste case sono perfetta-mente identiche, ma sembrano diverse'," *Lotus* 9 (1975): 162–71, 234–35; Nicholas J. Habraken, "Tre principi fondamentali per l'abitazione/Three R's for Housing," *Lotus* 9 (1975): 172–93.

an order that could include the impedimenta of daily life that Le Corbusier had wanted to exorcise from the bourgeois dwelling.[57] But the accouterments they listed were, like the flower pot in the window of Guild House, lower-middle class knickknacks rather than haute-bourgeois paraphernalia: "Behind the geometric facades our washing, our china dogs and aspidistras look out of place. Life in action cannot be forced behind the netting of imposed pattern."[58] Held in common by all of these theorists was a belief that art is not separate from the rest of culture, that "*there is only one world in which we all live and in which all our activities take place...our sense of any single activity can only be made rational by our sense of the whole.*"[59]

The conviction that architecture must participate in a common "meaning-world" that could be understood both by artistic elites and ordinary persons was basic both to *Learning from Las Vegas* and to *Signs of Life.* This concern with popular meaning had activist roots. A belief that architecture ought to serve "the people" was part of Scott Brown's modernist architectural training at the Architectural Association, but her planning professors at the University of Pennsylvania—Paul Davidoff (the originator of advocacy planning), David Crane, and Herbert Gans—had questioned architects' assumptions about their role, the populations they served, and the sources of their forms.[60] These planners' sophisticated understanding of the composition and characteristics of "the people" constituted an important foundation for Venturi and Scott Brown's view about architects' service to the public.

Moreover, underlying both their position and their disagreement with Frampton about the degree of agency manifested by lower-middle-class consumers was a protracted exchange between American and European social thinkers centered around the nature of "the people," of mass or popular culture itself (even the term itself was contested), and of the mechanisms of its reception. This debate had been active since the mid-'30s, and its vicissitudes were central to the difficult reception of *Signs of Life.* The choice of material for

57] Alison and Peter Smithson, *Ordinariness and Light,* 58, 60.

58] Ibid., 21.

59] Goetze et. al., "Architecture of Democracy," 354. Italics in original.

60] Scott Brown, "Between Three Stools," in *Urban Concepts.*

the exhibition actually owed much to Herbert Gans's six-part categorization of taste cultures, each with its own coherent system of aesthetic standards and appropriate content, each equally valid within its own sphere. Gans was a student of David Riesman, a sociologist well-known for his studies of the effects of mass culture on the public. Riesman's 1950 article "Listening to Popular Music" constituted a direct challenge to European and American left intellectuals' pessimistic views of the effects of the media in particular. After discussing the contributions of the "gifted Europeans, horrified by the alleged vulgarization of taste brought about by industrialization," Riesman stated that what actually matters in the study of popular culture is not its level of bad taste, but "who says what to whom with what effect," that is, how information is communicated from one person to another.[61]

Gans himself was something of an expert on popular culture in the United States. In the mid-'60s, he had engaged in "participant observation" of Levittown (living in a house bought for him by the Ford Foundation), and he had documented his findings in the book entitled *The Levittowners*.[62] His best-known contribution to the debate on the role of the media in American society was his 1966 article "Popular Culture in America: Social Problem in a Mass Society or Social Asset in a Pluralist Society?," later expanded into the book *Popular Culture and High Culture*.[63] Gans's article began with a detailed examination of the evidence for the validity of contemporary critiques of mass or popular culture. He found the evidence of most studies to contradict the claims of "administered control" made by critical theorists such as Theodor Adorno and Max Horkheimer.[64] Gans's most important point was that there were actually a number of different popular cultures, which he proposed to call "taste cultures"—sets of cultural products and practices that were created in conformance with coherent sets of values. Each taste culture served its own "taste public"; each had its own art, music, literature, magazines, films, TV programs, furnishings,

61] Harold Lasswell, cited in David Riesman, "Listening to Popular Music," *American Quarterly* 2 (1950): 408.

62] Herbert J. Gans, *The Levittowners: Ways of Life and Politics in a New Suburban Community* (New York: Pantheon Books, 1967).

63] Herbert J. Gans, *Popular Culture and High Culture: An Analysis and Evaluation of Taste* (New York: Basic Books, 1974); "Popular Culture in America: Social Problem in a Mass Society or Social Asset in a Pluralist Society?," in *Social Problems: A Modern Approach*, ed. Howard S. Becker (New York: John Wiley and Sons, Inc., 1966).

64] Gans, "Popular Culture in America," 554–57.

architecture, foods, and cars. Each had its own institutions for meeting its aesthetic needs.

Gans described six of these taste cultures. While the lower-middle taste public, as the largest group, was dominant in terms of economic power, the upper-middle taste public had the most political power over public allocations of funds for cultural products, and the producers of high culture had the most prestige.[65] Two taste cultures, creator high culture and lower-middle culture, are particularly important to an understanding of Signs of Life. Creator high culture was that of the serious artist, the scholar, and the critic. It was exemplified by original art distributed in galleries, books published by subsidized presses, the "little magazines," off-Broadway theater, European and underground cinema, public radio and television stations. Cultural goods were judged on the basis of creator standards such as the relationship between method and content, the subtlety of content, depiction of mood and feeling, expression of the personal values of the creator. The taste public for these products was a small one that valued exclusiveness. More status was given to creators than to performers, and critics had almost as high a status as performers.[66] Lower-middle culture, on the other hand, had its public in the lower-status professions and other white collar jobs. This group's preferred culture was traditional, and it rejected the sophistication of upper-middle culture. Substance or "content" was emphasized, and form was required to serve substance. Cultural products ought to uphold lower-middle-class values, and conflicts with these values ought to be resolved within the art form. Heroes were ordinary persons. The lower-middle group was the major audience for the mass media; its tastes in architecture and furniture were traditional; it was more interested in performers than in writers or directors, and it paid little attention to critics, relying instead on the judgments of family and friends.[67]

Without the idea of six equally valid taste cultures it is difficult to understand the thrust of Signs of Life. For Venturi and Scott Brown at least, Gans's work answered the question "who are the people?" But although the imagery of Signs of Life, squarely located within Gans's category of

65] Ibid., 579–97.
66] Ibid., 584–86.
67] Ibid., 589–90.

lower-middle culture, was presented in the realistic tradition of aesthetic shock, in fact there was little shock or "oddness" in this material. Rather it was all too disturbingly familiar, too "close to home." Whereas Le Corbusier had attacked the stuffy bourgeois architecture of the academy, Venturi and Scott Brown were using (petit)-bourgeois architecture to attack the beliefs of a profession that felt itself to be revolutionary. And whereas the Smithsons had maintained, along with their frank enjoyment of American ads, an artistic or ironic detachment toward their material, Venturi and Scott Brown seemed to be advocating for theirs. In the section of the manuscript entitled "Manipulative Capitalism and the Critics," Venturi and Scott Brown addressed architectural critics certain that "everyone" hated what they themselves disliked. They observed that, although Levittown had been extensively renovated over the almost thirty years since its creation, most of the renovations had been symbolic, and the symbols tended to intensify rather than to nullify the imagery put in place by the developer. They concluded:

> How far can you take the argument "It was rammed down their throat?" Many of suburbia's critics live in suburbia, but they can generally afford a higher "class" of suburbia than Levittown. Why should critics deny people of lower income their own version of the suburban environment?[68]

Thus Venturi and Scott Brown's answer to Frampton's critique was that, given the chance to express themselves through their dwellings, Levittown's residents had shown that they actually preferred its lower-middle imagery to high art. It therefore behooved architects to pay serious attention to this imagery.

In many ways, understanding Venturi and Scott Brown's use of Gans's theory of taste cultures also provides the key to the difficult reception of *Signs of Life* within the architectural community. In following Gans, the exhibit conflated two incompatible kinds of formal analysis: the socio-

68] Venturi and Scott Brown, "Conclusion, Manipulative Capitalism and the Critics," in "Signs of Life," 1.

logical method of content analysis, and architectural explorations of aesthetic possibilities. Added to the one visually stimulating and shocking example, there were twenty not-so-dramatic ones. These large samples, necessary to a rigorous sociological analysis, were, however, presented more as a casebook, grouped under headings but without extracting either compositional or analytic principles. As sociological or anthropological data, the exhibition functioned to expose architects to material they thought they were familiar with, but in a way that implicitly revealed the aesthetic principles behind this material. However, also implicit in the presentation was a valorization, not only of lower-middle culture as the culture of "the people," but of the aesthetic principles of this group, a position most architects could not accept. For architects unfamiliar with this sociological method, the case study was all too easily construed as an aesthetic message. The exhibition also presented material laden with "content" and conventional moral messages that violated artistic avant-garde strictures against figuration as well as its demand that art be original. Stated in terms of Gans's schema, the exhibit transgressed the principles of the high-art taste culture of which Venturi and Scott Brown were members and to whose taste public they spoke. This combination of high-art method and lower-middle content pleased almost no one.

In addition, Venturi and Scott Brown's "deadpanning" was confusing to architects. Was it ironic or not? Venturi and Scott Brown themselves seem to have been undecided about this, caught between the avant-garde paradigm of revolution through art, and pop art's detached observation and commentary. Indeed, the exhibition did not make clear what architects ought to do. Whereas it was easy to make direct connections between the theory of *Complexity and Contradiction* and the Guild House, for example, or between the ideas in *Learning from Las Vegas* and the National Football Hall of Fame (1967) or the Thousand Oaks competition (1969), such connections were less obvious for *Signs of Life*. They were to be found less in their well-known projects than in decisions to engage in certain less high-profile, high-art projects such as the

Philadelphia Crosstown Community study and the Chinatown Housing project for the Philadelphia Redevelopment Authority (1979).

The residue of the confusion and misapprehension Venturi and Scott Brown encountered in applying high-art expertise to the task of providing an architecture for "the people" leaves a number of questions unresolved. Their definition of lower-middle culture as the common culture, although it made sense in terms of Gans's analysis of its numerical majority, did not correspond to architects' belief in the cultural dominance of high art. Further, their work raised the question of whether it is possible to design forms valid for social groups other than the designer's own. Put in Gans's terms, could one taste culture design for another? Caught between the ironic, high-art stance of the pop artists and realism's impulse toward nonjudgmental display, the exhibition did not present the forms of lower-middle culture in a way that made sense either to architects or to their lay audience. And despite their clarity about their position as high-culture artists, Venturi and Scott Brown's hope for an architecture valid for all taste cultures led them to design an amalgam of high and popular art forms that often alienated the "average person."[69] On the other hand, their recent museum projects, which have been popular successes, have not always been well received by architectural critics.

Venturi and Scott Brown's conviction that the mechanisms of reading were common to all segments of American culture was, in *Signs of Life*, transformed into a search for a commonly understood set of symbols to be derived from lower-middle taste culture but subjected to the transformations of high art. Venturi and Scott Brown believed that a common language and common mechanisms of reception for architectural messages could be developed, and they gave the baroque as an example of an architecture that had appealed on many different levels to all of the diverse sectors of its society.[70] But their belief that "reading" architecture by means of association to other known forms provides the basis for a commonly understood language of architecture seems belied by current practice. While the concept of architecture as communication is accepted by many practitioners as the

69] Scott Brown, *Urban Concepts*.

70] Robert Venturi and Denise Scott Brown, lecture, Princeton University, 9 December 1991.

In our mass society, the suburbs have come to stand for the country life.

"THEMES AND IDEALS OF THE AMERICAN SUBURB, THE RURAL IDEAL," ILLUSTRATION FROM "SIGNS OF LIFE," 1976.

principle underlying the design of forms, the content of the communication is often designed to disturb rather than confirm commonly held cultural patterns. Thus Venturi and Scott Brown's contention that lower-middle culture is acceptable on its own terms still controverts architects' conceptions of their role.

Finally, the most difficult question raised by the work of Venturi and Scott Brown is whether the forms of the everyday can attain a legitimate public role. Can this unconceptualized realm of experience be represented in the public realm by means of architecture without destroying its diffuse, "practical" character? Venturi and Scott Brown's attempts to represent the internal structure of the everyday world in *Signs of Life* must be accounted only a partial success. Their instinct for its intellectual form did not translate into a presentation comprehensible to architects, nor did their built work find a way out of this contradiction. The question raised by the work of Venturi and Scott Brown—can the public art of architecture succeed in displaying the ordinary, unmarked events of everyday life in its forms, or can it only accommodate and shelter them?—remains unresolved.

TOM'S GARDEN

MARGIE RUDDICK

My neighbor Tom planted a vegetable garden a few years ago. I can see it from my study window, and I can also see, at very close range, the decoy owl that is planted on a stake above the garden to frighten predators. While I can't say that the owl has done a good job of repelling pests, it has become something of a personal emblem, a token that indicates to me, by the very fact that I have grown to like it, a change in the way I perceive the world around me.

Tom's house was built in the early 1960s, on a less than half-acre plot of dune overlooking the Atlantic on the eastern end of Long Island, next to the beach house my parents bought in 1957. When we moved there, ours was one of a handful of beach cottages strewn along the dune that had survived the hurricane of 1938. The original owners of Tom's house—Procter and Gamble heirs from Cincinnati—built it as their beach cabana, a place to retreat to when they wanted a vacation from their immense stucco mansion a mile away, atop the bluff that is the very end of the terminal moraine of the glacier that created Long Island. Several owners later, in the early 1980s, the house still stood peacefully, a Japanese inspired structure on the neutral ground of beach grass and sand. Then Tom bought it.

Tom was a player in the junk bond fields of the 1980s. He bought the house as a beach house, but after a career reversal that included testifying against his boss, Tom moved out to the house full-time, making this neighborhood of small beach houses and contemporary bungalows his year-round world. Soon a young woman with a very young child moved into the house with him. Things on his land started to change.

I should have anticipated what Tom would slowly begin to do to his house and dune when he enlarged his oceanfront deck. Challenging the legality of his extension, the building department asked Tom to delineate his property, for reference. With customary bravado, he fenced off his property on all sides, and for the first time the linear swath of dune was segmented along property lines, one of which runs perilously close to my house. The dune became ours versus his, a suburban overlay on a shore landscape. Over the years the rugosa roses have grown up and the split-rail fence has weathered. Inevitably, the harsh beach climate blurred the hard lines of fence and ownership.

When my family moved to Long Island in 1957, there probably was no building department to speak of. Our house sits at the ocean's edge of a beach development started in the 1920s, laid out on a grid of two blocks parallel to the water, with eight lanes running perpendicular to the ocean. The tiny plots—most are a quarter of an acre—could be purchased with model plans for small anonymous cape houses with names like "Nantucket" and "Sconset." The scrub landscape of shad, bayberry, beachplum, scrub oak and Japanese black pine provided a soft medium for the modest cottages that began to spring up over the low-lying back dunes. When I was small, the straight dirt roads had a wild character despite their layout: a tangle of trees, shrubs, vines, and native grasses screened the houses that nestled in the growth. Many people, however, had carved small gardens out of their back yards, and you could catch a glimpse, around the corners of the houses, of small emerald green patches, proper gardens with wisteria, hydrangea, and daylilies. While the face toward the road was often unkempt and chaotic, the small private world behind the house was often lush and well groomed; each of these gardens was different from the next.

In the 1960s, the dunes to the west of our neighborhood, which had stretched unbroken from the bluff to the ocean, were surveyed, cleared of their scrub, and built on. The roads, rather than following the grid of the 1920s development, were laid out in serpentines, winding lanes that were, by code, wider than their predecessors, and asphalted. The character of this neighborhood bore little resemblance to the older settlement: whereas that original neighborhood was organized around narrow, straight dirt roads, this new development had to conform to minimum widths for fire trucks, and required more durable materials for roads; whereas the grid of the older neighborhood appeared wild and rural, this new subdivision, laid out in a pastoral, meandering plan, appeared artificial, new, and garish. This was not merely the product of road layout: new contemporary houses, each a unique architectural statement, loomed from atop sandpiles, rather than nestling in hollows. It is not coincidental that Charles Gwathmey's studio and house for his parents sits atop the bluff, overlooking this precinct. His experiment in pure geometric form on a residential scale seems to have spawned legions of offspring tumbling down the dune toward the ocean. Whereas the old neighborhood was a diverse landscape with somewhat anonymous houses tucked into it, the new neighborhood became a collection of gregarious houses, with a single remaining component of the landscape, sand, tucked under it.

Tom's house predates the new development, but in some ways, in its original form, it was similar—a lone figure on a ground of dune, sited close to other houses. What it has become is certainly a less clear and austere vision. A big blank lawn cut out from the grasses; trees jammed up against the house; a basketball hoop; the vegetable garden, slipped into a bank of scrub next to the driveway. Some people who come over to my house ask me what the landscape idea is over there at Tom's. In order to appreciate Tom's landscape, it is essential to understand what it looks like with people in it; it is necessary to see Tom, his family, and his friends in it. Without them, it is an array of unlike spaces, materials, and objects. With them, it is a gathering place; a series of gardens; a recreational place. Because Tom has added each of these features as he has seen fit, his landscape has never been conceived through the lens of an overall plan.

If Tom's landscape were drawn in plan, it would probably look more like a collage than a cohesive whole, and would only start to make sense when the uses—people playing ball or sitting around a table, say—were overlaid on the plan. In the case of many of those landscapes that are studied and held up as monuments of design, it is the objects of daily life that begin to unravel the illusion of integrity. Most of the official canon of twentieth-century landscape architecture consists of remarkable places photographed at times when they appear most extraordinary: a horse drinking at a 100-foot-long trough, surreal against a luminescent back-drop, in a Luis Barragán landscape; the infinite grids of Dan Kiley; the sublime organic forms of Tommy Church and Henry Moore against the more earthbound meanders of a saltmarsh; the eerie grove of birches in Fletcher Steele's Blue Steps. Even Richard Haag's Gasworks Park, intended as a people's place, ends up in most photographs as an abstracted com-position of industrial shapes against the curvaceous regrading of a toxic site. But the landscape of the everyday is not terribly photogenic in the abstract; to attempt to orient oneself to the everyday in the landscape, to the ways in which one experiences a landscape from day to day, in prac-tical as well as conceptual terms, it is helpful to imagine people, and the ordinary objects that people bring with them, in these landscapes. By peopling the landscape, one can begin to introduce various conflicting uses and meanings into one landscape, as well as to imagine a landscape as occurring not over the course of one photo shoot but over many years' time.

In practice, it is relatively easy to create a landscape that, sealed off from the visual noise of people and their things, seems beautiful, arresting, of a piece. The training of most landscape architects in Amer-ica often begins with the assumption that there's no one home—the work of design begins with the plan, with a few supporting sections or perspectives into which ghostly figures are inserted at a height of approx-imately five-foot-eight. It is more difficult, or rather goes against a tradi-tional formalist training in a more disquieting way, to create a landscape that is accepting of the evidence of the commonplace, and accepting of more ideas or facts than can fit within an overall, unified, formal gesture. Tom's design by accretion—his insertion of the functions that he wanted into the landscape—took the opposite approach to the professional's overall strategy. Rather than being a ground onto which the objects of every day are placed, his landscape is the objects of every day, arrayed side-by-side. A beach ball does not merely provide atmosphere; it is the atmosphere. Tom's landscape admits of the present, of the facts of daily life, in a way that a professionally prepared landscape rarely does. And the reason that it admits of the present is that it is constituted by change—the things that occur over seasons, over time—and by fragments. Lacking a cohesive overall plan, the landscape can accept new additions, as there is no pure intention as to the landscape's formal integrity with which to interfere. There is no consistent whole to Tom's landscape; it resists objectification because it is composed of incidences, all unrelated except in that they result from Tom's needs.

On a recent trip to Stourhead, I was disheartened to discover that my visit coincided with the yearly *fête champêtre*, which required that many of Stourhead's lawns, lakes, and numerous follies be outfitted with soundstages, lights, ferry slips, and other festival paraphernalia, including workers scurrying around in preparation for the evening's spectacles. These would follow an "oriental" theme. After a few attempts to avoid photographing light standards emerging from the lake, stages, and microphones, I began to appreciate what an opportunity this coincidence provided for me: while I could always buy magnificent slides of an unblemished (and almost nonexistent) Stourhead, when could I ever have captured such a demonstration of scale, of occasional use, an example in the landscape of both ends of Aldo Rossi's spectrum of propelling versus pathological permanences? I would imagine that Rossi would classify Stourhead as the latter, a monument frozen in the era of its construction, incapable of adapting to new meanings and uses. But as a monumental landscape so clearly resistant to admitting the present, it was doing a pretty good job of assuming new functions, at least for that week. By contrast a landscape that is the product of tinkering, of adding one thing, then the next, has a great advantage over the canonical monuments of landscape design created out of whole cloth, in that, as a product of accretion, it can accept new uses and meanings with less friction, less tension between an identifiable whole and the dissonant parts that are added on, shoehorned in, or laid over. The world that the designer creates, through addition, subtraction or substitution, has as its organizing principle the will of the designer. The degree to which the landscape becomes a closed system—with a limited vocabulary and a cohesiveness that is sometimes referred to as harmony—often corresponds to the power of the designer to subsume the client's interests, and the facts of everyday life, within the overall conceptual drive. A landscape that is the product of tinkering, of adding and adjusting, can suggest the possibility that design can be the product of many confluences, in three dimensions, of many different streams of life.

I have come to see Tom as a great tinkerer. The first thing Tom built was his deck. What had been a small overlook perched above the ocean became a large outdoor living space. Tom has many friends, and the deck became a gathering spot for barbecues, cocktails at sunset, and family reunions. The house began to grow—a garage, a maid's room, an enlarged upstairs master bedroom, among other amenities, were added. The house changed from a beach bungalow, a simple bar building with a hexagonal common room, to a split-level. Tom didn't hire an architect—he and the builder designed exactly what he needed, a new room here, windows there for views. The result is what would be called a builder's house if it weren't for the quirkiness of the old cottage poking through the utilitarian additions. The rooms became bigger, the surfaces more slick, and the character moved from beach to suburb—nothing effects this shift as quickly as baseboard heating. Because there were so many people visiting Tom on a regular basis, he enlarged his parking area—from a small gravel turnaround to an ample lot. Then came the basketball hoop above the new garage door. After a few rounds of gravel dribbling, he ordered the asphalt truck to come asphalt the whole driveway. And so, incrementally, Tom's lot came to be dominated by the structures needed for the way he lives. The effect to me, next door, was that my serene baseline—the dunes, the ocean, the quiet—was receiving an increasing amount of static from the precinct of Tom's house. Literal noise intruded when his older kids would visit and pump out rock music into the salty atmosphere. But there was a lot of aesthetic noise happening too: fences, asphalt, basketball hoops. Over the next few years I watched my unease change in character, from suspicion of Tom's every move (will he be installing a bowling alley? A giant TV screen over the deck?) to suspicion of my own training, my own expectations, and my own conception of my role in the landscape, all of which conspired to judge Tom's tinkering with his landscape as something to be suppressed.

My own set of values when it comes to my own landscape is based on an assumption, widely held in the area in which I live, at least until recently, that the highest level of art involves manufacturing the appearance that nothing has been done, acquired, or forced. To Tom, this might seem outlandish. To spend large sums of money on work that is not evident once it is completed could seem the height of perversity. In fact, my level of wariness of the signs of consumption has led me to award high value to work that eliminates all signs of consumption, in the process commodifying the look of austerity, or of casualness. But I have been raised in and have passed through educational and cultural systems that have trained me to consider my landscape as inevitable and unambitious, and, in this beach environment, to consider a landscape in which the signs of construction and acquisition are evident as jarring and unnatural. If Tom and I had passed through the same systems, I would not spend so much time thinking about his landscape, and only imagining what he must think of mine; we would probably get together once every so often for a drink, on one of our decks, overlooking the ocean.

But Tom comes from a culture different from the amalgam of cultures that my parents and environment provided me. His mother's house, down the road and away from the beach, is a modest builder's house, a two-story box that would look familiar in a suburban neighborhood. She has, over the years, adapted the house and its small landscape, sitting on the edge of the new, winding subdivision, to its seaside setting with beachy perennial plantings, gravel, buoys, and welcoming signs. Like houses along the Jersey shore, which often do not differ from houses in the suburbs in form or style, the house does not rely on architecture to tell you that it is a beach house, but rather on signs in the landscape. My house, with its diminutive size, shingled gables, and white trim, fits into the rural tradition of the eastern end of Long Island, a small farm out-building that happens to be a beach house. My mildly neglectful attitude toward the house and the landscape fits in with an ethic that is common in the area, an attitude of *laissez-faire* that keeps the place casual and nat-ural-seeming. No space reads as very important: a small kitchen garden, a deck, and a terrace provide places to be out of doors, but the dominant landscape is the dune and the ocean. I was not aware that my own land-scape carries with it the messages of a culture until I began to try to understand Tom's next door. I did not recognize that the plantings I have put in over the years—native grasses, bayberry, thyme—are as much a sign to my visitors, a message that it is better to enhance what is already in place, as the buoys that line Tom's walkway to the beach, or the ban-ners that have sprouted on his deck—first an American flag, then an Irish flag, and, more recently, the Scottish flag—are messages about Tom. The fact that I have spent considerable time and money to achieve the desired effect of naturalness belies my own intentions.

In the upper-middle-class culture that until recently dominated this particular area of eastern Long Island, and along the margins of which I was raised, it is considered unseemly to make a big deal out of oneself. I don't know where Tom grew up, but I can imagine that for him, it is acceptable to let people know where you have come from and where you are going. In a suburban neighborhood, the garage and the car are not necessarily things to hide; in a rarefied summer community that had existed for a century on the eastern end of Long Island, proudly dis-playing one's acquisitions was traditionally perceived as a sign that one had arrived very recently, and had not yet developed a sense of humility. Once, when I attended a church service in the town at a congregation originally formed by the soap heirs who lived on the bluff, the sermon topic was humility; I heard from a friend who attended another service that that Sunday's theme was hospitality. The messages of the culture are clear: although you get to live in this place, which is heaven on earth, remember that there are people less fortunate; don't speak too loudly; don't flaunt your success. In this particular region, when people not born into this culture have reached a level of achievement that affords them a house on the ocean, they have more often than not jettisoned the landscape style of their origins, opting for the impressive yet understated landscape mode of hedges, scaled-down Victorian carpetbedding (that is what all that *impatiens* is, after all), and large shade trees. A client once railed at me, after I had placed plants far enough apart so that they could grow well, with earth still visible, that I had made his property "look like an *immigrant's* house," an odd choice of words, I thought, to be passed from one child of immigrants to another. But Tom has brought his landscape with him—a landscape that signals not that a very important personage lives here, but that a family lives here, a family with a specific history of enjoying being outdoors, and being together. That said, even to discuss the signals Tom is sending is to deny a major factor in Tom's makeup, one that distinguishes him from many people who aspire to have houses in this community: Tom does not really care what other people think of him.

One day I drove up to my house and noticed a wooden frame sprouting from the small patch of scrub between my driveway and Tom's. "Hey, Tom, what're you building?" I asked, trying to mask any sign of desperation in my voice, for what more could he do? "A vegetable garden," came the answer. Tom was clearing away grasses and native shrubs to make way for corn, tomatoes, and squash. His answer caught me short, and I found myself rethinking my assumptions about Tom, about his house, and his land. As with the house and the driveway, Tom was carving out exactly what he needed. He had no image in mind; while neighbors down the road pulled out acres of grasses and bayberry to put down perfect lawns and long lines of *impatiens*, Tom did not seem guided by a concern for what anybody would think when driving past or to his house. The first year of the vegetable garden, Tom could not have been a more anxious parent. He cultivated, watered, coddled, staked, paced around, smoked, looked some more, adjusted a leaf here, cut back a stalk there. As his first crop matured, I began to take an interest. It didn't hurt that he would give us the odd cucumber. I noticed the snowfence less, and the height of the corn more. I enjoyed seeing the owl as I entered my study. I liked the sound of water from the hose on hot days.

So the garden came, and I assimilated it into the things that are good in my purview. Gone were the *Panicum virgatum* and the *Andropogon scoparius*, but the cabbage and rhubarb weren't dismal replacements. Tom was not finished with his landscaping, however. One day a Bobcat appeared and began tearing up the grasses, shrubs, and other "weedy" growth in front of the house on the other side of Tom's circular driveway. This had been happening elsewhere in the neighborhood: as property values have skyrocketed to the point at which a tiny bungalow can fetch a small fortune, new homeowners have come to feel that their grounds, even if they occupy less than a quarter-acre, should appear appropriately stately. The grasses are ripped out, as are the bayberry, beach plum, and vines—the cover that is home to dove, quail, snipes, rabbits—and instant lawn is installed. The aesthetic of wild dirt roads and tangled front yards is vanishing. The inevitability of the desire for lawn—the folly of it, given the conditions of our region, and the maintenance it requires—are as integral to our regional character as cold winters. In my neighborhood, despite zoning regulations that require homeowners to retain at least half of their land in its original state, lawns do seem to creep from one lot to the next, as a peculiar peer pressure seeps like runoff across property lines. The grasses that grow along the roads have their aesthetic as well as ecological merits—tender green in spring, golden in late summer, clouds of seed heads in fall, yellow against the snow in winter. But they are, to many homeowners, weeds: they look unkempt, unmanaged, and unciv-ilized. When I saw Tom's landscaper begin to tear out the grasses, I imag-ined that the lawn seepage making its way through our neighborhood had finally reached my doorstep. But he did not, in fact, clear out to the road. He left the grasses and Russian Olives that screen him from the road, and cleared a patch only about 20 feet in depth, maybe 60 feet in length. After the lawn was laid, a hammock appeared, and a huge beach ball. Once the roots had taken, I began to see the child who lives with Tom out on the lawn, sometimes with a caretaker, rolling around on the huge ball, or playing with a badminton racquet. I realized that this swath of lawn was a present from Tom to this boy—a soft, green carpet where he can play and be watched from the house. He has special needs, and plays on his own mostly, so this was his own playground, replete with activities that he can do alone or with one of the adults who care for him. The lawn, far from being a symbol, as it is for people who want the look of the pastoral English park landscape at the beach, is simply a useful surface. And it is one of a series of landscape moves that have transformed Tom's dune from a cabana on a spare, neutral ground to a compound, with many activities and uses.

What Tom has done over the years has transformed the figure-ground relationship between his house and the land in ways that, despite the style or form the landscape was adopting, actually bring his house closer in line, at least in the way land is used, with the modest houses of the older neighborhood. When Tom bought it, the house stood alone amid the beach grass, but it now forms the boundary between front and back, and fits into a compound of scrub, dune, garden, and lawn. Front and back differ in their materials—lawn, scrub, and vegetables in front; deck and dune in back. But Tom's use of what should be considered his front, the approach, is actually what occurs in the backyards of the older houses—gardening, tossing a ball around—and it has occurred to me that a beach house actually has two fronts; Tom's erection of an Irish, a Scottish, and an American flag atop the dune, visible from the beach, and his installation of a figurehead atop a piece of play equipment overlooking the ocean are as much a statement about who lives there as the things one usually sees at the entrance to a house. Tom's landscape reworking has varied, distinguished, and reclassed the parts of his landscape according to the things he likes or needs to do outdoors. His place has shifted from picturesque scene to a working landscape, from view to place. The changes that Tom has wrought have transformed the neighborhood: a summer beach colony, its faded and shingled structures blown across a dune, now has in one small corner a place that looks rooted year-round, with evergreen trees that become a light garden at Christmas. When I discovered this latter effect one December as I stopped by to check my closed-up house, I understood why Tom had planted such seemingly out-of-place spruces along the road.

By now it is fairly common for the lay person to understand that the landscape, or its components, are constituted of change: ecosystems comprise a dynamic process of competition, shifting equilibriums, of the movement of water, soil, plants, and animals across space and time. What is less easy to accept is that one's neighbors act as agents in this system, that changes in the culture of the land next door are as natural and inevitable as a change in the water table, or the death of an old oak. Although we can easily comprehend that nature "out there" is a constantly shifting mosaic of forces, it is less comfortable to acknowledge that our own back yards are engaged in this process, and that new neighbors, new modes of acting within the landscape in daily life, are what keep a place in motion, propel it, as it were, in time.

So, after understanding that the process of change is inevitable, that Tom's landscape is as natural to the area as mine, the question still remains: just what is the landscape idea over there at Tom's? What am I to make of the form it has taken? My interest in, and appreciation for, Tom's garden is not innocent; the fact that his landscape looks disjointed, that the building is, to my eyes, less than beautiful, feeds into a quarrel that has been taking place within me for a long time, the tug-of-war between form and content. The first thing a designer will do is attack the plan—it is to the plan that we turn in trying to organize space and program. But many landscapes that are widely held to be successful or satisfying, certain English gardens or the Ramble in Central Park for example, read as somewhat disjointed, chaotic, or awkward when viewed in plan. Often a landscape that is considered to have too much going on is dismissed by the professional as confusing. But landscapes with overlappings, shifts of direction, interruptions, and, not least of all, signs of the matter and detritus necessary for people to inhabit a place are often landscapes that are dear to the people who live with them. The impulse, after years of training, to justify, rectify, organize, and simplify often enforces one mode of action in a place; unanticipated or even subversive uses, the kinds of activities that can give a place an identity of its own beyond the way it looks, can be preempted by the overarching desire to make things work out formally, in plan. On Tom's land, things happen; the place becomes.

As the designer of his landscape, Tom has an economy of his own, with little regard for impressing his guests or appropriating a look or collecting plants. As a landscape architect, I find the whole hard to decipher, but as a neighbor I find its parts beautiful—the changing colors of the vegetable garden, the sound of a ball being bounced on asphalt, people waving hello and goodbye. And Tom's changes have not ended at his property line; I have to confess to a small amount of landscape seepage that is occurring at my own house, as I have begun to interfere more seriously with our tiny plot of beach landscape. This year I put in a one-zone irrigation system so that our front walk will be green; and for next year we are planning a small vegetable garden, south of a big pine, where a huge pokeweed has grown undisturbed for the past few years, next to a bank of pink Seven Sisters roses planted by my father, a tinkerer himself, thirty-five years ago.

JAMES CASEBERE

TOILETS, 1995

TOWARD A THEORY OF

NORMATIVE ARCHITECTURE

JOAN OCKMAN

1]

In their book *Kafka: Toward a Minor Literature* (1975), Gilles Deleuze and Félix Guattari identify three characteristics that make Franz Kafka's writing radical.[1] The first is *deterritorialization of language*. A citizen of Prague, Kafka spoke and wrote in German, the language of high culture for the educated bourgeois Czech-Jewish minority in the years prior to World War I. Yet the Jews of Prague had only a marginal claim to German culture. Kafka's language reflects his minority status, both within the Czech nation in which he lived and with respect to the historically anti-Semitic Germanic culture in whose language he wrote. His linguistic deterritorialization, as Deleuze and Guattari suggest, is analogous to that of African-American authors writing in English. The second characteristic is the inherently *political* nature of such language. Because of the self-consciousness that typifies the relationship between the deterritorialized individual and society, political questions, which might remain in the background for others, immediately come to the fore. The deterritorialized author always bears the burden of intensified political consciousness. Third, following from the previous two, such writing represents the experience of the outsider. Language is a shared property, a form of membership in a community. Not belonging by birthright to the community of German letters, Kafka is unable to write in its language as a "master." He comes to its tradition without standing, unauthorized. Hence his characters are generic; they are known by their initial (K) or their species (dog,

[1] Gilles Deleuze and Félix Guattari, "What Is a Minor Literature?" in *Kafka: Toward a Minor Literature*, trans. Dana Polan (Minneapolis: Univ. of Minnesota Press, 1986), 16–27.

mole, mouse, etc.). As nonpersons, they constitute an undifferentiated class of "others" related simply by virtue of being excluded, estranged, homeless. In representing these outcasts in his writing, Kafka gives expression to that which is "not yet given." His fiction is in this sense anticipatory, *the collective enunciation* of those whose voice has not yet been heard.

These three characteristics constitute Deleuze and Guattari's definition of a minor literature. "A minor literature doesn't come from a minor language," they state; "it is rather that which a minority constructs within a major language." As such, it is the seedbed of subversion and transformation. "There is nothing major or revolutionary except the minor."[2] With this seeming paradox, Deleuze and Guattari dramatize that their reading of Kafka, as original a contribution to literary criticism as it is, is ultimately also the pretext for a strategy of cultural transformation.

But at the same time a less utopian corollary is suggested. Might it be possible, by reversing Deleuze and Guattari's terms, to derive the reciprocal definition: that is, the opposite, or counterrevolutionary, process of transformation? If a minor architecture—and here let us make the move into our own field—may be defined by deterritorialization, intensified political consciousness, and the anticipatory assemblage of new cultural forces, then might a *major architecture* be defined as *territorial, apolitical, and conservative of the status quo, or normative*? Such a definition seems to offer a useful description of the evolution of American architecture after World War II and of the process by which the international style achieved hegemony. The following is an attempt to apply this theory of becoming major to those developments and, briefly, their aftermath. More generally I wish to suggest that such an analysis can offer a dynamic explanation for the emergence of new or revisionist ideologies within architectural culture. It must be stressed that the relationship between minor and major architecture that is being proposed is to be understood as a historical condition in which that which is major is constantly redefining itself in relation to that which is minor, and that which is minor is always potentially challenging or hybridizing that which is major.

2] Ibid., 16, 26.

2]

As is well known, Henry-Russell Hitchcock and Philip Johnson's exhibition at the Museum of Modern Art in 1932 was effective not only in bringing European modern architecture to the consciousness of architects in the United States, but in removing from it the revolutionary social and political content that characterized it in the context of European socialism. William Jordy has called the *International Style* show "one of the most breathtakingly successful educational enterprises of the twentieth century."[3] Shifting the meaning of the new architecture from social reform to aesthetic style, Hitchcock and Johnson's canonic formulation went a long way toward making modern architecture "safe for capitalism," as Colin Rowe was later to put it, or, as Catherine Bauer said at the time, "safe for millionaires."[4]

This initial move bore fruit in the warm institutional receptions given European modern architects forced to flee their homelands for the United States during the 1930s and early '40s. Foremost among them were those who had been leading figures at the Bauhaus in Germany. In its successive incarnations in Weimar, Dessau, and finally Berlin, the Bauhaus existed at the margins of society. Some of its faculty and students were left-wing radicals; a large number were immigrants and foreigners. Although the school's ambition was to enter into a full-scale alliance with German industry, its finances were constantly precarious and the political climate surrounding it increasingly hostile. For Walter Gropius, Marcel Breuer, Ludwig Mies van der Rohe, Laszlo Moholy-Nagy, and the others who ended up in the United States, schools like the Harvard Graduate School of Design, the Illinois Institute of Technology (IIT), and the New Bauhaus in Chicago afforded far more hospitable working and living environments. Years later, Breuer looked back on the "Bauhaus idea" as a specific product of its time:

The Bauhaus was starting at zero. Everyone knows about the basic design course, and that was important. It

3] William H. Jordy, "The Aftermath of the Bauhaus in America: Gropius, Mies, and Breuer," in Donald Fleming and Bernard Bailyn, eds., *The Intellectual Migration: Europe and America, 1930–1960*, vol. 2 of *Perspectives in American History* (Cambridge, MA.: Charles Warren Center for Studies in American History, 1968), 493.

4] Colin Rowe, Introduction to *Five Architects: Eisenman, Graves, Gwathmey, Hejduk, Meier* (New York: Wittenborn, 1972), 4; Catherine Bauer to Lewis Mumford, 29 January 1932, cited in *The International Style: Exhibition 15 and the Museum of Modern Art*, ed. Terence Riley (New York: Rizzoli, 1992), 209.

changed visual education. But the basic design approach wasn't the Bauhaus. The Bauhaus belonged to society, and to its time. It was made for a destroyed society. Germany had lost the war. The inflation was terrible. Uncertainty was everywhere. The Bauhaus student was no professional. When I came to the Bauhaus [in 1920] I had no idea what I would become. In those conditions you didn't think about what you would become. The Bauhaus student was nobody. The Bauhaus ideal was starting from zero.[5]

To start from zero and aspire to a new cultural totality was to dream of creating a new world in the ashes of a tired and war-damaged Europe. In contrast, as the German architectural refugees realized, the United States was already a "new world," young and vigorous. An institution like Harvard was its academic centerpiece, richly endowed, its students from affluent backgrounds and professionally oriented. It is hardly surprising, then, that Gropius's approach to architecture underwent a transformation in the new circumstances: from "totality" to "team," from a vision of modern architecture as a synthetic world view potentially capable of broadscale cultural transformation—as he had envisioned in the first, idealist phase of the Bauhaus—to an affirmative notion of the architect as a team player collaborating with a diverse group of specialists. In America, Gropius saw the architect's role as professional servant to the democratic state, coordinator and aesthetic arbiter of its building program.[6]

Mies, operating in the context of a technical rather than a liberal arts school, was now in a position to institutionalize and propagate his own architectural philosophy. This occurred at IIT without ostensible sacrifice of aesthetic rigor, but at the price of academicization. In the cases of both Gropius and Mies, however, what must be emphasized is their ready adaptation to normative American building practice and their successful integration into the American professional

5] Cited in Jordy, "The Aftermath of the Bauhaus in America," 506.

6] See "The Architect Within Our Industrial Society" and "Architect—Servant or Leader?" in Walter Gropius, *Scope of Total Architecture* (New York: Harper & Brothers, 1955), 76–98.

milieu. Gropius's first projects in this country reflect his appreciation for New England wood-frame construction, while Mies's vocabulary of steel and glass appeared a natural successor to the Chicago frame as it had developed since the last quarter of the nineteenth century. To quote Jordy again:

> Despite differences in approach between Gropius's and Mies's programs, they both believed in a visual language of simple, clear, elemental forms as the "objective" basis for architectural education. They both emphasized structure and technology which was normative and standard rather than radical and extraordinary.... Both programs accepted what is laconically given in modern American society and made this the starting point for their programs.[7]

Such accommodation was, in any event, essential for European architects desirous of acceptance and opportunities to work in the United States. Cultural elitism, no less social radicalism, could only prove counterproductive. A xenophobic attack by Robert Moses on the new wave of foreign architects, published in the *New York Times Magazine* in 1944 under the title "Mr. Moses Dissects the Long-Haired Planners: The Park Commissioner Prefers Common Sense to Their Revolutionary Theories," sent a crude message:

> Let's have a general look at the "Beiunskis." A Beiunski is usually a refugee whose critical faculties outrun his gratitude to the country which has given him a home. He is convinced that we are a pretty backward people and doesn't mind saying that they ordered things better in the old country. "Bei uns," he says, they did it this way. The fact that we happen to like our awkward and primitive ways will not turn any genuine Beiunski from the stern task of teaching us how really cultured folks should behave. You have to be quite humorless to be a good Beiunski.[8]

7] Jordy, "The Aftermath of the Bauhaus in America," 515.

8] Robert Moses, "Mr. Moses Dissects the Long-Haired Planners: The Park Commissioner Prefers Common Sense to Their Revolutionary Theories," *New York Times Magazine*, 25 June 1944.

In short, the ideological reduction performed by Hitchcock and Johnson was hardly challenged by the émigrés themselves. Like their American colleagues, the transplanted architects were for the most part eager—whether out of new convictions or simply acquiescence—to realign the agenda of modern architecture with the imperatives of American capitalist society. Nor did this entirely insulate them from the attacks of the likes of Moses, especially after World War II, when the inception of the Cold War caused formerly left-leaning intellectuals to gravitate to the politics of consensus.

At the same time, on the wings of the victory delivered in World War II by United States military technology, mechanization took command of the American imagination—to evoke the title of Sigfried Giedion's book of 1948, *Mechanization Takes Command*. Despite resistance from a building industry entrenched in its traditional practices and a profession founded on aesthetic conservatism, the discipline of rational planning, having "won the war," was now seen as the prerequisite for continuing productivity and economic prosperity. The functionalist ethos infused the industrial process, increasingly becoming the chosen aesthetic of American big business. Even more importantly, at least from the standpoint of the present argument, this approach now became transformed from a merely accepted fact into a symbol of American cultural policy, an efficacious ideological tool. In other words, modern architecture stopped being an American import and became an export. If the term *international style*, when it was invented by Hitchcock, Johnson, and Alfred Barr, had designated, on tendentiously constructed premises, a common aesthetic denominator for diverse European movements—from Le Corbusier's Esprit Nouveau to the Bauhaus, from Dutch neoplasticism to Russian constructivism—by the 1950s *international style* betokened the increasingly homogeneous architectural imagery that was being transmitted back to Europe and throughout the world by a triumphalist American culture.

LEFT: **JACKSON POLLOCK AT WORK, 1950.**

RIGHT: **SKIDMORE, OWINGS & MERRILL, HEADQUARTERS FOR CONNECTICUT GENERAL LIFE INSURANCE COMPANY, BLOOMFIELD, CONNECTICUT, 1954–57. PARTNER IN CHARGE OF DESIGN, GORDON BUNSHAFT; SENIOR DESIGNER, NATALIE DE BLOIS.**

3]

In recent years revisionist art historians have sought to explain the success of abstract expressionism during the Cold War as a function of not just its undeniable formal vitality, but also its absence of disturbing sociopolitical content.[9] The new art proselytized in the 1950s by the ex-Marxist art critic Clement Greenberg, dubbed the New York School and institutionally backed by the Museum of Modern Art, was predicated on a celebration of the "intrinsic" qualities of the painterly medium—flatness of surface, the brushstroke, the fluidity of paint. Nonrepresentational and autonomous, it effectively served the apolitical politics of the "vital center," the new liberal-centrist thinking that became dominant in the United States by the late 1940s.

It is possible to characterize the dominant architecture during the same period analogously: as sheer technical power and formidable material presence conjoined with an ideologically neutral aesthetic. The abstract, laconic, and highly refined glass and steel facades of the international style harbored no explicit critical messages. In this sense, the "hot" abstraction of Jackson Pollock's painting and the "cold" abstraction of Skidmore, Owings & Merrill's architecture functioned simi-

9] See especially Serge Guilbaut, *How New York Stole the Idea of Modern Art: Abstract Expressionism, Freedom, and the Cold War,* trans. Arthur Goldhammer (Chicago: University of Chicago Press, 1983).

larly.[10] Both, intentionally or not, forwarded the cultural policy of the United States government. The intensive program of American embassy building undertaken around the world in the 1950s and early '60s exemplifies the symbiosis between Cold War propaganda and the new architectural style.[11] As historian Godfrey Hodgson has suggested, what the government sought from its professional elites during the period after World War II was "a maximum of technical ingenuity with a minimum of dissent."[12] This characterization would seem to apply as much to the arbiters of culture—painters and architects, among others—as to the captains of industry, science, and public policy.

At the same time, abstract expressionist painting and international style architecture manifestly differed as styles of self-presentation. Deriving its mythos from the romantic cult of genius and its modernist successor, the cult of originality, abstract expressionism glorified the individual artist, who enacted his American birthright of freedom in machismo gestures. Greenberg presented the New York School as a new American avant-garde, an artistic elite capable of transcending the leveling kitsch of mass culture. The architects of the postwar international style, on the other hand, aspired less to avant-garde heroics and aesthetic autonomy than to integration within the mainstream of capitalist production. Both Gropius and Mies, as already stated, saw their respective aesthetics as rooted in the givens of American industrial building practice. Moreover, while Gropius emphasized the team aspect of the design process, Mies saw architectural production even less individualistically, as the result of an impersonal and objective historical process. The architect, exalted as his calling might be, was ultimately the Zeitgeist's agent: "The individual is losing significance. His destiny is no longer what interests us. The decisive achievements in all fields are impersonal, and their authors are for the most part obscure."[13]

10] On "hot" and "cold" abstraction (although without reference to architecture), see several contributions to *Reconstructing Modernism: Art in New York, Paris, and Montreal, 1945–1964*, ed. Serge Guilbaut (Cambridge, MA: MIT Press, 1990), including Jean Baudrillard's "Hot Painting: The Inevitable Fate of the Image," a suggestive linkage of the metaphor to hot and cold war as well as to Marshall McLuhan's hot and cold media.

11] See Jane C. Loeffler, "The Architecture of Diplomacy: Heyday of the United States Embassy-Building Program, 1954–1960," *Journal of the Society of Architectural Historians* (September 1990): 251–78. Also see "US Building Abroad: In Doing Its Share of $100 Billion Postwar Job, the Building Industry Has Become a World-Wide Ambassador," *Architectural Forum* (January 1955): 98–119.

12] Godfrey Hodgson, "The Ideology of the Liberal Consensus," in *America in Our Time* (Garden City, NY: Doubleday & Co., 1976), 97.

13] Ludwig Mies van der Rohe "Baukunst und Zeitwille!" in *Der Querschnitt* 4, no. 1 (1924): 31; translated (differently) in Fritz Neumeyer, *The Artless Word: Mies van der Rohe on the Building Art* (Cambridge, MA: MIT Press, 1991), 246.

But with respect to the relationship between aesthetic and political culture—and what is here described in terms of a relationship between major and minor cultural forces—the difference between hot and cold abstraction was largely just a matter of style, which in turn may be seen as a function of the differences between painting and architecture as aesthetic practices. Thus the former could be individualistic and gestural, while the latter strove to be universal and laconic. Nonetheless what made both abstract expressionism and international style architecture normative or major in the 1950s was that they were basically apolitical. Both affirmed American Cold War ideology by leaving it unchallenged. For this reason both could be annexed by the system and their imagery disseminated around the world.

4]

If the impersonal approach of post–World War II architecture was strongly inspired by the work of Mies van der Rohe—beginning with his designs for the campus at IIT, executed from 1942 on—it was quickly synthesized and elaborated by a new generation of American practitioners. Above all it was the firm of Skidmore, Owings & Merrill (SOM) in its classic work of the 1950s and early '60s that defined and perfected the steel and glass aesthetic in the context of the large architectural office. Other firms—among them, those of Eero Saarinen, Pietro Belluschi, I. M. Pei, Victor Gruen, Wallace Harrison and Max Abramowitz, Vincent Kling, Edward Larrabee Barnes—were also successful propagators of the style. In Europe architects like Egon Eiermann, Arne Jacobsen, and Gio Ponti translated the American model, establishing, with local variations, the universality of the new architectural language. Apart from the formal characteristics shared by these various manifestations, however, what was most impressive about the postwar international style was its tectonic, programmatic, and professional refinement. The level of mastery and generalization it achieved could hardly have been anticipated from the isolated realizations of its prewar precursors. In these sophisticated and often beautifully articulated buildings, the glass "house" of the 1920s, repository of modernist culture's most utopian hopes, was transformed into a fully embodied expression of advanced capitalism, corporate bureaucracy, and big business. Architecture not only gave representation to these realities, but also partook of them in its professional structure and scale of operation. Postwar modern architecture absorbed the ethos of capitalism, disciplining it and giving it an aesthetic form.

Nor was this vision bereft of idealism, at least initially. On an intuitive level, an architectural image of transparency and openness was believed to embody values of democracy and freedom; "good design," it was expected, would join hands with enlightened capitalism to raise general standards of living. The soap company that commissioned SOM's Lever House in 1949 was motivated by such thinking, even if it also recognized the highly novel advertising impact of an all-glass facade in the traditional streetscape of New York's Park Avenue. But the reemergence, during the second half of the 1950s, of more eclectic and expressionistic impulses within architectural modernism is evidence of the crisis of this ideology. A new generation of architects like Philip Johnson, Edward Durrell Stone, Minoro Yamasaki, Paul Rudolph—many of them trained at Harvard under Gropius—as well as Gropius himself in the context of his firm TAC, quickly began to wring decorative variations out of the diagrammatic clarities of abstract functionalism, seeking to infuse architecture with the emotional and representational content it lacked.[14]

On the other hand, what today seems most remarkable about the normative "glass box" of these years is precisely its anonymity, its surrender of subjectivity. The language of reticence and rigor spoke of mastery and power, but without a traditional architectural master, without ego games. The buildings of the new international style were seemingly content to play a neutral role in the cityscape—even if they initially stood out in spite of themselves by virtue of their difference from everything around them. In SOM's case, the firm's collective signature and its emphasis on teamwork downplayed the identity of the individuals who were responsible for any design. The firm offered itself as comprehensive designer, from the

14] Cf. Klaus Herdeg, *The Decorated Diagram: Harvard Architecture and the Failure of the Bauhaus Legacy* (Cambridge, MA: MIT Press, 1983).

SKIDMORE, OWINGS & MERRILL, U.S. AIR FORCE ACADEMY, COLORADO SPRINGS, 1954–62. DIRECTOR OF DESIGN, WALTER NETSCH.

master plan to the ashtrays, but no longer in the sense of the *Gesamtkunstwerk*: more, rather, in that of being a "full-service" bureau of professionals. At the same time, the firm was sought out by elite and affluent clients who sensed, in both its organizational structure and highly controlled aesthetic, a productive capacity and a vision of the world mirroring their own.

The Museum of Modern Art undertook to exhibit SOM's work as early as 1950; Lever House was still only on the boards at this date and appeared in the show in model form. Founded by Louis Skidmore and Nathaniel Owings in 1936, SOM had received its decisive boost during World War II, when it received a government commission to design Site X of the Manhattan Project, a *tabula rasa* town at Oak Ridge, Tennessee, where the atomic bomb was secretly being developed. In this contribution to the incipient American military-industrial complex, which occasioned an exponential enlargement of the firm, as well as other early projects like Lake Meadows housing in Chicago for New York Life Insurance Company (1949–60), SOM honed its characteristic methodology and aesthetic. The exhibition curators stated:

> When a museum exhibits a painting, a piece of sculpture, an architectural drawing or model, the first question in the minds of both the staff and the public is "who is the painter, the sculptor, or the architect who designed it?" In the past, all of the architectural shows the Museum of Modern Art has exhibited have been designer's shows—the work of individuals like Le Corbusier, Ludwig Mies van der Rohe, Frank Lloyd Wright....
>
> When the Museum invited Skidmore, Owings and Merrill to exhibit its recent buildings, it did so because this

firm, composed of a group of single designers working exclusively in the modern idiom, produces imaginative, serviceable and sophisticated architecture deserving of special attention. The single designers who function within this organization have no fear of a loss of individuality. They are able to work within their corporate framework because they understand and employ the vocabulary and grammar which developed from the esthetic conceptions of the twenties. They work together animated by two disciplines which they all share—the discipline of modern architecture and the discipline of American organizational methods.[15]

In an article written three years earlier entitled "The Architecture of Bureaucracy and the Architecture of Genius," Henry-Russell Hitchcock had identified two opposite categories of architecture that he saw as coexisting at midcentury.[16] One of these was *bureaucratic architecture*, which he defined as "all building that is the product of large-scale architectural organizations, from which personal expression is absent." Hitchcock cited the work of Albert Kahn's firm in Detroit as an example: "the strength of a firm such as Kahn, or for that matter of a state architectural bureau, depends not on the genius of one man…but in the organizational genius which can establish a fool-proof system of rapid and complete plan production." Hitchcock specifically noted that he was using the term *bureaucratic* "without the pejorative connotation." Indeed, he stated, "Bureaucratic architecture can achieve in experienced hands a high level of amenity."

In direct opposition to bureaucratic architecture, according to Hitchcock, was *genius architecture*, "a particular psychological approach and way of working at architecture which may or may not produce masterpieces." Its qualities "depend on overall impact, just as the qualities of the more intensely expressive types of art such as poetry or painting or music do." Hitchcock considered this type of architecture an "artistic gam-

15] "Skidmore, Owings & Merrill, Architects, U.S.A.," *Museum of Modern Art Bulletin* (fall 1950): 5.

16] Henry-Russell Hitchcock, "The Architecture of Bureaucracy and the Architecture of Genius," *Architectural Review* (January 1947): 3–6.

ble," as likely to fail as to succeed. Although he acknowledged that "the world of the mid-twentieth century will need some buildings by architects of genius, for only thus can the necessary monotony and the low level of plastic interest of bureaucratic architecture be balanced and relieved," particularly when it came to "focal structures" like monuments, he also warned that in the hands of lesser architects, or applied to inappropriate programs or to very large and complex projects, the architecture of genius could easily lead to "pretentious absurdity." Forecasting that in the future the emphasis would more likely be on the architecture of bureaucracy than of genius, he cited as the two supreme and exceptional figures representing the latter tendency Frank Lloyd Wright and Le Corbusier, whose Guggenheim Museum and Marseilles housing block respectively, neither yet realized at the time, offered ample evidence of the power of the modern architectural imagination in the hands of masters.

It is significant that Hitchcock did not mention Mies at all in this article. I shall suggest why shortly. Meanwhile, not surprisingly, Wright vehemently took the opposite position. His book *Genius and the Mobocracy* (1949), a belated tribute to his *lieber Meister* Louis Sullivan, was an implicit assault on Hitchcock's argument. Bemoaning the death of the "great master," he denounced the standardized architecture of the "code-made and code-making expert." A typical subchapter in his book is entitled "Incapable of Conception They Are Masters of Appropriation."[17]

5]

Meanwhile, in Britain, a somewhat different model of bureaucratic architecture emerged at the same time that deserves to be considered here in passing. This was elaborated in the architectural department of the London County Council (LCC), an office responsible for a vast program of rehousing, and town and school building for the new British welfare state, some of it, despite the economic asperities of the day, of high quality. In the climate of postwar Britain, dispirited and greatly weakened by the war, the LCC and other county councils throughout the nation succeeded in striking a

17] Frank Lloyd Wright, *Genius and the Mobocracy* (New York: Duell, Sloan and Pearce, 1949), 7.

HERTFORDSHIRE COUNTY COUNCIL, KINDERGARTEN AT GARSTON, HERTS, ENGLAND, 1951–52. ARCHITECT IN CHARGE, C. H. ASLIN.

compromise between the orthodox positivism of CIAM (the Congrès Internationaux d'Architecture Moderne) and the empirical, populist, and domestic qualities that the English so much admired in the social welfare architecture of Sweden, a country that, having remained neutral during the war, had continued to build uninterruptedly throughout the 1940s. Through the councils, a domesticated modernism became normative in Britain, implementing what Maxwell Fry, a founding member of the British wing of CIAM, was to call "the ideal of a comprehensive architecture for the use of a highly technical and reasonably integrated society."[18]

As a broadscale program of state-implemented modernism, the work of the county councils bears comparison to that undertaken in major German cities in the 1920s, for example under the auspices of Ernst May's Neue Frankfurt administration or Martin Wagner and Bruno Taut's GEHAG in Berlin. But within the postwar period, as Hitchcock pointed out, the production of an office like the LCC may only be compared to a private firm like SOM in terms of size, scope of undertakings, and quality of work. The two may be seen as representing alternative models—public and private—of the "enlightened architectural bureaucracy."[19]

Also exemplary of the unprecedented hopes placed in a universal modernist language after the war was the discourse surrounding the development of the curtain wall. Two issues of the British *Architectural Review*, the first published in December 1950, the second in May 1957, bracket a changing attitude toward American culture, marking Britain's shift away from the "new humanist" sentimentality evoked by the war. In the 1950 issue, entirely devoted to "the mess that is man-made America," the editors roundly condemned the United States as a "hygienic but *visually* scrofulous waste-land which is the universal embodiment and symbol of Progress, twentieth century

18] Maxwell Fry, "Twenty-Five Years of Modern Architecture in England," *Architectural Design* (November 1955): 341.

19] Henry-Russell Hitchcock, introduction to *Architecture of Skidmore, Owings & Merrill, 1950–1962* (New York: Frederick A. Praeger, 1963), 10.

style."[20] They portrayed its expansionist ambitions as a dangerous threat to European culture: "Technocracy, as we see it, is the pistol the U.S. holds to the stomach of Western civilization."[21] In the second issue, published seven years later and entitled "Machine Made America," this verdict on American technical achievement was reversed; as Charles Jencks later remarked, the captions got changed. An enervated, postimperial Britain now looked longingly at the dynamism and prosperity of its former colony, a "success story" celebrated on the magazine's cover by Independent Group artist John McHale's proto-Pop robot head.

Above all, the *Architectural Review* of 1957 attached importance to the development of the curtain wall in the United States. In an argument reminiscent of Hitchcock's earlier article on bureaucracy and genius, and also echoing Gropius's homilies at this date, the editors stated that "America is beginning to give promise that a vernacular of modern architecture may be developing." They noted:

> It is an awkward but inescapable truth that the architecture of an age is judged by its weak as well as its strong links. Ever since the breakdown of classical discipline in the romantic movement and right up to the present, architecture's weak links have been very weak indeed. An age or nation may or may not produce its geniuses, there is nothing at all you can do about it, but if the average man is left without terms of reference, codes of practice, vocabulary or pattern book, he flounders. And the average man, architect, builder, handyman and client has been left to flounder now for nearly a hundred and fifty years without any clear architectural terms of reference....
>
> The curtain wall is the first sign of such a discipline presenting itself to modern architecture and being generally accepted. It has been observed that it has a "low emotional content." Is this a matter, though, for complaint? One of the most unpleasant aspects of our environment today is the litter of buildings attempting to express an emotional content

20] *Architectural Review* (December 1950): 339, 414. Italics in original.

21] Ibid., 416.

that their designers were neither capable of feeling nor understanding....[22]

The next forty pages of the *Review* contained a detailed survey of American curtain wall construction, presented historically, syntactically, and typologically. The editors concluded,

ALISON SMITHSON AND PETER SMITHSON, SUGDEN HOUSE, WATFORD, ENGLAND, 1956.

> After all the arguments for standardization have been run through, many architects are still disquieted at the thought that the specialization it implies may mean a lowering in status. But this is true only for those who still think of themselves as the old-time-all-around Gentleman Architect, whose status anyway descends daily because it fails to take account of today's needs. Only a very brief look at the situation here and in America is enough to show that where the architect gains respect and raises his status, he does so by delivering the goods, and what is more, delivering them on time; the goods in this case being efficient, economical, weathertight, comfortable and good-looking buildings; much more than that the average man doesn't ask.[23]

Earlier in the century, the desire to breach the divide between architecture and everyday building, between elite and mass culture, had manifested itself in the revolutionary projects of the Soviet avant-garde and manifesto-like projects and writings of architects like Le Corbusier, Bruno Taut, and Hannes Meyer. It was now reframed in the pragmatic terms of normative building practice. For those positioning themselves in the lineage of the modern movement, the curtain wall—appearing in *Sweet's Catalogue* as a separate category for the first time in 1956—held the promise of becoming a "new vernacular," a common language of architectural components. As such, it offered an antidote to the tendencies of undisciplined eclecticism and egoism

22] *Architectural Review* (May 1957): 307.

23] Ibid., 335–36.

that were resurfacing. The midcentury modernists envisaged that the contemporary kit of parts would make it harder to design a bad building and at the same time, like the old lingua franca of classicism, give the built environment coherence. Unlike an architectural language based on imitation of the past, however, the curtain wall aesthetic was bound up with ongoing technological development and oriented to the future. In their "Letter to America," written in 1958 after a first trip to this country, Alison and Peter Smithson questioned the use of the term *vernacular* to describe the new curtain wall architecture, but embraced the concept:

> Although the application of curtain-walls cannot be called a vernacular (as that implies a language), buildings which use them are undoubtedly better than they would have been if their architects had had to develop a brick and stone facade of their own.

The Smithsons also found aesthetic virtues in the new technology:

> Glass and metal faced buildings give the maximum light reflection into the street and this in itself is a contribution to the city. And there are, moreover, magical distortions when two straight-up-and-down buildings are opposite one another. A blue glass city, no matter how organisationally banal, is never optically boring.

Following this endorsement of "organizational banality," however, they drew a distinction: "Seagram, of course, in dark brown glass and bronze, plays it so cool that everything else looks like a jumped-up supermart."[24]

Likewise a year later the Smithsons would note after a trip to Chicago, "Mies van der Rohe's work in Chicago has both...normality *and* light-filled poetic space."[25] Hitchcock, it will be remembered, had failed

24] Alison Smithson and Peter Smithson, "Letter to America," in *Ordinariness and Light: Urban Theories 1952–60* (Cambridge, MA: MIT Press, 1970), 141.

25] Smithson and Smithson, "Chicago," in *Ordinariness and Light*, 143. Italics in original.

to mention Mies in his article on bureaucracy and genius. Mies simply did not fit into either category. The 1957 issue of *Architectural Review* also took pains to qualify Mies's work as both typical and exceptional with respect to the curtain wall's development. Mies's architecture, that is, both defined the normative aesthetic and at the same time contradicted it. The exquisite refinement of his facades pushed the aesthetic to such a point of intensity, nearly obsession, that it exceeded its origins in normative technology and construction to become a form of poetry.[26]

Indeed, Mies presents the determinate exception with respect to a theory of a normative architecture. Returning to the definitions of major and minor architecture, to which category does Mies's postwar architecture belong? Is his architecture territorializing or deterritorialized? Was he political or apolitical? Does his architecture affirm the status quo, or is it a herald of the not-yet in the sense of Deleuze and Guattari?

The answers remain ambiguous. On the one hand, Mies was one of the foremost representatives of international architecture during the postwar period. He was among its most admired and widely imitated exponents, an indisputable master, creator of a steel and glass classicism. On the other hand, he remained a permanent foreigner in the United States. A high-school-educated son of a stonemason in the position of heading an American institution of higher learning, intellectually formed in the 1910s and '20s by his German Catholic culture, he was uncomfortable speaking English and claimed to have little architectural affinity for his adoptive city of Chicago. With respect to politics, Mies served clients wherever he found them—always with a certain Olympian detachment. In the 1930s, he put his rigorous aesthetic in the service of the Nazi government, just as he would put it in the service of the American developer afterward. In the end, his stance was probably more apolitical than aligned with any particular ideology. Manfredo Tafuri, however, accords Mies a rather more critical politics, reserving a privileged position for the German architect within his history of modern architecture. He interprets Mies's architecture, especially the Seagram building, as a

26] For a similar argument, see Peter Blake, "The Difficult Art of Simplicity," *Architectural Forum* (May 1958): 126–31.

LEFT: **LUDWIG MIES VAN DER ROHE (IN ASSOCIATION WITH PHILIP JOHNSON), SEAGRAM BUILDING, NEW YORK, 1958.**

RIGHT: **DEVELOPER HERBERT GREENWALD AND LUDWIG MIES VAN DER ROHE, ARCHITECTURAL FORUM, MAY 1958.**

27] Manfredo Tafuri and Francesco Dal Co, *Modern Architecture* (New York: Harry N. Abrams, 1979), 339. Reyner Banham, while in no way detracting from Mies's achievement, expressed an opinion opposed to that of Tafuri: "A commercial context needs to be emphasized. So much has been written (largely European wish-fulfillment) to make Mies van der Rohe out as a detached aesthete pursuing a platonic ideal of abstract, immaterial space-sculptures, philosopher of 'less is more' . . . that there is still a salutary and refreshing shock in being reminded that he was purveying a saleable product in a buyers' market . . . . [that] his significant patrons have always tended to be the apparatchiks of the US power elite." Reyner Banham, "The Last Professional," *New Society* (18 December 1969): 968.

quintessential expression of withdrawal and alienation, glacially "other" with respect to its context, a sublime and eloquent protest against the laissez-faire urbanism of the capitalist city. Apropos of Seagram, Tafuri quotes Karl Kraus: "He who has something to say, step forward and be silent."[27]

It would seem that the work of Mies leads a double life. It engages pragmatically with existing institutions while pursuing an idealist, perfectionist concept of *Baukunst*; it negotiates the profane world of power while striving for the transcendent *nemo me fecit* of the Gothic cathedral. Where should Mies be located in the theoretical framework we are advancing here? Perhaps he can best be characterized as a genius of the prosaic, a poet of architectural bureaucracy.

6]

The ambiguity presented by Mies's American work reflects one of the central intellectual problems of the postwar period (albeit in highly aestheticized form): the sense of alienation and lack of personal agency experienced by individuals in a highly bureaucratized and technological mass society, a society shadowed, moreover, by nuclear disaster. The widespread anxiety of the 1950s was expressed in popular novels like Sloan Wilson's The Man in the Gray Flannel Suit; in widely read works of sociology like David Riesman's The Lonely Crowd, William Whyte's The Organization Man, and Herbert Marcuse's One-Dimensional Man; and in the angst-laden philosophy of existentialism. The politics of consensus and conformism demanded by the ideological polarizations of the Cold War vastly diminished the average individual's sense of self, while the compensatory prerogatives of affluence undermined the idealistic foundations of rational planning. American society attempted to offset the anonymity of the corporate work world by preserving individual expression at home. City and suburb, Lever House and Levittown, were mirror images.

In view of what was to come, should the normative modernism of the period after World War II be considered "progressive" or "conservative"? As already suggested, the impersonal attitude toward authorship and the shift from the model of the genius-architect to that of the competent design team, represented a departure from the traditional humanist paradigm. The art world would also embrace a new objectivity by the 1960s, when the cooler aesthetics of pop and minimalism—exemplified by the work of Jasper Johns, Andy Warhol, Sol LeWitt, Agnes Martin, and Donald Judd—displaced the emotive, signature surfaces of abstract expressionism. In the hands of these artists, the grid emerged as a critical instrument rather than an instrumental affirmation of the status quo. It can be said, perhaps, that the "posthumanist" architecture of postwar modernism helped create the climate, or at least the backdrop, for this change in sensibility.

On the other hand, what marked the normative architecture of the postwar period as still within the paradigm of modernism rather than

CHARLES AND RAY EAMES, EAMES HOUSE, SANTA MONICA, 1949.

postmodernism was its continued pursuit of a unified formal language and a totalizing methodology. The architectural rhetoric of the period after World War II rings with calls for synthesis, integration, reintegration.[28] CIAM's formula "from the spoon to the city" summarizes the profession's aspiration to submit every scale of architectural intervention to standardized criteria, to suture the fragments of contemporary life by means of a grand design. Le Corbusier's Modulor, however idiosyncratically derived, epitomizes this universalistic mindset. At the same time, the kit of parts, the modular assembly, presents itself in these decades as an ideal compromise between totalization and diversity, law and choice, exactitude and flexibility.[29] It is perhaps the work of Charles and Ray Eames that most brilliantly effects this compromise in its balance of rationalism with more sensuous "California" inputs. Their work remains optimistically poised between the utopia of the modern movement and the cornucopia of postwar consumer culture, conjoining a liberal desire for "good design" with an affirmation of the "good life" as this prospect opens up in 1940s and '50s America.

Despite retrospective cynicism, the idea of modern architecture during the postwar era was connected, perhaps for the last time, with everyday ideas of goodness and happiness. This was so not only in the sense of the good life, or of design as the aestheticization of bourgeois commodities or "goods"—which is how the 1950s have conventionally been seen by leftist critics of a culture consumed with consumption[30]—but also in a more innocent sense of good design as having inherently ethical implications. However naive or manipulative such an ideology strikes us now, the romance of consumer capitalism and modernist design

28] See, for example, the classic texts by Sigfried Giedion, Laszlo Moholy-Nagy, Matthew Nowicki, Walter Gropius, and Richard Neutra, among others, compiled in Joan Ockman with Edward Eigen, eds., *Architecture Culture, 1943-1968: A Documentary Anthology* (New York: Rizzoli, 1993).

29] See Matthew Nowicki, "Origins and Trends in Modern Architecture" (1951), in Ockman, *Architecture Culture*, 154.

30] One of the most acute critiques of the contradictions between rationalist design and consumer society at the time emanated from the Hochschule für Gestaltung in Ulm; see, for example, Abraham Moles, "Functionalism in Crisis," *ulm* 19/20 (August 1967): 24. For a recent example of this critique, see Mark Jarzombek, "'Good-Life Modernism' and Beyond: The American House in the 1950s and 1960s," *Cornell Journal of Architecture* 4 (1989): 76–93.

had its benevolent side. Edgar Kaufmann's *Good Design* shows at the Museum of Modern Art, staged in conjunction with the Chicago Merchandise Mart, or Walter Paepcke's attempts to marry commerce and culture first at Moholy-Nagy's New Bauhaus and later at a "new Athens" in Aspen, were idealistic initiatives.[31] In the end, however, the attempt to establish a design elite whose mission was to elevate the taste of capitalist producers and consumers failed. It foundered precisely on the impossibility of sustaining an innovational and self-critical impulse in a modernist culture that had "become major." Increasingly an accomplice of big business and government, managerial rather than experimental, territorializing rather than critically distanced, postwar modernism could reproduce itself only in mannered and empty variations.

HARRISON AND ABRAMOWITZ, "XYZ" BUILDINGS FOR THE CELANESE, MCGRAW-HILL, AND EXXON CORPORATIONS, SIXTH AVENUE, NEW YORK, 1971–73.

7]

Yet if the more enlightened institutional attempts during the postwar period to normalize and universalize a progressive design culture ultimately collapsed, it is nonetheless necessary to recall this chapter in mid-twentieth-century architectural history that too often has been dismissed as a record of compromise and conformity. After the heroic story has been told of how the socialist dream of modernism came to grief in the 1930s, that of how the capitalist vision of a benevolent modernism receded by the 1960s affords more than an anticlimax. To formulate it this way is not to reinforce, once again, a sense of déjà-vu with respect to the tragic relationship between modern architecture and the "project of the Enlightenment"—the construction of a society on rational foundations—but to uncover the dynamics of major and minor: of territorialization and deterritorialization, of the apolitical and the political, of the normative and the transformative.

31] See James Sloan Allen, *The Romance of Commerce and Culture: Capitalism, Modernism, and the Chicago-Aspen Crusade for Cultural Reform* (Chicago: University of Chicago Press, 1983).

SUPERSTUDIO, **THE CONTINUOUS MONUMENT**, ARIZONA DESERT, 1969.

Indeed, by the 1960s the collapse of hopes in an enlightened normative architecture gave rise to a resurgence of architectural criticism. Emanating from very different quarters, it ranged from the passionate journalism of the "nonprofessional" Jane Jacobs to the paper projects of a younger generation of architects like Archigram in England and Superstudio in Italy, from Bernard Rudofsky's vernacular photographs for the exhibition *Architecture without Architects* to architect Robert Venturi's "gentle manifesto" for complexity and contradiction. Ironically, at the same time as political protests intensified over issues like civil rights and the war in Vietnam, a new discourse of autonomous architecture crystallized within the architectural profession. Led by the most theoretically and formalistically inclined architects, like Aldo Rossi and, later in the decade, the New York Five, it amounted to an emphatic retreat from an "insupportable present." Thus the radical and in some cases brilliant innovations proposed by the new avant-garde of the 1960s—John Hejduk, for example—had only a very mediated or negligible impact on everyday life. Unlike the critique of Jacobs, their failure to engage the built environment marginalized their critique and left it untested.

At this point it is necessary to distinguish between "avant-garde" or "neo-avant-garde" architecture and the concept proposed here to replace it, minor architecture. A minor architecture is necessarily political; it is always minor *in relation to* a major architecture, which in turn serves the interests of a dominant system of power. The problem with the term avant-garde is that it has been used in contradictory ways over the course of this century. Movements or individuals described as avant-garde have variously occupied the entire political and aesthetic spectrum: they have been progressive aesthetically and liberal-left politically, progressive aesthetically and apolitical, progressive aesthetically and right-wing politically, conservative aesthetically and left-wing politically. This diversity makes Peter Bürger's definition of the avant-garde as an attack on bourgeois art institutions seem too vague, while Tafuri's history of avant-garde architecture as a succession of linguistic transgressions becomes—paradoxically—politically ambiguous. In the end, "avant-garde" seems to connote any kind of rebellion whatever, or else any kind of newness—which brings it ambiguously close to that other cultural phenomenon that is also defined by novelty, namely fashion.

It is possible, in fact, that the whole category of avant-garde, and with it neo-avant-garde, is not very meaningful in architecture anymore, and should be consigned to the dustbin of outdated modernist ideas. On the other hand, if there is still some efficacy in this once heroic concept, then it is useful to consider that in military terms *avant-garde* refers to the forward line of an army, the part that goes out front in order to reconnoiter for the main body behind. It is deputed by that main body to report back with information about future conditions of march, not to mount internal attacks upon its host. Its job, that is, is less to subvert and overturn than to precede and guide an army safely through a foreign environment. In my view, a definition of the avant-garde in architecture—like a definition of the minor—can only be framed with respect to the way any group or movement operates within a highly specific context of both internal (linguistic, formal) and external (social, political) relations. It is escapism or solipsism to speak of the avant-garde's innovations exclusively in relation to its own disciplinary tradition.

Of course, this is ultimately the argument that Tafuri makes himself, even if *The Sphere and the Labyrinth*, published in 1980, concludes more in the spirit of Theodor Adorno than Walter Benjamin. The trajectory of the avant-garde he traces in that book, "from Piranesi to the 1960s," takes the debate over engagement versus silence to a largely negative conclusion with respect to both strategies. Yet in his overarching project, the critique of architectural ideology, Tafuri remains dedicated to provoking confrontations between the discipline of architecture and "reality." What he characterizes as "architecture in the boudoir" in his 1974 essay of that title refers to the flight taken in the late 1960s by the leading international architects—his prime examples being Rossi, the New York Five, and James Stirling—from reality into "language."[32] Tafuri sees this flight as a defense mechanism by architects against fears of their own irrelevance and of architecture's status as a "negligible object." Tafuri borrows the metaphor of his title from a book by the Marquis de Sade, *Philosophie dans le Boudoir*: in the boudoir, where sex is at stake, everything must be focused exclusively, cruelly, on sexuality, as Sade shows. Likewise, argues Tafuri, where the discipline of architecture is at stake, only maximum formal terrorism, the "supreme constraint of a geometric structure,"[33] can give architects a sense, however illusory, of their own potency and freedom. Tafuri concludes "L'Architecture dans le Boudoir" by reprising Walter Benjamin's argument in "The Author as Producer," enjoining architects as well as critics to rethink architecture as part of the cycle of economic and technical production rather than outside it: "to discover the tricks of a magician it is often better to observe him from behind the scenes rather than to continue to stare at him from a seat in the audience."[34] The resulting "explosion of architecture out towards reality" can in turn lead architects to shift their energies from "form to reform." The historical tradition he cites in support of such a reformist approach is entirely different from that of the master form-givers. Among the protagonists he names are Clarence Stein, Charles Whitaker, and Henry Wright in the United States; Fritz

32] Manfredo Tafuri, "L'Architecture dans le Boudoir," *Oppositions* 3 (May 1974): 38.

33] Ibid., 53.

34] Ibid., 57.

Schumacher, Martin Wagner, Ernst May, and Hannes Meyer in Germany; as well as "technicians who today choose to work in contact with cooperative organizations or public agencies." Contrary to the pessimism generally assumed to pervade his view of architecture, Tafuri hazards that even if such technical-administrative activity has an ambiguous relationship to the political and economic system within which it operates, and even if such efforts often fail in their reformist ambitions, they "without doubt make for alternatives other than those followed by people desirous of preserving a linguistic 'aura' for architecture."[35]

In effect, Tafuri is postulating here a *critical-normative* practice of architecture as an alternative to an avant-gardist, or purely linguistic, one. He implies that such a practice is likely to be the most realistic mechanism for affecting the built environment given architecture's relatively modest capacity to bring about social change. We are herewith returned to our earlier discussion of the "enlightened architectural bureaucracy," and led to raise the question of whether there is any possibility of this kind of reformist practice in large-scale architectural practice today, in either the public or private domain.

8]

Despite his pessimism, however, Tafuri does not rule out the necessity for formal experimentation and innovation in architecture. Rather, it is always a matter of balancing "project" with "criticism," of submitting language to ideological critique. To Tafuri's theory and history of the avant-garde, two other radically counter-avant-garde discourses that have emerged since the 1960s can be compared. These bear on the present discussion inasmuch as they too concern themselves with the problem of architectural "realism" or normativity. One such discourse is associated with the Italian architect Giorgio Grassi and his theory of continuity, or of architecture as *mestiere*, a

35] Ibid., 56–57. It may be noted that the Marxian concept of "the real" on which Tafuri relies in his opposition of "language" and "reality" in this essay is contradicted or qualified by the definition of architectural realism that he proposes in a later essay entitled "Realismo e Architettura." There Tafuri treats realism entirely as a historically constructed concept. Taking Italian neorealism and Soviet socialist realism as points of departure, he traces the meaning of the term with reference to a number of twentieth-century manifestations, including the building programs of Red Vienna and Roosevelt's New Deal, associating realism with a rhetoric of populism, community, and construction rooted in the natural landscape. This later essay also contains some observations on the relationship between realism and avant-gardism that are relevant in the present context. Tafuri's essay is in Vittorio Magnago-Lampugnani, *L'Avventura delle idee nell'architettura, 1750–1980* (Milan: Electa, 1985), 123–45.

profession or craft rather than an art. Grassi proposed this theory most polemically in the mid-1960s (when he was also closely associated with Rossi). According to Grassi, the discipline of architecture is about the transmission of an ongoing tradition of building practice.[36] The architect's role is to construct lasting monuments by building upon a typology of forms sanctioned by history. Grassi's exemplars include such architects as Heinrich Tessenow and Adolf Loos, as well as J. J. P. Oud, Ludwig Hilberseimer, and Mies van der Rohe. The work of these architects might well be described as critical-normative in the sense just proposed. Yet Grassi's insistence on the persistence of architecture's techniques and forms and its internal continuity as a discipline; his desire to pit a rule-governed building practice against the flux of history; and his predisposed hostility to experimentation make his position reactionary. His unabashed nostalgia for a strong sense of order breathes suffocatingly through his highly didactic, rigidly determined formal repertory.

To Grassi's theory a more opposite approach could hardly be imagined than that of Robert Venturi and Denise Scott Brown. Yet they too propose what is in some sense a critical-normative theory of contemporary architecture, undertaking to address collective social and symbolic needs. But instead of venerating timeless forms, they adopt a more ironic stance toward history and recommend learning lessons from the ordinary, the everyday, and the ephemeral—the Las Vegas Strip, the Levittown housing tract, and other examples of the architecturally *déclassé*. The attitude that they take to these environmental facts is to "defer judgment" in the interests of "receptivity" and the overcoming of elitist cultural prejudices.[37] This suspension of value judgments about the status quo has led, in their own architecture, to pleasurable games of populist referencing, historical pastiche, disjunctive juxtaposition, and studied kitsch. Paradoxically, the approach becomes a rationale for exploiting the shock value of a deliberately iconoclastic taste—an avant-garde strategy in itself. Despite the social critique from which especially

36] See Giorgio Grassi, *La Costruzione logica della architettura* (Padua: Marsilio, 1967); and Grassi, *L'Architettura come mestiere e altri scritti* (Milan: Franco Angeli, 1980).

37] Denise Scott Brown, "Learning from Pop," *Casabella* (December 1971): 23.

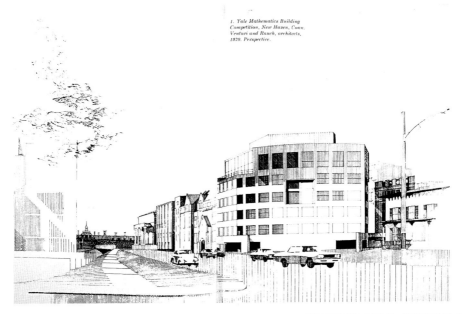

VENTURI AND RAUCH, ARCHITECTS, COMPETITION PROJECT FOR YALE MATHEMATICS BUILDING, NEW HAVEN, 1970. STREET PERSPECTIVE.

Scott Brown began, the result is, once again, formalism, which is where Venturi began, only now with a new set of "low" references to inflect and contaminate architecture's "high" jinks. Colin Rowe's critique of the Yale Mathematics Building, published in 1976, remains incisive:

> The ideal of the "ordinary" has led to a manifestation that is supposed to be the equivalent of Main Street but which is not that equivalent because it assumes towards Main Street a sentimental attitude. It has led to a building that, in its refusal to communicate, in its determination not to reveal, in its assumption of the primitive and the banal, in its supposed innocence and its very great formalism, in the profession it makes of being addressed to the "average" man, is, externally, supremely affirmative of the pathos, the unassuming beauty, and the hopelessness of a matter-of-fact pragmatism. It has led to a building that both celebrates and calls into question a

Rotarian ethos; and that, in its supposed rejection of quality, becomes almost ostentatious.[38]

Contrary to the approaches of both Grassi and Venturi/Scott Brown, I do not believe that it is possible to "design" a normative architecture. On the one hand, the project of repeating forms endlessly according to timeless laws that assume architecture's stability and continuity as a discipline fails to acknowledge architecture's accelerating sense of crisis within contemporary culture; on the other, as Rowe points out, the attempt to design what already exists is a conceit. What I wish to suggest, then, by a critical-normative architecture is a critical theory or critique of normative architecture that can in turn lead to a critical practice. Inasmuch as architectural theory, in allying itself with avant-garde projects rather than addressing itself to issues of normative practice, has too long evaded the challenge of taking on the real and pressing problems of the designed environment, I believe that this represents a necessary new program. Indeed, it is the only hope of mending the breach between theory and practice, of overcoming the discipline's present-day marginalization.

Avant-garde architecture has reached an impasse. By enclosing themselves in seductive boudoirs, by staking their claim within elite cultural and academic ghettos, so many of the most critically minded architects today end up by remaining deterritorialized, homeless, "minor." But this is so only in a passive or negative sense, not yet in the revolutionary and constructive one posited by Deleuze and Guattari. Venturing out into the real world on rare occasions when invited to solve an everyday problem—housing, for example—the self-appointed representatives of the contemporary avant-garde tend to do a signature building and return to their ghettos. In a final degeneration of the romantic concept of originality, the phenomenon of the signature building today, a term with its origins in fashion (scarves, jeans), only bolsters the system's ability to coopt genuinely experimental or innovative work and turn it into its own ornaments (in the most trivial sense). A project by Frank Gehry on the outskirts of Frankfurt, completed

38] Colin Rowe, "Robert Venturi and the Yale Mathematics Building," *Oppositions* 6 (fall 1976): 16.

in 1996, is worth citing as an interesting exception, especially within the recent oeuvre of a "signature architect." A low-cost residential complex produced by a partnership of public and private interests, it manages to be not just formally inventive but socially sensitive.[39]

9]

Let us return one last time to Deleuze and Guattari's essay on Kafka. Recall their insistence that a minor literature does not come from a minor language; it is that which a minority constructs within a major language. As we have suggested, their essay is written more in the polemical spirit of cultural politics than in the interests of promoting a particular literary style. But given that the essay arises out of a study of Kafka, it is not surprising that the authors should have in mind a specific mode of construction, of deterritorialization. This mode is intensification. Writing in a language never fully his own, Kafka pushes that language further and further in the direction of his own deterritorialization, to the point where it shakes free of all literariness, taking on a concrete but strange— surreal? hyperreal?—materiality. Deleuze and Guattari actually characterize Kafka's mode of writing as a "new sobriety."[40] They contrast the rigorous strangeness of his form of literary enunciation with the esoteric and kabbalistic mysticism of Max Brod, his friend and fellow Czech-Jewish writer, the latter attempting to effect a symbolic reterritorialization by artificially enriching the appropriated German language with arcane signifiers. Likewise, citing the parallel instance of two Irish writers, James Joyce and Samuel Beckett, Deleuze and Guattari compare Joyce's excessive, polyglot Irish-English with Beckett's parsimonious English and French: "The former never stops operating by exhilaration and overdetermination and brings about all sorts of worldwide reterritorializations. The other proceeds by dryness and sobriety, a willed poverty, pushing deterritorialization to such an extreme that nothing remains but intensities."[41]

Certainly the kind of intensification that arises from an absolutely disciplined and minimalist style of

39] On this project, see Herbert Muschamp, "In the Public Interest," *New York Times Magazine*, 21 July 1996, 39–41.

40] Deleuze and Guattari, "What Is a Minor Literature?" 25.

41] Ibid., 19.

articulation is only one strategy among others, and it would be absurd to draw a value judgment on this basis between Joyce and Beckett, for example. Nor is the desire for a "new sobriety" lacking in a certain nostalgia of its own, recalling the purist dreams of modernism. And beyond such qualifications, we must also distinguish between architecture and literature as kinds of critical practices. Literature functions solely through the manipulation of language; this is because its reality, its sphere of action, is language. In architecture, on the other hand, "language" is largely a metaphor for a visually perceived order. The full meaning of architecture is far more complexly—i.e., extralinguistically, experientially—constituted.

Nonetheless, what Deleuze and Guattari's theory of minor literature can suggest to those who have long been excluded from the major territory of architecture—groups like women and African-Americans, for instance— is a different strategy from either the nostalgic reterritorializations of recent postmodernist practice or, on the other hand, the shock tactics associated with the militant tradition of the avant-garde. These tactics are not only exhausted by now but sadly misdirected. Instead, the strategy of a minor architecture might be incremental, subtle, and persistent. Like the deterritorialized literary imagination of Kafka, it might entail a process that begins within the major, little by little appropriating it and making it strange, until the normative, the familiar, becomes something new, the inception of a different consciousness:

Since the language is arid, make it vibrate with a new intensity.[42]

42] Ibid.

Kafka instructed the publisher of his story *The Metamorphosis* that the main character, the transformed "bug" Gregor Samsa, should never be illustrated. He felt that to do so would limit the reader's ability to imagine him. Likewise, while some architecture being done today has already moved in the direction I am proposing, I think it best—for the sake of the suggestiveness of the argument—to refrain from citing specific examples.

This paper was presented at Columbia University Graduate School of Architecture, Planning and Preservation and Yale University School of Architecture in November 1994 and February 1995 respectively. I am grateful to Bob Slutzky and Mary McLeod for their valuable comments on its further development.

GECEKONDU

MARY-ANN RAY

WITH MEMBERS OF STUDIO TÜRKIYE

ANKARA, TURKEY, EARLY SPRING 1993

We arrived in Turkey having caught wind of the structures called *gecekondu* [ge-ja-kàn-dü], which roughly translates to "house built in one night." We knew that the builders of these homes took advantage of a Turkish law that allowed those who could build quickly enough (in one night) to remain. If, by sunrise, the walls and roof enclosed a shelter that could keep bedding dry, and if water for tea was boiling, Turkish law gave rights to the quick builders.

For us, the notion of the "up-overnight house," conjured up images of temporality—of makeshift structures clinging, attaching, and hanging off of other buildings; of structures perched precariously on stilts, built of sticks and stones, cloth, cords, and papers—as fantastical as one of Italo Calvino's Invisible Cities.

An initial disappointment set in after discovering that the *gecekondu* were actually built of substantial, (mostly) legitimate, and even standard materials, and that they took their weight more strongly and directly to the ground than we had hoped.

However, at the end of our first full day spent in the neighborhoods and interiors of *gecekondu* in Dikmen and Balgat (two districts at the edge of the city of Ankara), we came away astonished by what we had found. We saw an architecture that had not been called architecture before, an architecture that was quick and nimble on its roaming feet. As it turned out, it was an architecture that the thing we had always called architecture before had a lot to learn from. For example, we learned that rooms could be

Members of Studio Türkiye: Jody Albert, Juli Brode, Greg Slowik, Evelyn Tickle, Catherine Venart, Robert Adams, Heidi Schenker, Vic Liptak, Alexander Kitchin, Debbie Mackler, Mehmet Kutükcuoglu.

RAGGED OUTSIDES/ TAUT INSIDES

EXTERIOR RAGGEDNESS FORMALLY JOINS THE GECEKONDU TO THE EARTH ON/IN WHICH IT SITS. TAUT AND SIMPLE INTERIORS PROVIDE FOR A "LIGHTNESS OF BEING"—AN UNCLUTTERED LIFE THAT FLOATS ABOVE THE EXTERIOR EARTH.

ILLUSION

COLOR APPLIED AS AN ECONOMICAL AND COSMETIC LAYER OF PAINT CAN ACHIEVE POWERFUL EFFECTS. SWABBED ON PAINT CONSTITUTES A YEARLY SPRING CLEANING, AND THE GECEKONDU GET A BATH OF FRESH COLOR EVERY YEAR. UNLIKE MATERIALS ARE UNIFIED, LIKE MATERIALS ARE PULLED APART, AND THE ENDLESS SPACE OF THE SKY IS PUT INTO THE INTERIOR OF THE GECEKONDU .

BUILDING IS A VERB

THE GECEKONDU ARE IN A CONTINUAL STATE OF CONSTRUCTION, FOR THE BUILDER IS THE INHABITANT AND THE INHABITANT THE BUILDER. WE HAVE FOUND AN ARCHITECTURE IN WHICH THERE EXISTS NO GAP OR SEPARATION BETWEEN THE MAKER AND THE MADE. THE HOUSE IS A FLUID, MOVING, AND CHANGING ENTITY— ALWAYS UNFIXED AND UNFINISHED, CHANGEABLE AT A MOMENT'S NOTICE (ESPECIALLY ON A DAY OFF FROM OTHER WORK).

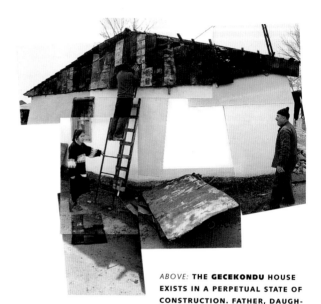

ABOVE: **THE GECEKONDU HOUSE EXISTS IN A PERPETUAL STATE OF CONSTRUCTION. FATHER, DAUGHTER, GRANDFATHER INFILL A GABLE WITH FLATTENED COLLECTED FOOD TINS.**

RIGHT: **ALCHEMY TRANSPIRES AS A BUILDING OF MANY MATERIALS IS PULLED TOGETHER BY A DOSE OF TURQUOISE PAINT.**

blind, gigantic space could be found in miniature rooms, and space could be constructed with almost nothing. In no particular order, our architecture began to learn from this architecture.

Accompanying the following illustrations are some notes made during and after our visits to the *gecekondu* in several districts on the outskirts and deep in the heart of Ankara.

MAKING SPACE WITH ALMOST NOTHING

THE GECEKONDU *BUILDER MAKES PERGOLAS AND FENCES—PRECINCTS AND DOMAINS—FROM STICKS AND WIRES AND VINES. BIG USE IS MADE OF VERY LITTLE MATERIAL.*

MOVING HOUSE

EVERY ROOM IN THE GECE-KONDU *IS CALLED* ODA *(NO LIVING ROOM, DINING ROOM, BATHROOM, BED-ROOM DESIGNATIONS APPLY), WHICH IS PRO-GRAMMATICALLY SPECIFIC AND GENERIC (OR DO-IT-ALL) AT THE SAME TIME. BECAUSE OF THE LACK OF FIXTURES (EXCEPT FOR THE ISOLATED SPIGOT BUILT INTO THE WALL AND THE DRAIN ON THE FLOOR OF EVERY* ODA*), THE FLEXIBIL-ITY AND MOVEABILITY OF THE FURNITURE, AND THE PROPORTIONAL AND DIMENSIONAL SAMENESS OF THE SPACES, THE ROOMS OF THE* GECEKONDU *(AS IN THE TRADITIONAL TURKISH HOUSE AND BEFORE THAT, THE TENT) TAKE ON SIMUL-TANEOUS ROLES AS ROOMS TO WORK, PLAY, EAT, SLEEP, BATHE, OR DO OTHER THINGS IN AS TIMES OF DAY, SEASONS, AND SIZES AND CONSTITUTIONS OF FAMILIES CHANGE. IN THIS WAY, THE HOUSE HAS THE ABILITY TO "MOVE" AGAINST THE INHABITANTS AT THE SAME TIME THAT THE INHABITANTS MOVE AGAINST THE HOUSE, AT A MOMENT'S NOTICE, ALLOWING BOTH TO BE NOMADIC.*

SPACE MAKING WITH ALMOST NOTHING—
A DOMAIN OF STICKS AND WIRES.

INFILL

ONE SINGLE MATERIAL DOESN'T HAVE TO DO ALL OF THE WORK IN THE GECEKONDU. ANOTHER MATERIAL MAY STEP IN AT ANY TIME TO FILL IN AN OPEN GABLE OR A GAP BETWEEN STRUCTURES, AS MONEY AND TIME PERMIT.

ATTACHMENT

ANYTHING BUILT AS PART OF THE GECEKONDU LEAVES ITSELF OPEN AS A BASE FOR ATTACHMENT AND DISPLAYS ITSELF AS AN OPPORTUNITY TO TAKE ON MORE.

MIRROR

MIRRORS, PLATED TRAYS, AND ARTIFACTS POPULATE THE GECEKONDU. THEY HANG OR LEAN AGAINST A WALL SWABBED TURQUOISE OR A GREEN/BLUE "SKY" COLOR. TO SEE THE REFLEC-TION OF A SKY UPON A SKY UPON A SKY INSIDE OF A VERY SMALL ROOM BUILDS A LARGE SPACE WITHIN A MINIATURE CONFINE.

WRAP

IN THE TAUT INTERIOR OF THE GECEKONDU, THE "GOODS OF LIFE" ARE DRAPED, WRAPPED, AND COVERED FOR PROTECTION FROM DUST AND DIRT. CAR-PETS SLIDE FROM FLOORS UP ONTO SOFAS AND FROM SOFAS UP ONTO WALLS. IN THE SPACE OF THE HOUSE, THE TACTIC OF THE WRAP HAS THE EFFECT OF BLUR-RING OR DISSOLVING THE LINE BETWEEN FURNITURE AND ROOM, WALL AND FLOOR, OBJECT AND SPACE.

MIRRORS AND PLATED TRAYS (MOVEABLE TABLE TOPS) POPULATE THE GECEKONDU.

A PLACE ON ITS WAY TO BECOMING ANOTHER INTERIOR ROOM.

**USE OF OTHERWISE
UNWANTED MATERIALS**

*THE APPROPRIATION OF
OTHERWISE UNWANTED
OR DISCARDED MATERIALS
LIKE FORMWORK (USED TO
BUILD THE CONCRETE
FRAMES FOR NEARBY OR
ADJACENT GOVERNMENT
HIGHRISE DWELLINGS),
FOOD CANS, THE FIRST
SHAVINGS OFF LOGS IN
THE MAKING OF "REAL"
PLANKS, ETC., IS ONE
PART OF THE PALETTE OF
MATERIALS FOR THE
GECEKONDU. SALVAGE
YARD BUSINESSES CALLED
ARDIYE SPRING UP ALONG
ROADS LEADING TO
GECEKONDU NEIGHBOR-
HOODS.*

**USE OF THE MOST
STANDARD MATERIALS**

*THE ADOPTION AND ACCEP-
TANCE OF SOME OF THE
MOST STANDARD BUILDING
MATERIALS—LIKE TERRA-
COTTA ROOF TILES AND
CONCRETE BLOCK—ARE
THE OTHER PART OF THE
GECEKONDU BUILDER'S
PALETTE. THIS OFTEN
LEADS THESE BUILDERS
TO CHOOSE SITES NEAR
MAKESHIFT AND TEMPO-
RARY FACTORIES (USUALLY
ESTABLISHED FOR GOVERN-
MENT HOUSING CONSTRUC-
TION) WHERE STANDARD
MATERIALS ARE PLENTIFUL
AND TRANSPORT IS RELA-
TIVELY EFFORTLESS, THUS
KEEPING COSTS LOW.*

THE "GOODS OF LIFE" ARE DRAPED, AND
CARPETS SLIDE FROM FLOORS ONTO
CUSHIONS ONTO WALLS. THE LINES
BETWEEN FURNITURE AND ROOM, WALL
AND FLOOR, AND OBJECT AND SPACE ARE
DISSOLVED.

SPLICE

BIG SURFACES ARE ACHIEVED AT TIMES IN THE GECEKONDU THROUGH THE LAMINATION OR SPLICING OF SMALLER PARTS—SOMETHING BIG AND SUBSTANTIAL IS MADE FROM MANY SMALL AND INCONSEQUENTIAL PARTS.

BLIND ROOM

THE "BLIND ROOM" IS THE ROOM OF THE GECEKONDU HOUSE THAT DOES NOT RECEIVE LIGHT. OFTEN, IT IS CONSTRUCTED ALONG A RETAINING WALL AGAINST THE EARTH, LEAVING IN A DAMP SPACE. THIS FREES THE ROOM TO BECOME THE CONTAINER IN WHICH THE CLUTTER OF LIFE IS COLLECTED, ALLOWING THE OTHER ROOMS TO REMAIN AUSTERE AND ALMOST BLANK—UNINTERRUPTED BY STUFF. THE BLIND ROOM ALSO MAKES IT POSSIBLE TO INVITE A PASSERBY TO STAY FOR THE NIGHT (AND IT WAS OFFERED TO US AT MANY GECEKONDU, AS WE WERE TRAVELERS PASSING THROUGH).

FLOOR OF TOPOGRAPHY

MULTIPLE CARPETS ARE LAYERED OVER THE FLOORS AND ARE FELT UNDERFOOT. STREET AND LAND SHOES ARE TAKEN OFF AND LEFT OUTSIDE OF THE THRESHOLD, AND WITH BARE OR STOCKINGED FEET, THE FLOOR OF THE HOUSE FEELS LIKE THE WILD SURFACE OF THE EARTH OF THE FIELD OR THE SAND OF THE DESERT.

CARPETS SLIDE FROM FLOORS UP ONTO SOFAS AND FROM SOFAS UP ONTO WALLS.

THE CENTER OF A NARROW HOUSE FOR
FOUR OR FIVE FAMILIES. THE HOUSE
OCCUPIES A SLIVER OF LEFTOVER CITY
LAND BETWEEN TWO FORKS OF A ROAD.

(ROO[F)LOOR]

*WITH A SLIGHT OF HAND,
THE GROUND PLANE OFTEN
GIVES WAY, FOLDS, OR
BEVELS UP TO BECOME A
ROOF.*

SEIZING OPPORTUNITY

THE GECEKONDU *BUILDERS
DEFTLY TAKE ADVANTAGE
OF WHAT IS LAID BEFORE
THEM: UNUSED LAND, IN-
PLACE PRODUCTION (IN
THE FORM OF OPEN-AIR
FACTORIES) ESTABLISHED
FOR "LEGITIMATE" BUILD-
ING PROJECTS, LEFTOVER
MATERIALS FROM THE SAME
PROJECTS, A LAW WORDED
IN SUCH A WAY SO AS TO
MAKE AN OVERNIGHT CON-
STRUCTION A QUICK CLAIM
OF LAND.*

*THE PART OF THIS OPPOR-
TUNISM WE LIKED BEST WAS
THE ABILITY TO ACT
QUICKLY, TO GERRY-RIG,
TO DESIGN, AND TO MAKE
ARCHITECTURE SWIFTLY.
THIS WAS SOMETHING
OFTEN DISCOURAGED
FROM WITHIN THE THING
WE WERE USED TO CALLING
ARCHITECTURE, IN WHICH
WE WERE USUALLY TOLD
THAT WE NEEDED TO TOIL
OVER AND CONSIDER AND
RECONSIDER EVERY MOVE
WE MADE. A DESIRE TO
WORK THIS OTHER WAY
WAS SOMETHING WE
ACQUIRED IN THE OPEN
AIR OF THE* GECEKONDU.

**A RAGGED EXTERIOR AND A ROOF
BENDING DOWN TO BECOME A
FLOOR.**

A VISIT TO WOMENHOUSE

PAT MORTON

HOME PAGE

WOMENHOUSE
WomEnhouse is located on the World Wide Web at the
URL http://www.cmp.ucr.edu/womenhouse/

EDITORIAL BOARD: Annie Chu, Amelia Jones, Karen
Lang, Christine Magar, Pat Morton, Joanna Roche
CONTRIBUTORS: Lynn Aldrich, Dana Cuff, Amy Ger-
stler, Betty Lee, Lauren Lesko, Catherine Lord, Kathleen
McHugh, Laura Meyer, Yong Soon Min, Alessandra
Moctezuma, Harryette Mullen, Susan Narduli, Mary-
Ann Ray, Susan Silton, Lynn Spigel, Erika Suderburg,
Faith Wilding.
TECHNICAL CONSULTANTS: Jacalyn Lopez Garcia, Terry
Hudak, Anita Moryadas

I would like to thank the editors and Henry Urbach for
their perceptive and constructive criticism and suggestions regarding this essay.

WOMENHOUSE

WomEnhouse is a collaborative, multiauthored
Web site that explores the politics of domesticity and gender relations through virtual
"rooms" and conceptual domestic "spaces" created by twenty-four artists, architects, poets, art
historians, and cultural theorists.

    WomEnhouse takes its initial inspiration
from the 1972 *Womanhouse*, a groundbreaking
feminist project by Judy Chicago, Miriam
Shapiro, Faith Wilding, students in the Feminist
Art Program at the California Institute of the
Arts, and artists from the local community. *WomEnhouse*
contains collaborative creative work that, like that in
Womanhouse, dissects the ways in which domestic environments are constructed, perceived, and occupied
within gendered power systems.

    WomEnhouse moves away from conceptualizing
domestic experiences in terms of the literal architectural spaces of the house. It explores, through the virtual language of the World Wide Web, the intersecting
issues of race, class, gender, and sexuality as they are
articulated in the psychic arena of the home. The
domestic is thus posited as the primary site of the

FIRST ITINERARY   **THROAT**

intersection of the public and the private realms. These realms have collapsed into one another with the penetration of commodity culture and men's (as opposed to domestic, or women's) labor into the home by means of direct mail marketing, television, and telecommuting devices.

WomEnhouse proposes that, just as the domestic sphere is no longer separated from the public world of capital, so the "feminine" (and feminism) must expand into a cyberpolitics that addresses the multivalent vicissitudes of identity formation and domesticity at the turn of the millennium.

WHAT IS A HOME?

"Home is where the heart is," and "there's no place like home," but "a house is not a home." It isn't the building that makes a home, but the life residing in the house or apartment or tent or whatever other shelter. *Webster's Dictionary* defines the home as "a family's place of residence"; "the social unit formed by a family living together"; "a congenial environment"; " a place of origin."[1] Today, there's another kind of home, the home page.[2] Home is where the server is or the place from which one browses. In this context, to go "Home" on the Internet cannot be an atavistic return to the *heimat*, since the home page has none of the attachment to tradition and soil as defined by Martin Heidegger. Yet Internet lingo is sprinkled with the language of domesticity (home page, chat room, mailbox). This domestic idiom is apparently so entrenched in our culture, and we have such a strong need for the panacea of origins, that even the radically deterritorialized World Wide Web is embedded with references to "home."

1] G. & C. Merriam Company, *Webster's New Collegiate Dictionary* (Springfield, MA: G. & C. Merriam Company, 1977), 546.

2] This home terminology is so new that neither the *American Heritage Dictionary*, Third Edition CD (1993) nor the hypertext *Webster* interface (a searchable Web dictionary) have definitions for "home page" or "Internet."

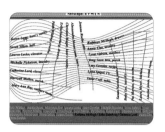

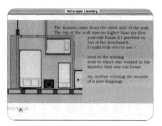

HYMEN

LAUNDRY

LAUNDRY

The home seems to be the most "normal" of architectural creations, something about which every person has an intuitive, psychologically-loaded conception. To the degree to which the house is taken for granted as a "neutral" container for domestic activity, it is invisible in the public eye, a given of the built landscape. And yet an "unconscious" of domestic space underlies our collective and individual assumptions about "home": self-identity, safety, permanence, comfort, urbanity, community, justice. Even the most banal tract house is weighted with psychic freight, shipped from tradition and from personal history. By contrast with the psychological imperative of the domestic, the historical composition of the house as a realm separate from work and as an isolated domain of femininity is no longer strictly applicable to current patterns of use and need. The elision between inside and outside, public and private, and the unconventional hierarchies among spaces and among inhabitants of the Internet parallel changes in the "real" domestic environment, which is increasingly permeated with work and public spaces. With the penetration of commodity culture and productive activity into the home (for example, with home shopping networks, modem and computer connections), the domestic sphere is no longer separated from the public world of capital. The house is a productive environment, both in terms of traditional "women's work" and of new employment patterns; and of the accompanying changes to the physical structure of the house.

Within architectural traditions, the house is simultaneously the most basic and the most reviled of programs. Although twentieth-century modernism was founded on domestic explorations by a handful of architects for a few wealthy clients, today the house is denigrated in favor of

  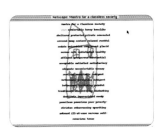

FENCE   FENCE   PORCH

more monumental, public building. The limitations and restrictions of the house, the products of preconceptions and conventions as well as clients' stubborn desires that often oppose architects' zeal for abstract solutions, have made it seem a less "pure" design problem or one too closely associated with the personal, the feminine, and the eccentric. The passions, fears, and desires with which we invest the house are neglected. The unspoken conventions that govern domestic spaces can produce neuroses and repressions that erupt in nightmares and feminist rage.

THE DOMESTIC MYSTIQUE

The problem lay buried, unspoken, for many years in the minds of American women. It was a strange stirring, a sense of dissatisfaction, a yearning that women suffered in the middle of the twentieth century in the United States. Each suburban wife struggled with it alone. As she made the beds, shopped for groceries, matched slipcover material, ate peanut butter sandwiches with her children, chauffeured Cub Scouts and Brownies, lay beside her husband at night—she was afraid to ask even of herself the silent question—Is this all?

Betty Friedan, The Feminine Mystique[3]

In her analysis of postwar femininity, Betty Friedan chronicled the rise of a "a mystique of feminine fulfillment" after World War II, when women's identity was exclusively defined in terms of fulfillment as housewife-mother.[4] Women were pressured to conform to the bland, unthreatening characters of wife and mother as defined in print and promulgated in TV sitcoms such as

3] Betty Friedan, The Feminine Mystique (1963; reprint, New York: Dell, 1983).

4] Ibid., 38.

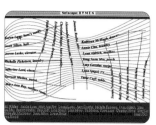

DRESS UP FOR DADDY

ATTIC

HYMEN

Father Knows Best, *Make Way for Daddy*, *Ozzie and Harriet*, *Leave It to Beaver*, *The Lucy Show*, *The Honeymooners*, and *The Donna Reed Show*. The suburban housewife became the "dream image of the young American woman and the envy...of women all over the world."[5]

Phyllis Rosser, who lived that "dream," saw another reality behind this "image of perfect happiness" in "anger and even insanity (mental breakdowns) brought on by the loss of identity that came from being relegated to and isolated in the home....Raising three children in suburbia was the most depressing work I've ever done."[6] Contributing to women's depression and anger was the fact that the woman's role in the home was not held in high esteem, that housework was considered menial and childrearing intellectually unchallenging. Friedan found that educated women who left cities where they were professionals, could take university courses, or have access to day care, were taking tranquilizers to suppress the feeling that their lives were pointless.[7] There was even a medical condition dubbed "housewife's fatigue" that was caused by boredom, the repetition of tasks, the monotony of the suburban setting, its isolation, and the lack of stimulation of life in the suburbs.

5] Ibid., 18.

6] Phyllis Rosser, "There's No Place Like Home," in *New Feminist Criticism: Art, Identity, Action*, ed. Joanna Frueh, et. al. (New York: HarperCollins, 1991), 60–61.

7] Friedan, *Mystique*, 244, 250.

8] On feminist art in this period, see Lucy Lippard, *From the Center: Feminist Essays on Women's Art* (New York: Dutton, 1976); and Arlene Raven, Cassandra L. Langer, and Joanna Frueh, eds. *Feminist Art Criticism: An Anthology* (Ann Arbor, MI: UMI Research Press, 1988).

WOMANHOUSE

Certain aspects and works of feminist art in the 1960s and '70s evolved out of women's dissatisfaction with the "feminine mystique" and as a response to the denigration of women's work, especially housework.[8] Feminist artists used domestic techniques and materials in their work as a means of expressing what they called "woman's experience," which usually meant the lives of white, middle-class, American women. The most notorious feminist art work of this period, Judy Chicago's monumental *Dinner Party*, employed "feminine" arts such as china painting and embroidery to celebrate both the ordinary dinner party and the achievements of women in history.[9] *Womanhouse* was one of the manifestations of feminist artists' search for appropriate, alternative means and venues for representing what Chicago called "a woman's struggle" to overcome her conditioning as a woman and to develop strong personal identities.[10]

Womanhouse was created within the Feminist Art Program of the California Institute of the Arts by teachers Chicago and Miriam Shapiro and a group of their art students, joined by local feminist artists Wanda Westcoast, Sherry Brody, and Carol Edson Mitchell. In 1972, the *Womanhouse* participants completely renovated a house near downtown Los Angeles and transformed it into a feminist environment in which they critiqued what they saw as the patriarchal oppression of women within the contemporary domestic sphere. They taught themselves construction skills—a part of the empowerment agenda of the Feminist Art Program—and rebuilt the dilapidated structure. They then refashioned each room of the house and produced installations that exposed the ways in which women have traditionally been contained and disempowered by the "feminine mystique" of domesticity. "The isolation and anger that many women felt in the single-nuclear-family dwelling in every suburb of America were flung out at the public who came to see [*Womanhouse*]," according to feminist art critic Arlene Raven.[11]

In the *Womanhouse's Nurturant Kitchen*, the walls were entirely painted in pink—a color that its creators associated with the color of women's flesh—and covered with fried-eggs that metamorphosed into breasts, evocative of the very flesh of the woman associated with the kitchen. One bathroom was painted white, marred only by a shelf of feminine hygiene products and a wastebasket overflowing with bloody tampons. Another bathroom contained the body of a woman trapped in a sand-filled bathtub; a third was covered in

9] See Amelia Jones, ed., *Sexual Politics: Judy Chicago's Dinner Party in Feminist Art History* (Berkeley: University of California Press, 1996).

10] Judy Chicago, *Through the Flower: My Struggle as a Woman Artist* (1975; reprint, New York: Penguin Books, 1993), 65.

11] Arlene Raven, *At Home* (Long Beach, CA: Long Beach Museum of Art, 1983), 5.

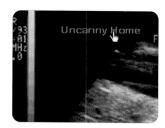

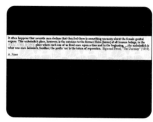

SECOND ITINERARY   **HYMEN**   **WOMB ROOM**   **WOMB ROOM**

brilliant red paint (the color of lipstick or nail polish), a garish testament to ideals of female beauty. A linen closet swallowed up a female mannequin, while another closet was choked with hundreds of shoes. The feminists who constructed *Womanhouse* saw the house as the physical site where established myths of femininity became instantiated, where femininity was constructed and performed. In response to the commodification of the domestic, they made radical interventions into the house that exposed the taboos of what Friedan called "the problem with no name" and the anger, frustration, and despair of women enmeshed in the feminine mystique.

WOMENHOUSE

Postface. The building or any other artifact of the creative impulse seen as offspring, is clean, whole, and ordered. It appears, complete and fullblown, at the end of an uncertain period of gestation. The "real thing" is not only a triumphant production...but a messy, bloody, erotic event. An other architecture is an architecture of abjection (the thrown away). At the moment of birth, the body gives forth excrement, vomit, blood, mucous, as well as a human being. Abject offerings, gifts, they are the products of flows. The abject products of the body might be metaphorized in the abject products of the body politic—detritus of street and home— toward a project of positive fetishizing, supplementing excrement, vomit, and blood to the phallus.

Jennifer Bloomer,
"Abodes of Theory and Flesh: Tables of Bower"[12]

12] Jennifer Bloomer, "Abodes of Theory and Flesh: Tables of Bower," *Assemblage* 17 (April 1992): 27.

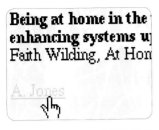

WOMB ROOM

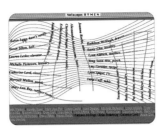

HYMEN

WomEnhouse takes its inspiration from the insights of *Womanhouse*, while rethinking the domestic in light of the massive demographic and theoretical shifts in women's "identities" and in the idea of the house during the last twenty years. The purpose of *WomEnhouse* is to increase discussion and awareness of the ways in which domestic environments are constructed, perceived, and occupied within gendered power systems, and to sponsor the type of collaborative creative work spawned by the original *Womanhouse* project. *WomEnhouse* provides a forum for a broad spectrum of investigations into the politics of femininity and both its traditional and unconventional associations with the house. The very title of the project, which pluralizes "woman," opens out the assumptions within the earlier *Womanhouse* project, which presumed a unified female experience of the home.

Whereas *Womanhouse* defined and contested the house primarily in terms of its conventional function as a space in which to construct femininity in isolation from the public sphere, *WomEnhouse* looks at the domestic as that realm where the public and the private meet in the 1990s. In late capitalism, the strict division between the public and private, which has operated in modern Western culture as a means of subordinating women and disallowing them access to the empowerments of the public sphere, is dissolving.

The public/private realm of cyberspace forms the principle site of exploration, a realm that tends to exclude women's participation. The early history of the Internet as the exclusive province of defense contractors, scientists, and others with access to advanced computer and communications technology—a largely male group—established the phallocentric character of cyberspace.[13] The utopia of the Internet as the realm of

13] For several case histories in early cyberspace, see Roseanne Allucquere Stone, "Will the Real Body Please Stand Up?: Boundary Stories about Virtual Cultures," in *Cyberspace: First Steps*, ed. Michael Benedikt (Cambridge, MA: MIT Press, 1991), 81-118.

unfettered democratic communication and individual freedom coexists with the actuality of the Internet as a misogynist, racist domain of elite privilege.[14] The Guerrilla Girls "proclaim the Internet too male and too pale" on their Web site. As they point out, "the Internet is 84.5% male and 83.2% white."[15] *WomEnhouse* as virtual domain encourages women to occupy and engage in cyberspace as an alternative realm that potentially disorients traditionally gendered roles and spaces.

FIRST ITINERARY[16]

WomEnhouse is initially entered through a home page, the *heimlich* introductory Web space that instructs the visitor in the basics of *WomEnhouse*'s structure and navigation. This is the public, conventional facade of *WomEnhouse*, the place where the cybervisitor can feel most at home.

From this customary "home," the visitor travels through the *Throat*, a dark birth passage or womb space.

After the Throat, the visitor enters the *Hymen*, a permeable, GIF-mapped web of links, where she can pass to and from most of the rooms and spaces of *WomEnhouse*. This web of participants' names is the main threshold for *WomEnhouse*, a more private, concealed entry than the home page/front door. There are two veiled places—the *Closet* and the *Drawer*—that are inaccessible from the *Hymen* and must be entered by links with other spaces, following their creators' desire that these spaces appear in unexpected locations within *WomEnhouse*. The nonlinear organization of *WomEnhouse* requires a correlative noncorporeal movement through its virtual spaces, conforming to the Web's hyperlinked filaments rather than to the literal promenade through a "real" house's rooms.

From the Hymen, we go into the *Laundry*, a collaboration of Annie Chu, Betty Lee, and Michelle Fickeisen. A "documented memory" of Betty Lee's childhood home, the Chinese laundry is a site of business and home, "where commercial washers and dryers coexisted with children's toys and the kitchen stove."

14] Cameron Bailey, "Virtual Sin: Articulating Race in Cyberspace," in *Immersed in Technology: Art and Virtual Environments*, ed. Mary Anne Moser (Cambridge, MA: MIT Press, 1996), 29-49.

15] The Guerrilla Girls, World Wide Web site, URL: http://www.voyagerco.com/gg/internetposter.html.

16] These itineraries are not comprehensive. They do not travel through the whole of *WomEnhouse*, nor do they represent all the possible ways of visiting this site. They are a personal selection of links and spaces.

The *Laundry* leads us to Alessandra Moctezuma's *Fence*, the border between the private front yard and the public street. Moctezuma contrasts the fortified, unused front lawn of Anglo Westside Los Angeles with the Latino neighborhoods where the front yard and fence are extensions of the house.

The *Porch*, a collaboration between Harryette Mullen and Yong Soon Min, forms another transitional space between the home and the public realm that is increasingly mediated by women. In "Mantra for a Classless Society," they move us from cozy to tense in a chant of homey, comforting words that metamorphose into paranoia.

Embedded in the "Mantra for a Classless Society," there is a link to part of Catherine Lord's *Closet*, "Dress Up For Daddy." In this and three other lesbian porn vignettes, Lord inserts what she calls a "leaking homosexuality" into traditional American domestic spaces.

From the *Closet*, the visitor can link herself to the *Attic*, Joanna Roche's exploration of the peripheral space where the "miraculous chaos of childhood" is stored.

This itinerary then repenetrates the *Hymen* and comes to a contingent resting point.

SECOND ITINERARY

On a second journey through *WomEnhouse*, the visitor links from the *Hymen* to the *Womb Room* by Amelia Jones. This womb space as "home" brings into contact the womb as a signifier of "essential" femininity, as the creators of *Womanhouse* conceived of it, and the womb as a site of public intervention, including antiabortion legislation and biotechnology.

The *Uncanny Home* contains Freud's formulation of the womb and female genitalia as uncanny, *unheimlich*. This, in turn, is penetrated by *Welcome Home*, a text on returning home by Faith Wilding.

From this welcome space, the visitor returns to the *Womb Room* and, hence, weaves back to the *Hymen*.

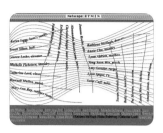

| THIRD ITINERARY | HYMEN | DINING ROOM TABLE | SUBURBAN DYKES |

THIRD ITINERARY

The visitor begins the third trip through *WomEnhouse* at the uncanny and yet *heimlich* Hymen.

This time, the visitor can sit at the *Dining Room Table*, provided by Dana Cuff to illustrate the conflation of "work" and "home" spaces for the career Superwoman. "A woman's work is never done."

This text is linked to another of Catherine Lord's *Closet* pieces, *Suburban Dykes*, in which a video porn scene is "flatfootedly" translated into well-known lesbian porn narrative, without commentary.

The link from the *Closet* to *Kant's Vanity* is an easy one. Karen Lang and Christine Magar's make-up table features the physiognomy of beauty, taste, pleasure, and the sublime and their philosophical links with femininity and masculinity.

A link with vanity takes the visitor into the *Teen Room*, a vision of adolescent feminine norms by the author. Using images and text from teen magazines, this space articulates the mixed messages that girls receive about their bodies, their sexuality, and from sexually ambiguous teen idols.

The last link in the visit conveys the visitor to the *Drawer*, a series of concealed aphorisms created by Erika Suderburg and Kathleen McHugh on models by *Hints from Heloise* and Friedrich Wilhelm Nietzsche. Morality and the moral mingle in a warped domestic interior where "political language is grafted awkwardly onto everyday experience and the objects that one employs to act out domestic dramas and the spaces that contain them."

Closing the *Drawer* behind her, the visitor slips home to the *Hymen*.

VANITY

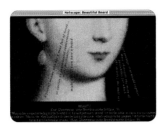

VANITY

TEEN ROOM

CONCLUSION

Joshua Meyrowitz claimed that television helped create the women's liberation movement of the 1960s by bringing the male public world into the female private world. This is an essentialist notion of space. Public spaces like the office or the theater are not simply male; they are organized according to categories of sexual difference. In these spaces certain social positions and subjectivities are produced according to the placement of furniture, the organization of exits and entrances, the separation of washrooms, the construction of partial walls, and so forth. TV's incorporation of the public sphere into the home did not bring "male" space into female space; instead it transposed one system of sexually organized space onto another.

Lynn Spigel, "The Suburban Home Companion"[17]

While the early 1970s could be said to mark the beginning of the end for the mythology of domestic femininity, the 1990s continue that trend and embrace refashioned experiences and concepts of the domestic and notions of femininity. If the "Ozzie and Harriet" model privileged the role of the housewife who did not work, the contemporary ethos promotes the myth of the Superwoman and the support services that enable her to work (high-paid, white-collar career, nanny, housecleaner, supportive mate, etc.). Just as *Womanhouse* dissected the repression inherent in the housewife model, *WomEnhouse* critiques the subterranean repressions operating in the domestic realm of the 1990s. The feminization of labor and poverty (as

17] Lynn Spigel, "The Suburban Home Companion: Television and Neighborhood Ideal in Postwar America," in *Sexuality and Space*, ed. Beatriz Colomina (New York: Princeton Architectural Press, 1992), 209.

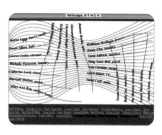

TEEN ROOM **DRAWER (APHORISM)** **HYMEN**

insecure, marginal, and underpaid), the permeability of boundaries between the public and the private, and the eradication of "public life" and the substitution of privatized, technological spaces are subjects under investigation in the "spaces" of *WomEnhouse*.

In spite of conservative rhetoric appealing to a traditional conception of "family values," the assumptions underlying such "values" are no longer the norm, if they ever were. Women participate in the workforce at a rate of at least 72 percent, many families are led by one parent or by nontraditional partners, and men play a larger role in housework and child rearing. Whereas the home is commonly associated with heterosexual, nuclear-family life and queer, unconventional lives are relegated in the popular imagination to "other" spaces (bathhouses, bars, parks), everyday domestic spaces, in fact, shelter a broad range of households that do not fit the "[heterosexual] married couple with children" norm.[18]

> If it was ever possible ideologically to characterize women's lives by the distinction of public and private domains...it is now a totally misleading ideology, even to show how both terms of these dichotomies construct each other in practice and in theory. I prefer a network ideological image, suggesting the profusion of spaces and identities and the permeability of boundaries in the personal body and the body politic.
>
> Donna Haraway, "A Cyborg Manifesto"[19]

WomEnhouse delves into the uncanny aspects of domestic space—the personal, the feminine, and the

18] See Mark Robbins, "Building Like America: Making Other Plans," *Assemblage* 24 (August 1994): 8-11.

19] Donna Haraway, "A Cyborg Manifesto: Science, Technology, and Socialist-Feminism in the Late Twentieth Century," in *Simians, Cyborgs, and Women: The Reinvention of Nature* (New York: Routledge, 1991), 170.

"deviant"—in order to expose the neglected psychology of the house, to find ways of expressing the hidden life of the house, and to explore a cyberhome that dissolves the spatial, material, psychological, and technological limits of conventional domestic space. Its creators have aspired to construct a new domestic space in which nontraditional identities and practices can be performed, without concretizing or effacing difference. The nonlocalized, multilinear paths and spaces of *WomEnhouse*, linked through the permeable *Hymen*, form a place where difference is maintained while boundaries are blurred, where the psychic and corporeal inside and outside of the house flow into a messy, if cozy, "home."

JAMES CASEBERE

GEORGIAN JAIL CAGES, 1993

THE LEVITTOWN LOOK

ROBERT SCHULTZ

The name Levittown evokes the mass-built suburbia of the United States following the Second World War. For its critics, Levittown epitomized the humdrum, vinyl-coated world of middle America—the "Split-Level Trap" and home of the "Organization Man," to borrow the titles of two well-known studies of the time.[1] Despite its singular, mythical status, Levittown was actually not one but three vast and considerably heterogeneous housing developments built between the late 1940s and the late 1950s in Long Island, Pennsylvania, and New Jersey.

The brothers William and Alfred Levitt produced houses at a scale never before seen. At the first Levittown, on Long Island, over seventeen-thousand houses were built during a period of six years. The Levitt company was essentially a manufacturing operation that used assembly-line techniques and aggressive marketing to move its product quickly into the hands of the consumer. Like their counterparts in the automobile industry, the Levitts modified the package of standard features included in their houses year by year. They discarded unpopular elements and restyled exteriors to keep ahead of the market's tastes. In the two later developments in Pennsylvania and New Jersey, the Levitts offered a choice of three or four models to appeal to different budgets and to give variety to the Levittown street.

A chronological study of Levittown houses between 1947 and 1958 reveals the Levitt brothers' efforts to codify the aspirations of their ideal home buyer. The accompanying drawings show ground-floor plans, front eleva-

1] Richard E. Gordon, Katherine K. Gordon, and Max Gunther, *The Split-Level Trap* (New York: B. Geiss Associates, 1961); William H. Whyte, *The Organization Man* (New York: Simon and Schuster, 1956).

tions, and various analytical diagrams of the least expensive Levittown house from selected years. The first set of diagrams shows the location of living areas within the house. The second series gives an inventory of the appliance package. The third group shows the size, location, and degree of enclosure of the garage and kitchen, two spaces that were designed for "dad" and "mom" respectively. The last series of diagrams gauges the relation between front and rear facades. In general, the drawings reveal a shift—over the course of a decade—from efforts to modernize and advance the suburban house toward an arguably more retrograde production of traditional domestic spaces and images of home.

.   .   .

The 1958 Levitt house appears to be a tawdry conclusion to the Levitt Brothers' early attempts to develop the suburban house as an innovative, stylistically unified whole. The Levitts studied their market and saw a desire for modern convenience paired with a self-consciously historicist image. The modern functioning of the house was split from its modernistic appearance. The artifice involved in this split compels one to view the later Levittown houses as descending into kitsch.

Nevertheless, the Levitts' contrived use of style shows their pragmatism in the face of two realities of suburban life. First, in American suburbia, the front and back of the house do indeed take on different functions and meanings. The front yard, the front facade, and even the front rooms act as forums for display while the routines of the TV, the easy chair, and the backyard grill go on behind. Second, technology is welcomed into the house as a convenience but shunned as an image. Modern materials and devices are marketed to the home owner in the guise of something safe and familiar, leading to hybrid objects like wood-grained toasters—and microwave ovens—and faux-stucco vinyl wallpapers. These pasted-on images have a certain aesthetic consistency in their thinness and absurdity, fueled by a desire to make the one-of-a-kind reproducible and the technological feel right at home.

$ 6,9 9 0

image:: old shaker farm

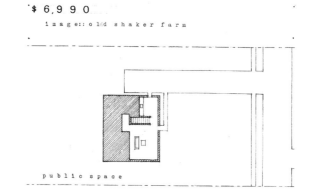

1947

*BASIC AND FRUMPY, THE FIRST
LEVITT HOUSE FEATURES A BUILDER'S
STANDARD "CAPE COD" FLOOR PLAN
AND A PLAIN SYMMETRICAL FACADE
THAT HAS OVERTONES OF BOTH
GRANDMA'S FARMHOUSE AND
WARTIME WORKERS' HOUSING.*

public space

inventory

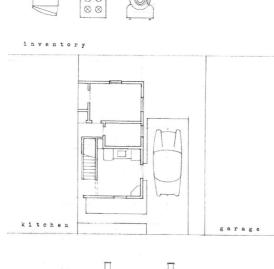

kitchen   garage

1947

front   back

unified

pretention index

$ 7,990

image: Frank Lloyd Wright moderne

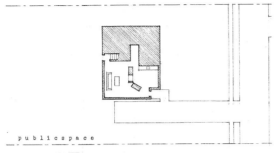

publicspace

inventory

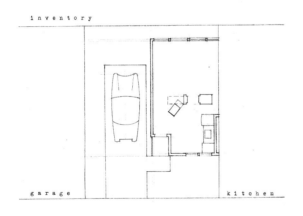

garage   kitchen

front   back

unified

pretention index

1949

THE LEVITTS EXPERIMENTED WITH MODERN STYLING IN THE 1949 HOUSE. THE CENTRAL "SEE-THROUGH" FIREPLACE HAS THE FLAVOR OF FRANK LLOYD WRIGHT, AS DOES THE HORIZONTALLY BANDED ELEVATION. THE PIVOTING STORAGE CABINET ATTACHED TO THE FIRE-PLACE ALLOWS THE HOUSEWIFE TO KEEP THE KITCHEN OPEN FOR DAILY USE AND TO CLOSE IT FOR PRIVACY WHEN COMPANY COMES.

1949

1950

*THIS HOUSE RETAINS A MODERN-
ISTIC IMAGE. HERE, THE DEVELOPERS
HAVE DELETED THE PIVOTING CABI-
NET AND ADDED A NEW FEATURE: A
TELEVISION BUILT INTO THE LIVING
ROOM WALL. LIKE THE 1949 HOUSE,
THIS ONE HAS FLOOR-TO-CEILING
WINDOWS THAT LOOK OUT ONTO A
NEW FAMILY SOCIAL SPACE, THE
BACKYARD.*

$ 7, 9 9 0

i m a g e :: f u t u r o - c o m f y

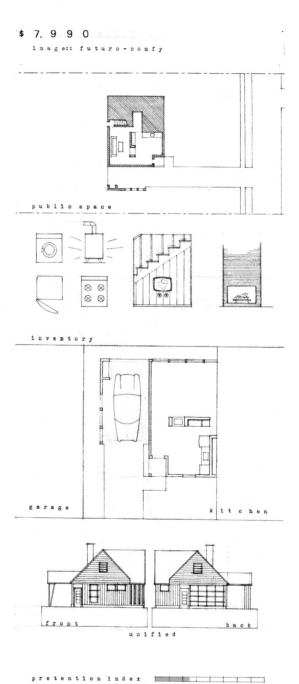

p u b l i c s p a c e

i n v e n t o r y

g a r a g e   k i t c h e n

1 9 5 0

f r o n t   b a c k

u n i f i e d

p r e t e n t i o n i n d e x

$ 8, 9 9 0

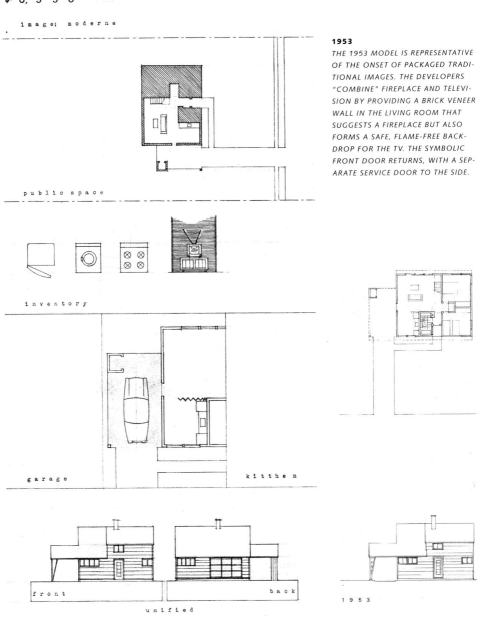

i m a g e ; m o d e r n e

p u b l i c s p a c e

i n v e n t o r y

g a r a g e   k i t t h e n

f r o n t   b a c k

u n i f i e d

p r e t e n t i o n i n d e x

1953

THE 1953 MODEL IS REPRESENTATIVE OF THE ONSET OF PACKAGED TRADITIONAL IMAGES. THE DEVELOPERS "COMBINE" FIREPLACE AND TELEVISION BY PROVIDING A BRICK VENEER WALL IN THE LIVING ROOM THAT SUGGESTS A FIREPLACE BUT ALSO FORMS A SAFE, FLAME-FREE BACKDROP FOR THE TV. THE SYMBOLIC FRONT DOOR RETURNS, WITH A SEPARATE SERVICE DOOR TO THE SIDE.

1 9 5 3

$ 1 0, 9 9 0

image: moderne-taste of colonial

1955

THE 1955 HOUSE ADDS ANOTHER INNOVATION, THE FULLY ATTACHED GARAGE. THE GLOOMY PRESENCE OF THE GARAGE DOOR IS OFFSET BY CUT-AND-PASTE FACADE STYLING, WITH PATCHES OF BOARD-AND-BATTEN SIDING AND BRICK VENEER TRIM COMPLETING THE HOUSE FRONT. IN THIS HOME THE DEVELOPERS NO LONGER PROVIDE A SPECIFIC SETTING FOR A TELEVISION, INDICATING THAT THE APPLIANCE HAD ALREADY BECOME A STANDARD PIECE OF FAMILY FURNITURE TO BE PROVIDED AND PLACED BY THE OWNER.

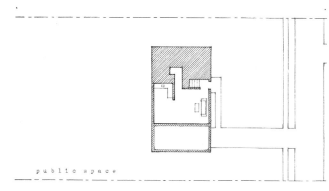

public space

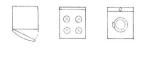

inventory

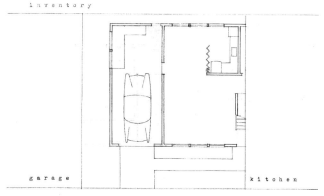

garage   kitchen

1955

front   back

slightly off

pretention index

$ 1 4 , 5 0 0

image: modern yet traditional

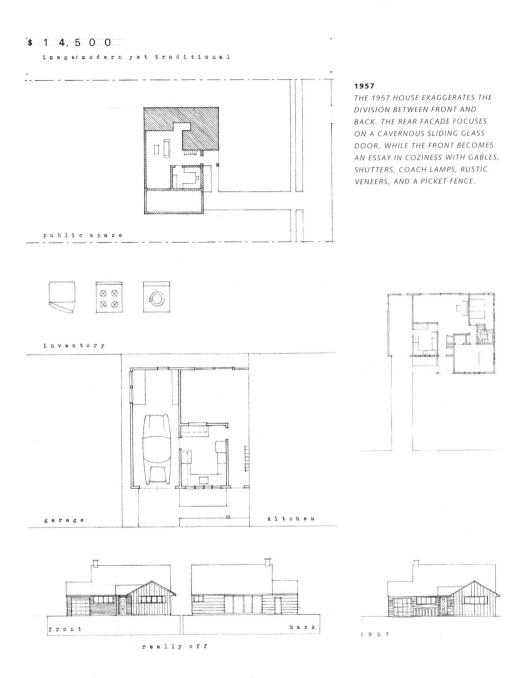

public space

inventory

garage · kitchen

front · back

really off

pretention index

1957

THE 1957 HOUSE EXAGGERATES THE DIVISION BETWEEN FRONT AND BACK. THE REAR FACADE FOCUSES ON A CAVERNOUS SLIDING GLASS DOOR, WHILE THE FRONT BECOMES AN ESSAY IN COZINESS WITH GABLES, SHUTTERS, COACH LAMPS, RUSTIC VENEERS, AND A PICKET FENCE.

1 9 5 7

$ 11,990

image: olde Cape Cod-medieval England?

1958

THE 1958 HOUSE SHOWS A DECREASE IN SIZE AND A RETURN TO AN ECONOMICAL, SIDE-ENTRY FLOOR PLAN. AT THE SAME TIME, THE STYLISTIC ADD-ONS HAVE BECOME MORE EXPLICIT, WITH HANSEL-AND-GRETEL DIAMOND PANE WINDOWS, "OLDE-FASHIONED" PLANK SHUTTERS AND AN ARCHED CANOPY DISGUISING THE GARAGE DOOR.

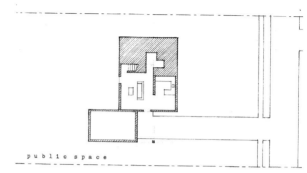

public space

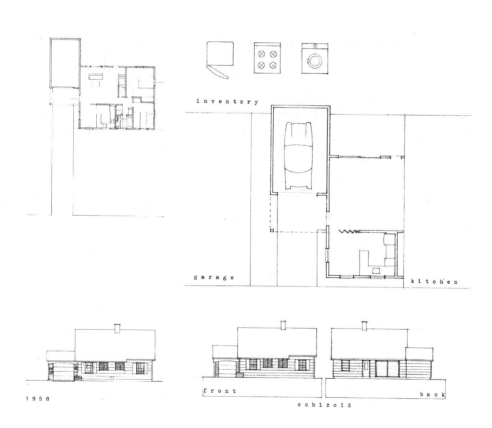

inventory

garage   kitchen

1958

front   back

schizoid

pretention index

THE EVERYDAY TODAY:

EXPERIENCE AND IDEOLOGY

PETER HALLEY

There are two versions of the everyday that exist today, though the two seem contradictory. In one, the everyday is understood as an aesthetic experience tied to democratic values. In the other, the everyday becomes a signifier for the identity of a powerful class. Can these two phenomena exist side by side? Can we claim one to be an ideological construct and the other a product of unmediated experience?

In the first version, the everyday embodies a common democratic culture with a modernist preference for experience over display and ceremony. It reflects the values of a culture that has taken the kitchen out of hiding and made it the most public room in the house. In the second version, the everyday becomes the sometimes cruel pretension of a hugely powerful and wealthy class. It expresses the desire of that class both to hide its existence with an anti-iconography and to claim its connection to an earlier industrial materiality whose reality it has effectively usurped. The make-up of this class is itself open to question: is it comprised of those who have accumulated vast fortunes in the post-1960s high-tech meritocratic boom? or is it, more broadly, the United States in relation to the developing countries that supply it with factory-made goods produced under Dickensian conditions?

The first vision of the everyday is strongly rooted in twentieth-century American art. It is the everyday of Edward Hopper, Wallace Stevens, and the progressive American cinema of *The Last Picture Show*, *Midnight Cowboy*, and *Badlands*. It is the everyday of sunlight, of the periphery, of the unnoticed (in either the natural or constructed landscape). It is that moment, particularly valued by the creative mind of the twentieth-century American, at which time seems to slow down, daily concerns dissipate, and our senses become receptive to sight and sound. It is a kind of phenomenological intoxication in which details come into focus, textures are heightened, and sounds become disassociative but somehow meaningful.

The architecture that comes out of this sensibility has played an important role in American modernism. American architects have long been interested in how simple things are made—the exquisitely straightforward details of such materials as industrial steel, poured concrete, or plainly-joined wood. There is an identification with the independent craftsperson and with practical industrial technologies not intended for luxury use. The symbolism of public places is introduced into private life.

We associate this sensibility with the populism of American culture; we see America as an egalitarian country in which each one of us, in true egalitarian fashion, may know how a turkey is roasted or a transmission is fixed. There is an assumption that we know these things because America does not have a long-standing aristocracy in which cooking, laundry, carpentry, or gardening are labeled menial. On the contrary, it is presumed throughout our large middle class that today's middle-aged millionaire was once a short-order cook or carpenter, that everyone has some experience of the mechanical arts.

In borrowing from public iconography, American architecture also makes the assumption that the public realm is a popular, democratic place and the product of neither statist, aristocratic, nor corporate power. A Whitmanesque vision of America emerges in which the schoolhouse, the pool hall, and the diner can all be safely domesticated in the private realm as reminiscences of a shared benevolent culture.

The other version of the everyday is as mandarin and elitist as the first is luminous and democratic. It is premised on the idea that entrenched wealth and power need no longer assert itself aggressively. Extreme power may be clothed in a simplicity to which it can attach itself by choice rather than necessity. Wealth and power may be better off hidden in simple nostalgic styles than trumpeted by ostentatious display. In the current popularity of this everyday, we see a generation that has produced a new postindustrial universe of the intangible that embraces a vernacular of tangible effects. A generation whose status is built on creating entertainment and luxury goods now chooses to clothe itself in Spartan garb and Protestant self-denial. It seems ironic that this new multiethnic meritocracy has attached itself to the traditional White-Anglo-Saxon-Protestant identification with understatement.

It is the old WASP ruling elite that first identified itself with the everyday in its embrace of simple styles—in the Adirondack camps of the turn-of-the-century, the rediscovery of such historical areas as Cape Cod and Nantucket, the value given to Colonial furniture, and the naturalistic modernism championed after World War II by such figures as the Rockefellers. (Of course, we must keep in mind that these phenomena were embraced by only a minority of that ruling elite—many more built sprawling mansions on Fifth Avenue or in Newport.)

It is tempting to relate this desire for the everyday with the WASP relationship to the English aesthetic tradition, with its naturalistic gardens and Arts and Crafts movement. However, a more exact identification of the historical roots of the American WASP oligarchy may help us define its aesthetics differently. This oligarchy was embodied almost entirely by a contingent of Northerners who arrived at wealth and power in the triumphant post-Civil War era that spawned America's first great industrial boom in railroads, oil, and steel. It was a world in which the Northern self-made "man" had vanquished the power of the landed Southern aristocrat. This clique arose with the Republican world epitomized by Abraham Lincoln, the first Northerner to seize the power of the presidency from the Southern landed gentry, who rose from humble rural circumstances to political and professional prominence. It is the ideology of this Lincolnian Republicanism that precipitated the embrace of the everyday by the post-Civil War elite. For this group, the everyday was an ideological celebration of the newly-invented self-made man and his identification with his common roots.

Is today's ruling group only miming its identification with these earlier Republican values? Has the older everyday now become spectacularized and transformed into its own simulacrum? Or is today's meritocracy a continuation of that Lincolnian social landscape? If so, it is the trailer park or suburban subdivision that should replace the Nantucket cottage as its touchstone.

Can both these everydays exist at the same time? Roland Barthes has said that every signifier yields a multiplicity of signifieds. The everyday, as a cultural sign, also has not one but many meanings, meanings that are brought to it by the particular agendas of its users. Have the artist and the entrepreneur used the everyday for the same purposes or different ones? After all, the impulse of both to embrace the everyday comes from similar sociopolitical origins. But their use of the everyday is still at odds. For the artist, the everyday remains primarily an experiential state, a means of internalizing our culture's populist leanings. But for the rich the everyday is essentially an inert sociopolitical sign that serves as a coat rather than a skin, and like a coat it may be discarded and replaced at will.

THE EVERYDAY AND THE UTOPIAN

PEGGY DEAMER

> Architecture thus coincides ever more with existence: no
> more to exist sheltered by architecture, but to exist as archi-
> tecture. The time is gone in which tools govern ideas and also
> the time ideas created tools; now, ideas are the tools. It is with
> these new tools that life may be freely structured in a cosmic
> consciousness. In a society of nomads, the dream house may,
> according to circumstances, be found by the sea or in the
> hills, in the mountains or on the plain, remaining of calm
> exposed to the eyes of the post service); it will be the whole
> earth as a spaceship, seen from the bed.
>
> Adolfo Natalini, Superstudio[1]

The work of "visionary" architects in Europe during the 1960s—for
example, Archigram in England; Hans Hollein, Coop Himmelblau,
Raimund Abraham and Friedrich St. Florian in Austria; Superstudio and
Archizoom in Italy—is generally known for its futuristic and often monumental urban machines. But in actuality, this work was fundamentally
lodged in a utopian image of the body, one animated by visions of the
future yet bound by the concerns of the everyday. The particular formulation of this body—as technologically advanced but programmatically
primitive—defined a "new man" who was ideologically committed to
seeing the self as the safeguard of the values of ordinary life and the
defense against the co-opting of the everyday. This formulation suggested that the life of this new man could

1] Adolfo Natalini, "Le 'Dream Houses' di Raimund
Abraham," *Domus* 499 (June 1971): np.

never be aestheticized nor abstracted and could never be technologically sanitized. The new man was about the handshake and sleep, about talking and dreaming; he was about collecting garbage and making love. He was about identifying the body and the everyday as the last arenas in which a societal revolution could be contested.

This group, while more commonly known as visionary than utopian, operated in the context of "utopian" debates that permeated the politics of the '60s. It was this utopianism that united a group that, despite individual and national diversity, identified itself around the common goal of promoting irreverent architectural practices. Peter Cook of Archigram wrote reviews of the work of the Austrians;[2] Superstudio's Adolfo Natalini directly acknowledged the influence of Archigram, and also wrote reviews of the work of Raimund Abraham;[3] Hans Hollein contributed to the republication of Archigram's monograph *Archigram*;[4] the Italian magazine *Casabella* published the work of the Austrians, comparing it to that of Archizoom and Superstudio.[5]

The work of this group stimulates a question about the radical nature of utopian architecture: in what way can it be utopian—i.e., avoiding reality—and still be political—i.e., taking on reality in order to overthrow it? It is a question that Fredric Jameson raises about '60s art in general and one that he answers with assurance: utopian work of the '60s is not political but "proto-political." However, a close look at the particular nature of this utopian architecture—bound to the body and its everyday activities—raises issues that make such a judgment less secure and points to a more complicated set of relationships regarding the issue of how the "political" can be lodged in bodily art and architecture.

At the time that these architects were working in their visionary manners[6]—predominantly 1962–1972—modernism had displayed itself at its hegemonic worst. Modern architecture was increasingly aligned with developers, functionaries, business

2] Peter Cook, "The Mechanistic Image," *Architectural Design* 37 (June 1967): 288; and Cook, "Austria–Vienna: Graz," *A+U* (December 1988).

3] Natalini, "'Dream Houses'."

4] Hans Hollein, "A Comment from Hans Hollein," in *Archigram*, ed. Peter Cook (Basel: Birkhauser Verlag, 1991).

5] Franco Raggi, "Vienna Orchestra," *Casabella* 38 (1974).

6] Many, indeed most, of these architects went on to successful and more traditional practices in the '70s and '80s. These practices produced work antithetical to the radical positions held in the '60s.

monopolies, and politicians, and its visible effects throughout Europe, according to this generation of architects, were urban sprawl, highway networks, city grids, and high-rise development. The social aspirations of early modernism had been absorbed by a bureaucracy that it initially hoped to transform. In 1972, Hans Hollein wrote:

> The international style and the international scene had stag-nated, the great builders had little more to offer. The dogma had been formulated some time ago.... One was talking niceties and published a lot of buildings (if possible pho-tographed by Ezra Stoller).... Hardly ever discussed was new concepts and ideas.... [A new generation] questioned whether it should even enter this debate with buildings; more—whether the building was worthwhile discussing. One wanted to discuss subjects instead of object. Konzepte instead of Rezepte. One also wanted to discuss "city" and "life" in its widest sense.[7]

But unlike the overt formulation of postmodernism that would follow, there was, in this period, still a faith in a modernism that had (merely) gone wrong. Consequently, this generation of architects was less interested in replacing modernism—the hopes and aspirations of which they still believed in—than in critiquing what modernism had become. Modernism was not at fault, it was modernism's co-option that was.

What followed then was a dismantling of the apparatus of mod-ern architecture so that its social origins might be revealed. The technol-ogy, the machines, the systems of communication that had guided modern architecture were still viable, but their absorption into a capital-ist heritage was not. To resist this absorption, there was a literal transfor-mation of the object of architecture, not just in the sense of its new embodiment as image, manifesto, advertisement, or cartoon, but in terms of its content as well. If capitalism "objectified the world through

7] Hollein, "A Comment," np.

a false epistemology of positivism" and "distorted the concept of the individual by denying the difference between public and private," this generation of architects would make architecture not of buildings but of individuals. The object of architecture became the subject himself.[8] "To recover the dimension of oneself through behavioral operations... is a characteristic of the new operational spaces. The architecture of oneself before that of the thing;" wrote Franco Raggi, describing Austrian visionary architecture;[9] "Our architecture has no ground plane, but a psychical one,"[10] echoed the collaborative of Coop Himmelblau.

While this faith in the individual "subject" as a last bastion of incorruptibility appears to be naive today, it is important to realize that the reaction against modernization was not merely its link to capitalism and globalization but, in the aftermath of World War II, totalitarianism as well. Individuality was seen as the essential condition of a free society, and an ideological war was conducted over how to save an "authentic" individual able to recognize true, not produced, needs and desires. Thus these architects, in locating their work in the body of the human subject, hoped that such self-referentiality would secure, if not an authentic solution, at least an authentic debate.

PROJECTS

The motifs of the projects—the megastructures of Cook, Hollein, Abraham, St. Florian, and Superstudio; the pneumatic structures of Coop Himmelblau, Michael Webb, David Greene; the building as space/travel suits of Coop Himmelblau, Webb, and Greene; the calibrations of nature of Superstudio, Greene, Walter Pichler, and Archizoom—were diverse, but they were diverse less from nation to nation or individual to individual than within the oeuvre of a given individual or group. As the list above indicates, Archigram worked on the scale of the city and the scale of the body. Hans Hollein, for his part, worked on projects ranging from the city to sunglasses. These scalar dualities were

8] Hans Hollein, "Utopia as a Negative Dialectic," *Italian Architecture 1965-70* (Florence: Arti Grafiche Giorgi & Gambi, 1973), 60–66. Please excuse the male designation here and throughout. This is how they referred to themselves and unfortunately reflects the fact that they were indeed all men.

9] Raggi, "Vienna Orchestra," 42.

10] Coop Himmelblau, *Architecture is Now* (New York: Rizzoli, 1983). 182.

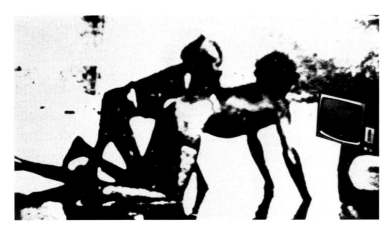

LEFT: **DAVID GREENE, THE ELECTRIC ABORIGINE, 1971.**

RIGHT: **DAVID GREENE, COLLAGE, 1972.**

matched by thematic ones, as indicated by work that was sometimes earth-bound and sometimes cloud-like; sometimes lodged in the essence of physicality and sometimes occupying "psychical space"; sometimes of the self and sometimes of the found and incidental object.

But the diversity of the projects and their apparent thematic contradictions dissolve when understood in the light of their underlying bodily theme. Four projects by architects of different nationalities demonstrate the common shift to a culturally inscribed, everyday body. *Gardner's Notebook*, a project comprised of small vignettes by David Greene of Archigram, mixes photographs of popular events and contemporary phenomena with speculative commentary.[11] Next to a photograph of naked men stooping toward a source of gratification—water? fire? an oracle? no, a television—is the title, "The Electric Aborigine," and the following paragraph:

> One meaning of the phrase "people are walking architecture" is disclosed when we carry our instrumentation around with us....e.g., the astronaut, or his terrestrial counterpart, the infraneuralelectricaborigine, who carries knowledge sensors with him/her.

[11] The work is entitled thus in the monograph, *Archigram*, which combines projects previously published in the journal also called *Archigram*—published by Archigram from 1961–1968—as well as later work.

In another project by Greene, *Video Notebook*, images ranging from the queen of a boat show to a group of astronauts were accompanied by the following inscription:

> Look at this picture. I feel it has something to do with architecture. Do you? It poses some questions . . . about reality. The basis of the modern movement is Judeo-Christian in that it upholds truth and the search for it formally as an architectural medium. But we know truth to be relative to available information and prejudices. The guerrilla camouflages himself and maximizes on available resources in a creative manner; the American army is more of a monument to technology. Its the difference between a portable videofax and the New York Public Library. Declare moratorium on building. . . .
>
> Our architectures are the residue of a desire to secure ourselves to the surface of our planet; if only they were on wheels, or if some slippery substance could be injected under them, our anchors to the planet, like aborigine's, should be software, like songs of dreams or myths. Abandon hardware, earth's-surface anchors. Electric aborigine makes for the moratorium on Buildings.[12]

Implicit in these texts was the description of a "new man" that rejected the machine age and all that it implied—mass-production, efficiency, standardization, repetition, the "machine aesthetic." In its place was the electric age, the age of the media switchboard, of instant transportation and transformation, of products that dissolved the distinction between physical and mental travel—an image of a high-tech future. And yet for all of the new-age equipment, this new man was an aborigine, a primitive nomad. Travel might be farther, it might be aided by synthetic products, but the meaning of the act—freedom and comfort—and the locus of its origin—the body—were unchanged. It was as if the shift from the machine age to the electric age no longer

12] Cook, ed., *Archigram*, 119.

propelled mankind and progress away from the limits of the physical self but threw that self into hyper-relief. The new man was the lone individual left to fulfill the most basic and ordinary of life's demands.

At the same time, the means of aesthetic production chosen by Greene—the photograph and the epigram—also suggest a similar duality between the technological and the corporal. Here, the architect's medium is no longer the building, nor the model or drawing, nor the photograph of the model or drawing, but the photograph of a televised portrayal of an enacted architectural situation. Moreover, the text that is associated with this image is not merely a caption

HANS HOLLEIN, AUSTRIENNALE: HANS HOLLEIN EXHIBIT, 1968.

identifying it, rather, it is a direct address to the reader from the author. Hence, the authorial voice that generally lingers tacitly within the object is explicitly foregrounded. The picture and the text, unlike a building, cannot stand on their own; they call attention to the authorial origin from whence they came.

Hans Hollein's project for the Milan Trienalle of 1968 was created in response to the theme of "The Great Number" (read: population explosion), Hollein made and described his installation in this manner:

> The visitor may pass through a shiny supermarket and end up in an area of garbage and waste. He may enjoy the refreshing coolness of Austrian Alps and pass through a snowstorm. (Snow—an Austrian mass product.) He may experience a particular sensation in a 20-ft.-high and 20-ft.-long corridor crammed on both sides, from top to bottom, with files of shelves…He physically experiences the population increase by passing through the corridor that edges in on him in a curve corresponding to that of the increase between now and 2000 AD. He experiences isolation and individuation—as well as the effect of crowding—as he has to squeeze through

a corridor lined with the "crowds."...He is frustrated in front of a door covered with door handles only one of which will open the latch. And finally, he may confront his own self—in a mirror.

In the exhibition, there was a display of Austrian products and a two-color injection molding machine that turned out a pair of Hollein designed sunglasses every fifteen seconds for the visitor to take with him or herself. The exhibition was "extended" as an event by the people wearing the glasses and also by the dispersal of the Hollein designed brochures that contained, amongst other things, a perforated and gummed sheet of "Austriannale" stickers for affixing to letters, walls, lampposts, etc.[13]

In this case, the installation worked in almost the opposite way as the work of Greene, who proposed equipment as weightless as electricity, luggage as thin as a mirror, and a subject as mobile as an astronaut. Here the subject—the visitor to the exhibition—was constrained and contained by the population machine. Indeed, like Rube Goldbergian contraptions, Hollein's exhibition was excessive and overdetermined in relation to what it produced: the tourist and the souvenir.

Nevertheless, the relationship between the body, the machine, and the activities of the everyday is similar in concept to that proposed by Greene. The machine, formerly assumed to liberate the body from its own physicality and its banal scope of activity, in fact only guarantees that the body becomes the privileged locus of life at its most banal—putting on sunglasses, walking in the city, and shopping.

Here, to borrow Marshall McLuhan's phrase, the medium is the message. The installation—part happening, part exhibition, part machine, and part concession—cannot simply be seen as a traditional object, aesthetic or otherwise. In fact, the object produced is less the installation, or even the sunglasses, than the subject participating in the Trienalle exhibit, uniformed and nationalized. Likewise, the aesthetic of the installation—sleek, smooth,

13] See description of this installation in *Architectural Forum* 129 (September 1968).

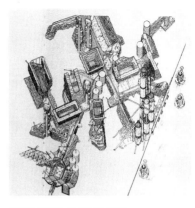

PETER COOK, PLUG-IN CITY (AXONOMETRIC), 1964.

polished, minimal—contrasts with the ordinary function of the factory machine. The "machine" aesthetic of modernism is invoked and mocked; the Trienalle-goers feel the tension of not knowing whether they as subject or the installation as object is the work of art. The dialectic between body and machine; futuristic aspiration and ordinary existence; designed and found object; and torture chamber or playground, yields a position of supreme irony, one that is as indebted to the humorous and playful as to the critical and trenchant.

Peter Cook and his *Plug-In City*, a series of ideas and images developed between 1962 and 1966, present a more complex example of emphasis being shifted to the body as an architectural object. As Cook writes, "The metal cabin housing was a prototype in the sense that it placed removable house elements into a 'megastructure' of concrete . . . It was inevitable that we should investigate what happens if the whole urban environment can be programmed and structured for change." He proceeds to offer this definition of a Plug-In City:

> The Plug-In City is set up by applying a large scale network structure, containing access ways and essential services, to any terrain. Into this network are placed units which cater for all needs. These units are planned for obsolescence. The units are served and maneuvered by means of cranes operating from a railway at the apex of the structure.[14]

While visionary architecture of the '60s is generally linked with this type of image from Archigram, as suggested at the outset of this essay, it is perhaps atypical. For the group itself, it represents early work. In fact, their latter efforts are better represented by the likes of Greene's *Gardner's Notebook*, in which architecture is worn as a survival kit. Nevertheless, Cook's project, and others like it by Hollein, Abraham, and St.

14] Cook, ed., *Archigram*, 36.

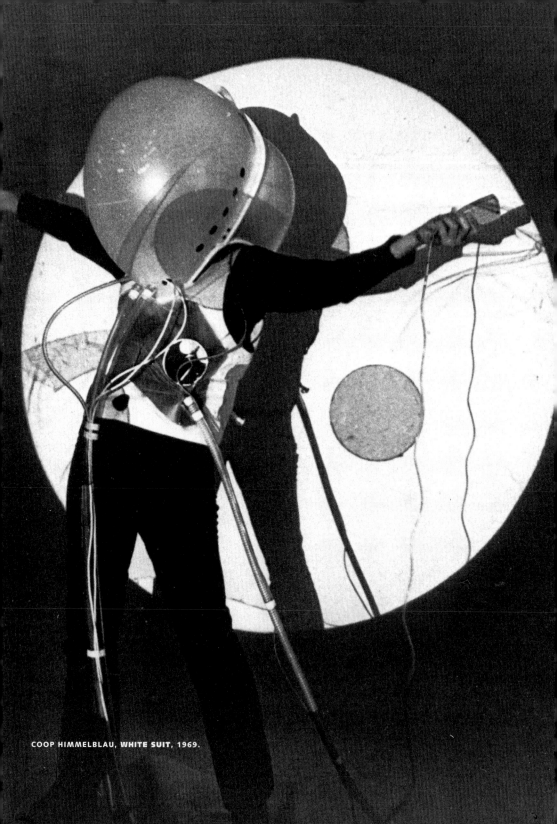

COOP HIMMELBLAU, WHITE SUIT, 1969.

Florian, seem too large, too monumental, and too object-like to be described as dissolving into the body as subject. But even here the work is not primarily about the monumentalization of the building or the scope of the architectural enterprise, but rather the dissolution of architecture into the everyday. "The most genuine architecture today," as it was put, "is anonymous buildings—machines, dams, factories, computer networks, surgical instruments." Moreover, this project explicitly rejects the city as object in favor of the city as a system of communication, and via this, a human tool. The megastructures were seen as devices in a larger network of dispersal and dissemination. Mobility was emphasized not merely for reasons of transportability and transformability, but to actualize the urban condition's movement away from its source. Architecture was "portable hardware." *Plug-In City* was less a city than a way of taking rooms with you as you abandoned the city, "a shift from the building to the device." The difference between this and an astronaut's suit was merely a matter of weight.

The overwrought and unnecessarily complex megastructures suggest a new subject whose gadgets are wonderful not because they indicate progress, but because they indicate that everyday life will always have new gadgets to envelop it.

The final project to be considered here in which the body becomes a locus of architectural emphasis is Coop Himmelblau's *White Suit* of 1969. Coop Himmelblau, the Viennese group founded by Wolf Prix, Helmut Swiczinsky, and Rainer Michael Holzer, described the project in the following manner: "The cold medium of TV is getting hot. The audio-visual information that appears on and in the projection helmet is supported by smells. And the pneumatic vest presents tactile information."[15] This project is, in a sense, the culmination and combination of the three projects previously addressed. Here the subject is postulated as a lone nomad preparing to survive in an overcrowded, polluted environment; a subject whose city/environment is so transportable that it can be worn on its own body. Architecture is constructed as portable hardware.

[15] Coop Himmelblau, *Architecture is Now* , 78.

The self-referential nature of *White Suit* is pushed to the extreme. The architects make their own bodies the subject of the work. The temporality of the moment in which the project is made public implies that it actually "lives" only through the reproduction of Coop Himmelblau's self-generated manifestos. The "object" of this piece is determined not merely by its elision with the subject, but ultimately and ironically, by the subject's own elusiveness as physical but not physical; as sensuous but denied sensual engagement; as operating in the environment but as the manufacturer of that environment.

McLUHAN

White Suit recalls the work of Marshall McLuhan, from whom the ideas of "hot" and "cool" media are directly appropriated. McLuhan was the ultimate theorist of the body as engulfed by electronic devices, of the individual as sensuous, centered, and desperately hanging on for control. Indeed, McLuhan was an enormous influence on leftist cultural and social thought of the '60s, and his effect on these architects is significant: not only Coop Himmelblau but Archigram, Archizoom, Superstudio, and Hans Hollein referred to McLuhan directly. To this generation McLuhan brought the essential idea that people are more shaped by technology than they are shapers of technology.

A dominant image throughout McLuhan's work is the extension of the bodily senses by technology and media: the body as metaphorically contorted, Frankenstein-like, by synthetic connections. McLuhan put this most succinctly in an interview with, ironically, *Playboy*:

> All media, from the phonetic alphabet to the computer, are extensions of the man that cause deep and lasting changes in him and transform his environment. Such an extension is an intensification, an amplification of an organ, sense or function, and whenever it takes place, the central nervous system appears to institute a self-protective numbing of the affected area, insulating and anesthetizing it from conscious awareness

of what's happening to it. It's a process rather like that which occurs to the body under shock or stress conditions, or to the mind in line with the Freudian concept of repression....Precisely at the point where a new media-induced environment becomes all-pervasive and transmogrifies our sensory balance, it also becomes invisible.[16]

McLuhan's idea that the body becomes mechanized and sensually transformed by changing technology is a theory of cultural change that privileges successively one sense over another and, with this, one type of community over another. Early tribal culture—preliterate and oral—was seen as living in an acoustical space that was all encompassing, ignored individuality, and both allowed for and demanded consistent reactions from everyone. All time is "now" in oral culture, and all space "one." In literary culture, communication is visual and the world is fragmented. Time is linear and sequential; mankind can, instead of reacting simultaneously, "act without reacting." In contrasting these two, McLuhan wrote:

> The man of the tribal world led a complex, kaleidoscopic life precisely because the ear, unlike the eye, cannot be focused and is synaesthetic rather than analytical and linear. Speech is an utterance, or more precisely, an outering, of all our senses at once, the auditory field is simultaneous, the visual successive.[17]

Within literary culture, there are also sensuous, technological, and cultural breaks. The first of these was the invention of the printing press by Johannes Gutenburg. The introduction of mechanical technology into our lives and bodies has transformed simple literary society into one that unfolds visual sequential culture into its essential form—repeatable, destined to pile individual upon individual, trance enduring, but also fragmented. The second, which McLuhan felt

16] Eric McLuhan and Frank Zingrone, eds., *Essential McLuhan* (New York: Basic Books, 1995), 237.

17] Ibid., 240. McLuhan links these sensory divisions to Freud's sexual phases, equating the preliterary, tribal period with the oral phase, the visual period with the anal phase. (See, "Oral-Anal," 191.)

characterized the '60s, was the transformation from mechanical technology to electronic technology. Unlike the previous conditions that "only extended a single sense of function..., i.e., the wheel as an extension of the foot, clothing as an extension of the skin, the phonic alphabet as an extension of the eye," electronic technology "enhanced and externalized our entire central nervous system."[18]

According to McLuhan, culture is no longer dominantly visual; it is characterized by nerve attenuation and sensual excess. Television, which he claims is more tactile than visual, terminated visual culture as we knew it and contributed to an era reminiscent of tactile, tribal society. "As youth enters this clan world and all their senses are electrically extended and intensified, there is a corresponding amplification of their sexual sensibilities. Nudity and unabashed sexuality are growing in the electric age because as TV tattoos its message directly on our skins, it renders clothing obsolescent and a barrier, and the new tactility makes it natural for kids to constantly touch one another.... The electric media, by stimulating all the senses simultaneously, give a new and richer sensual dimension to everyday sexuality."[19] Clearly the "regression" of electric man into the tribal primitive documented by McLuhan is represented by Greene's electric aborigine.

MARCUSE, JAMESON, AND UTOPIA

But if McLuhan properly describes the locus and content of the visionary architects, he nevertheless fails, for himself and for his followers, to provide a political response to the conditions he was describing. McLuhan claimed that he saw himself as a describer, not a prescriber, of the electric communications revolution, although it was clear that he viewed much of what he described with horror. His gut response was nostalgia for earlier periods of direct communal and bodily responses. Unlike McLuhan, the visionary architects did take a critical position in their architectural work; one that, to put it in the broadest possible terms (and in the discourse of the avant-garde) disrupted the institution of architecture. The manner in which it accomplished this and took a position in

18] Ibid., 245.
19] Ibid., 252.

cultural, economic, and political exchange relies more directly on the utopian philosophy of Herbert Marcuse.

To understand the utopian position of Marcuse, the term "utopian" as it was understood in the '60s and is now debated needs contextualization. Friedrich Engels contended, in his essay "Socialism: Utopian and Scientific,"[20] that the ideas of nineteenth-century utopian thinkers, such as Claude Henri de Saint-Simon or Charles Fourier, were necessary steps toward socialism, and he praised their essential insights. But they were themselves, he pointed out, inadequate models for historical revolutionary change because they were not "scientific" and "material" (i.e., economic) in their essence. The legacy of "utopian" thinking as it moved into contemporary political/social debate fluctuated to one side or the other of Engels' important if flawed evaluation of utopian thinking. On the right, in the midst of the Cold War, utopia was equated—in the West—with communism and Stalinism. On the left, in the '60s, critics like Manfredo Tafuri aggressively attacked utopian thinking as an agent of capitalist delusion. In his *Architecture and Utopia*, Tafuri argued that in modern architecture, ideology became overtly utopian and allowed the onslaught of rationalized, technocratic, multinational capitalism. Others, like Marcuse, saw utopian thinking as essential to radical politics. Unlike its nineteenth-century antecedents, contemporary utopian thought stated that the last hope for combating capitalist thought lay only in thinking the unreal.[21]

In contemporary thinking, Fredric Jameson has continued this debate and brought it more directly to bear on aesthetics and art criticism, attacking both Marcuse and Tafuri in various articles. In "Architecture and the Critique of Ideology," he addresses Tafuri's blanket rejection of "utopian" architecture, suggesting that there must exist "enclaves" of activities, thoughts, and hopes that keep alive a vision of post-revolutionary

20] Friedrich Engels, "Socialism: Utopian and Scientific," in *The Marx-Engels Reader*, ed. Robert Tucker (New York: Norton, 1972).

21] Other Italian architectural theorists of the '60s debated the conflict between the Marcusian outlook and the Tafurian one, in as much as both were Marxist and both were critical of existing modern conditions. In an essay by Andrea Mariotti entitled "Utopian as a Negative Dialectic," in *Italian Architecture 1965–70* (in which Mariotti is himself arguing for a positive interpretation of utopia but one contrasting with Marcuse's) the author traces utopianism in Italy in regard to the potential positive political value of utopia. He begins this lineage with the positive assessment of Ernesto Rogers in 1962, passes through the negative evaluation by Tafuri in 1966, and culminates in the exhibition/meeting in Turin in 1969 entitled, "Utopia and/or Revolution." At this gathering, Archigram, Paolo Soleri, Yona Friedman, and the Lefebvre-inspired group, Utopie, argued for and against utopianism as a political and revolutionary position.

The Italians were the most forceful in linking visionary architecture to utopian thought because they were (and are) more completely seeped in the Marxist/political current in utopian thought and hence the political dimension of this architectural project.

liberation.[22] In his article, "Postmodernism and Utopia" in *Utopia Post-Utopia*, Jameson makes the argument that some art of the '80s and '90s (for example, the work of Hans Haacke and Robert Gober), seemingly political and hence inconsistent with an "unpolitical" postmodernism, was in fact a throwback to '60s Marcusian utopianism; because of this, the work cannot properly be classified as political but, as described earlier, "protopolitical."[23] Jameson's alignment of Haacke, Gober, and the '60s with Marcusian utopian thinking, while admirable, implies the limitation of the work's liberatory effect. For what distinguishes the utopian from the truly political is that it is spatial and not temporal, bodily and not historical, fixed and not dialectical.

Marcuse's concept of utopia was one of his main contributions to Frankfurt School thought. As with other Frankfurt School thinkers, he criticized instrumental reason in the name of another kind of thought more compatible with sensuousness and authentic desire. For Marcuse, the critique of a totalizing and leveling social reality and of the deformations of consciousness that support it necessitated the attempt to uncover subjective experience.[24]

Marcuse's particular formulation of this rested on his description of contemporary society as "one-dimensional"; that is, constituted by "a comfortable, smooth, reasonable, democratic unfreedom." In one-dimensional society, every worry, every tension, is transformed into a positive amelioration. "Managerial modes of thought and research spreads into other dimensions of the intellectual effort," and "in this context, functionalization has a truly therapeutic effect. Once the personal discontent is isolated from the general unhappiness,...the case becomes a treatable and tractable incident."[25]

To combat this "pleasant" anesthetization to experience, Marcuse proposed a program of negation, the "Great Refusal," in which he demanded a refusal to rationalize the real. Thus negation in turn may or may

22 See Fredric Jameson, "Architecture and the Critique of Ideology," in *Architecture Criticism Ideology*, ed. Joan Ockman (New York: Princeton Architectural Press; 1985), 51-87.

23] This article is a basic duplication of the chapter "Utopia" in Jameson, *Postmodernism, or The Cultural Logic of Late Capitalism* (Durham, NC: Duke University Press, 1991).

24] See the discussion of Herbert Marcuse compared to Theodor Adorno in Shierry Weber Nicholsen, "The Persistence of Passionate Subjectivity: Eros and Other in Marcuse, by Way of Adorno," in *Marcuse: From the New Left to the Next Left*, ed. John Bokina and Timothy J. Lukes (Lawrence, KA: University Press of Kansas, 1994), 150–51.

25] Herbert Marcuse, *One-Dimensional Man: Studies in the Ideology of Advanced Industrial Society* (Boston: Beacon Press, 1964), 111.

not force change, but without it there is no hope. Until change comes, utopian thinking acts as the representation of the Great Refusal.

In *Essay on Liberation*, Marcuse admits that critical theory has been loath to embrace the concept of utopia "for fear of losing its scientific character." But, he says, this restrictive conception needs to be revised in and for contemporary societies. "The dynamic of their productivity deprives 'utopia' of its traditional unreal content. What is denounced as 'utopian' is no longer that which has 'no place' and cannot have any place in the historical universe, but rather that which is blocked from coming about by the power of established society." Utopia is not that which is impossible; it is the possible that rational society actively represses. But utopian thinking, likewise, is not the positive vision of the future, it is merely that which is not today. Marcuse was clear that his "utopia" was "not positively constituted, but meaningless outside of past traditions and current context."

THE BODY AND THE PROTOPOLITICAL

Marcuse's concept of a critical utopia—and its ability to "theorize" the work of the visionary architects—complicates Jameson's claim of utopia as protopolitical. For Jameson, the issue centers on the body as inherently apolitical (either universal and not operating as a product of culture, or completely culturally bound and too relative to resist culture.) In "Architecture and the Critique of Ideology," he writes:

> Yet arguments based on the human body are fundamentally a-historical, and involve premises about some eternal 'human nature' concealed within the seemingly 'verifiable' and scientific data of physiological analysis. If the body is in then the 'return' to some more 'natural' vision of the body in space...comes to seem ideological, when not nostalgic.[26]

But the body that is being presented here—operating in the realm of the everyday, but still primal—is somewhere between these two extremes: that is, a body that regis-

26] Jameson, "Architecture and the Critique of Ideology," 51.

ters cultural change but at some fundamental level remains uncorrupted and able to sustain authentic desires and judgment. Likewise, it is a body that is meaningless outside of its quotidian circumstance. As Marcuse states, the biological drive becomes a cultural drive; "there is sublimation and consequently culture."

For Marcuse, the body was the essential locus in which the dialectical battle between affirmation and negation, reality and utopia, society and self was fought. More than the other Frankfurt School thinkers, Marcuse studied Freud and used his psychological theories as a diagnosis of one-dimensional man. His goal was to replace a rational epistemology with a sensuous a one; to let the body think.

> Under the predominance of rationalism, the cognitive function of sensuousness has been constantly minimized. In line with the repressive concept of reason, cognition became the ultimate concern of the "higher," non-sensuous faculties of the mind.... Sensuousness, as the "lower" faculty, furnished at best the mere stuff, the raw material, for cognition, to be organized by the higher faculties of the intellect.[27]

Sensuous thinking, "far from destroying civilization, would give it a firmer basis and would greatly enhance its potentialities." The body and its sensuality must serve not the reality principle—given the nature of reality—but the pleasure principle—given its ability to register true desires.

A nonrational engagement with the world was not merely sensuous, but sexual. The body, "no longer used as a full-time instrument of labor, ... would be resexualized."[28] Instead of a sexuality that was (merely) genitally oriented, "the body in its entirety would become an object of cathexis, a thing to be enjoyed—an instrument of pleasure."[29] He emphasizes that this process "involves not simply a release but a transformation of the libido: from sexuality constrained under genital

27] Marcuse, *Eros and Civilization: A Philosophical Inquiry into Freud* (Boston: Beacon Press, 1956), 180.

28] Ibid., 201.

29] Ibid.

supremacy to erotization of the entire personality."[30] This is what Marcuse called "non-repressive sublimation" (as opposed to "repressive desublimation), because sexuality "spread" over the entire body "tends to its own sublimation."

This sensual/sexual body is also constituted in the everyday conditions of work and play. Play is sensuous, libidinal, and hence thoughtful and profound; work was to be modeled on play; work too could be sensuous and libidinal. Because the difference between work and play is one of purpose and not content—play serves gratification "in itself" and work serves "ends outside itself, namely, the ends of self preservation"—there need be no distinction between the two regarding their essential sensuous nature. No longer would pleasure in work be defined by forces of production but by forces of the libido.

> If pleasure is indeed in the act of working and not extraneous to it, such pleasure must be derived from the acting organs of the body and the body itself, activating the erotogenic zones and eroticizing the body as a whole; in other words, it must be libidinal pleasure....Certainly there can be "pleasure" in alienated labor too. The typist who hands in a perfect typescript...may feel pleasure in a "job well done." However, . . . such pleasure has nothing to do with primary instinctual gratification.[31]

Here, Marcuse is offering a version of a postmodern critical theory: postmodern in the sense that it doesn't have faith in the inevitable arrival of a revolution; that it sees the dispersal of ideology into the sense of daily life; and that the primary ideological question is that of subjectivity. But unlike postmodernism, it does not believe that irony is the only social option. Rather, it tracks the displacement of "politics" into realms previously considered nonpolitical in a manner that renders the political difficult to combat directly. Thus it envisions resistance arising from daily life experience, a politics of the personal. This might not be called

30] Ibid.

31] Ibid., 220–21.

"political" in the sense of promoting a revolution, but it is political in the sense that change, on different terms, is still fought for. Such a theory certainly isn't protopolitical; rather, it is, if not directly political, neopolitical.

This brings us to the larger question of how art (and the artistic activities of the visionary architects) operates in this "critical" postmodernism. To a certain extent, it must be acknowledged that art's relationship to politics is always in question, with purists contending that there can be no direct connection between the two. But there clearly is a complex and important connection between aesthetics and politics. For Marcuse, the same libidinal pleasure, the same emphasis on play, characterizes art. The aesthetic dimension is the mode whereby the individual can escape rational thinking and develop a sensuous, playful, engagement with the world. It is, he says referring to Alexander Gottlieb Baumgarten, "the science of sensuousness."[32]

In other words, the aesthetic dimension's inherent connection to the pleasure principle is the manifestation of utopian thought:

> The radical qualities of art, that is to say, its indictment of the established reality and its invocation of the beautiful image…of liberation are grounded precisely in the dimensions where art transcends its social determination and emancipates itself from the given universe of discourse and behavior while preserving its overwhelming presence. Thereby art creates the realm in which the subversion of experience proper to art becomes possible: the world formed by art is recognized as a reality which is suppressed and distorted in the given reality.[33]

With regard to the visionary architects, this position is both insightful and misleading. While the sensuous definition of art and the "subversion of experience" are matched by the content and intention of the architects,

32] Ibid., 181.

33] Marcuse, *The Aesthetic Dimension: Towards a Critique of Marxist Aesthetics* (Boston: Beacon Press), 6.

Marcuse's own vision of what art is, is not. For him, the master work hanging in the museum is still the operative paradigm, so that while his faith in the expressive content of the work is radical, the nature of that work remains unchallenged. (This actually goes hand in hand with a philosophy that privileges aesthetics as the principle activity of thought; that is, it valorizes aestheticism.) The architects examined here, on the other hand, were as skeptical about "art" as they were about building. Aesthetics itself was under siege in this backlash against high modernism and its connection to high culture. Thus the return to the body was a way of making visual the polemic of space/body/technology/nature/change/future without making an art object.

In the end, the visionary architects of the '60s actually express the utopian essence of Marcuse's philosophy more directly than his own aesthetic formulation. Because the aesthetic is the ultimate expression of Marcuse's utopian thought, it takes on the burden of a metadiscourse; it both promotes utopian thought and represents it. Therefore, it also takes on the obligation to represent the ultimate negative component of utopian thought. If utopian thought is to represent itself accurately, it must be the ultimate reminder that it is not a guide to the future but a protest of the present. It must be sensuous, but indicate that the experience of sensuousness is not the solution, it highlights the problem.

In this way, not only the "anti-art" art of these architects, but the self-referential quality seems especially apropos, as does the humor that at every turn undercuts the "serious" aesthetic project. The implications of these projects—that the artists rejected an architecture of things and replaced it with an architecture of themselves, and that they were designing their (physical) psyches more than they were designing art—indicate their awareness of the double burden of making art while representing art's ultimate negative capacity. In this way, exactly that which Jameson would argue against—an undialectic condition of self and body—becomes the expression, in a metalanguage, of the impossibility of dialectical success. It becomes, in other words, metapolitical.

**SUPERSTUDIO, VITA EDUCAZIONE CEREMO-
NIA AMORE MORTE, 1971–73.**

The negative agenda of Superstudio becomes, in this context, a provocative final offering. In works like *The Continuous Monument* and *Vita educazione ceremonia amore morte* Superstudio found humor and pleasure in its critical project. By pushing their critique of abstract, rational, totalizing imperialism, they made montages that simultaneously criticized both the world they operated in and the utopian one they imaged, a utopia of dystopic proportions. With beauty and terror in equal proportions, they evoked a world—both capitalist and utopian, both commodified and sensuous—that was coming to an end.

One must admire this not because it is a model for today's architecture but because it understood its own failure and still made it an object of both pleasure and necessity.

FAMILY VALUES (HONEY, I'M HOME)

MARK ROBBINS AND BENJAMIN GIANNI

Scanning the collection of garage-sale furniture in her living room, a friend joked about staging an interior decorating course for lesbians—the title: "Awaken the Fag Within You." Younger friends routinely "defag" their apartments in anticipation of parental visits. New York photographer Arne Svenson spent months photographing gay male subjects: friends, lovers, people he met at parties, whomever was willing to follow him to his studio. The men were shot clinically: standing straightfaced, eyes fixed on the camera, arms at their sides, feet on the same dot on the same floor against the same wall in the same space. The collection comprised an exhibit entitled *Faggots*, hundreds of photos in an identical 17 x 22 inch format. Imagine someone's (straight) parents scanning the gallery. What would they see? What conclusions could they draw?

For *Family Values*, we gathered data in an anecdotal way: placing ads in gay newspapers in Ottawa and Columbus (our respectively ordinary hometowns), posting on the Internet, asking friends to ask friends to document their domiciles. We sought to conjure an image of the private, ordinary realm of the everyday lives of purportedly extraordinary people: homosexuals. This data might support or dispel stereotypes, providing a glimpse of who we are and what we have in common, and suggest whether sexual orientation has a sensibility, whether gay lives have a style, whether homosexuality can be recognized, characterized, categorized, carried out.

The format—as straightforward as possible—is that of the real estate throwaway: grainy images on newsprint with descriptive captions.

Instead of advertising adjacency to schools or houses of worship, however, listed are the demographics of each household. Submissions vary
from a tasteful home in Silverlake, Los Angeles to a modest frame cottage
out of a Walker Evans landscape. The intent was to reflect the multiple
possibilities for the configuration of "home," in the expression of decor,
architecture, and household composition, i.e. men and women with children, living alone, or with lovers (One man wrote, beaming with civic
pride, about taking his partner and kids to Canada Day celebrations, and
participating in trash drives with the nonplused neighbors.). We hoped to
call into question the gay and lesbian community's assumptions about
itself as well as more widely-held conceptions about gay "lifestyles." Even
within this small survey, multiple codes of wealth, class status, and identity overlap with shifting degrees of consequence. Most of the signs are
commonplace and widely shared, others—such as rainbow flags—
though present, may not be readily apparent.

The neutrality of the presentation subverts assumptions; as such,
the data reveals as much about the viewer as the subjects it depicts. Some
will search for themselves among the images and statistics, seeking the
seeds of community and evidence of common experience. Some will
look to confirm stereotypes while others, fearing categorization, will
embrace the data as inconclusive. Some lesbians and gay men see being
recognized (both by themselves and by others) as a political imperative
tantamount to survival; others equate visibility with vulnerability. Some
will assent to the irreducibility of lives that comprehend all variations of
gender, class, race, and ethnicity, while for others to domesticate differences—to downplay the distance between "us" and "them"—misrepre-
sents something essential about the experience of being gay.

This project communicates something significant about the
everyday: how it differs from the statistics it engenders, how it expands
to embrace, invite, accept, and resist conclusions. Whatever the data
suggests about the lives of lesbians and gay men, those who view it
will come away better acquainted with their own assumptions about
homosexual life.

Columbus, Ohio has a population of
1.2 million

If one out of ten people are gay,
there are 120,000 homosexuals
living in Columbus

On a given night 5000 are in bars,
clubs or cruising areas

Where are the other 115,000?

Who are we? Where are we? How do we live?

We propose to place an ad in the classified sections of gay papers in two mid-sized cities: Columbus, Ohio and Ottawa, Ontario. In the ad we will ask members of the gay and lesbian community to send us two 3x5 snapshots of their homes—one exterior view and one interior view. We will also ask them to indicate their age, their gender, if they live alone, with roommates or a lover, and whether they consider their neighborhood to be urban or suburban. The photos will allow us to explore (and explode) stereotypes about the gay community, who we are and how we live. It will also allow us to examine certain assumptions—like the myth that gay men are urban dwellers while lesbians prefer suburbia.

We know that the demographics of the family have changed and that the "single family" house houses singles and many variations on the family. Census data is not specific, however, on sexual orientation. It is difficult to get a sense how gay men, lesbians and bisexuals are distributed throughout our cities. In gay ghettos, it is apparent, but the majority of gay people live among their heterosexual neighbors. Some of us react against normative symbols of domesticity, others of us embrace them.

For the exhibition on *Queer Space* we propose to present these photographs and the data we are able to collect about the gay household—either as a matrix on the wall or in a series of photo albums.

Benjamin Gianni, Ottawa, Ontario
Mark Robbins, Columbus, Ohio

OCCUPANCY: **LESBIAN**
AGE: **43**
DWELLING TYPE: **FIVE BEDROOM HALF HOUSE**
SETTING: **SEMI-URBAN**

HOUSEHOLD INCOME: **$70,000**
VALUE OF HOUSE: **$210,000**
NOTES: **CO-OWNED WITH EX-LOVER**

OCCUPANCY: **TWO GAY MALES**
AGES: **26 AND 27**
DWELLING TYPE: **CO-OP APARTMENT**

SETTING: **URBAN**
HOUSEHOLD INCOME: **$50,000**
RENT PER MONTH: **$800**

OCCUPANCY: **GAY MALE (LOVER LIVES ELSEWHERE**
AGE: **44**
DWELLING TYPE: **HOUSE**

SETTING: **RURAL**
HOUSEHOLD INCOME: **$20,000**
VALUE OF HOUSE: **$40,000**

OCCUPANCY:
AMBISEXUAL WOMAN
AGE: **41**
DWELLING TYPE:
LOFT CONDOMINIUM
SETTING: **URBAN**
DEPENDENTS: **PARAKEET**
HOUSEHOLD INCOME:
I SQUEAK BY
CURTAIN: **RED CHECK**
FURNITURE: **YELLOW METAL**

OCCUPANCY:	*DEPENDENTS:*
GAY MALE	**AN ENGLISH BULL**
AGE: **35**	**TERRIER, MAGGIE**
DWELLING TYPE:	*HOUSEHOLD INCOME:*
CONDOMINIUM	**$70,000**
APARTMENT	*VALUE OF APART-*
SETTING: **URBAN**	*MENT:* **$130,000**

OCCUPANCY: **TWO QUEER**	*SETTING:* **URBAN**
MEN, LOVERS	*HOUSEHOLD INCOME:* **N/A**
AGES: **43 AND 57**	*VALUE OF HOUSE:* **N/A**
DWELLING TYPE:	
TOWNHOUSE	

OCCUPANCY: **TWO GAY MEN**
AGES: **43, 40**
DWELLING TYPE: **HOUSE**
SETTING: **SUBURBAN**
DEPENDENTS: **TWO KIDS, 17 AND 15**
HOUSEHOLD INCOME: **$65,000**
VALUE OF HOUSE: **$170,000**
NOTES: **JOINT CUSTODY**

OCCUPANCY: **GAY MAN, LIVES WITH LOVER**
AGES: **40 AND 39**
DWELLING TYPE: **HOUSE**
SETTING: **URBAN**
DEPENDENTS: **TWO KIDS, 17 AND 15**
HOUSEHOLD INCOME: **OVER $150,000**
VALUE OF HOUSE: **$365,000**

OCCUPANCY: **GAY MAN AND STRAIGHT HOUSEMATE**
AGES: **29 AND 27**
DWELLING TYPE: **UPPER FLAT OF HOUSE**
SETTING: **URBAN**
HOUSEHOLD INCOME: **$63,000**
RENT PER MONTH: **$365**
NOTES: **WE'RE PAINTING**

OCCUPANCY: **LESBIAN OWNER AND TEMPORARY ROOMMATE**
AGES: **39 AND 30**
DWELLING TYPE: **HOUSE**
SETTING: **URBAN**
DEPENDENTS: **CAT NAMED MICRO**
HOUSEHOLD INCOME: **$85,000**
VALUE OF HOUSE: **$170,000**

OCCUPANCY:
TWO GAY MEN (LIFE PARTNERS)
AGES: **46 AND 42**
DWELLING TYPE: **SINGLE FAMILY HOUSE**
SETTING: **RURAL**
DEPENDENTS: **ONE ADULT DAUGHTER**
VALUE OF HOUSE: **$280,000**

THOUGHTS ON THE EVERYDAY

DEBORAH BERKE

We exist in a culture where heroes have been replaced by celebrities, and fifteen minutes of fame are valued over a lifetime of patient work. In this climate the architect must become a celebrity in order to gain the opportunity to build (or else must loudly proclaim a refusal to build in order to become established as a critical force). Those who do build tend to produce signature buildings designed to attract the attention of the media and sustain the public's focus, for under these rules architecture can only emanate from the hand of the name-brand architect. The built environment is strewn with these high-profile celebrity products—heroic gestures neither made nor commissioned by heroes.

What should architects do instead? A simple and direct response: acknowledge the needs of the many rather than the few; address diversity of class, race, culture, and gender; design without allegiance to *a priori* architectural styles or formulas, and with concern for program and construction.

We may call the result an architecture of the everyday, though an architecture of the everyday resists strict definition; any rigorous attempt at a concise delineation will inevitably lead to contradictions. Nonetheless, here are some points that may be related to it.

AN ARCHITECTURE OF THE EVERYDAY MAY BE GENERIC AND ANONYMOUS.

Much like the package in the supermarket with the black letters on the white ground that does not carry a brand name—but is still a perfectly good container for its contents—the generic does not flaunt its maker. It is straightforward. Unostentatious, it can lurk, loiter, slip beneath the surface, and bypass the controls of institutionally regulated life.

AN ARCHITECTURE OF THE EVERYDAY MAY BE BANAL OR COMMON.

It does not seek distinction by trying to be extraordinary, which in any case usually results in a fake or substitute for the truly extraordinary. In its mute refusal to say "look at me," it does not tell you what to think. It permits you to provide your own meaning.

AN ARCHITECTURE OF THE EVERYDAY MAY THEREFORE BE QUITE ORDINARY.

It is blunt, direct, and unselfconscious. It celebrates the potential for inventiveness within the ordinary and is thereby genuinely "of its moment." It may be influenced by market trends, but it resists being defined or consumed by them.

AN ARCHITECTURE OF THE EVERYDAY MAY BE CRUDE.

There is a freshness to things that are raw and unrefined. Buildings that are conceived without polish may be rough, but "rough and ready."

AN ARCHITECTURE OF THE EVERYDAY MAY BE SENSUAL.

The everyday world is sensual. It not only provokes sight but also touch, hearing, smell. The architecture of the everyday encompasses places known by their aroma, surfaces recognizable by their tactile qualities, positions established by echo and reverberation.

AN ARCHITECTURE OF THE EVERYDAY MAY ALSO BE VULGAR AND VISCERAL.

While vulgarity may seem the opposite of anonymity, both are often oblivious to external standards. This is not necessarily bad: standards of taste serve to legislate and perpetuate an approved set of objects. The vulgar rejects good taste and the unthinking obedience it demands.

In architecture, standards of good taste seem to dictate that the presence of the body not be acknowledged in or by buildings. Architectural photographs rarely show people, and the true user is often ignored by the architect. The result is sterility. Visceral presence cannot be denied.

AN ARCHITECTURE OF THE EVERYDAY ACKNOWLEDGES DOMESTIC LIFE.

There is poetry and consolation in the repetition of familiar things. This is not to romanticize dreary and oppressive routine; events need not be dictated and programmed by architects. An architecture of the everyday allows for personal rites but avoids prescribing rituals.

AN ARCHITECTURE OF THE EVERYDAY MAY TAKE ON COLLECTIVE AND SYMBOLIC MEANING BUT IT IS NOT NECESSARILY MONUMENTAL.

Without denying the need for monuments, it questions whether every building need be one.

AN ARCHITECTURE OF THE EVERYDAY RESPONDS TO PROGRAM AND IS FUNCTIONAL.

It is a form of design in which program contributes meaning, and function is a requirement to satisfy rather than a style to emulate. It resists debasement into winsome reproductions of another time in the name of "the vernacular" or simplistic contextualism.

AN ARCHITECTURE OF THE EVERYDAY MAY CHANGE AS QUICKLY AS FASHION, BUT IT IS NOT ALWAYS FASHIONABLE.

If the idea of an architecture of the everyday currently seems both a little too fashionable and a little too much like fashion, note that the real architecture of the everyday is subject to different forces of change from those that drive fashion. The forms, materials, and images of innovation in everyday life are often unpredictable. The next everyday cannot be discovered through focus groups and market analysis.

THE ARCHITECTURE OF THE EVERYDAY IS BUILT.

.　　.　　.

The initial impetus to search for a definition of an architecture of the everyday evolved from an ongoing conversation I had with Steven Harris as we traveled together to New Haven from New York City and back, twice a week, for nine years. Having been friends for almost twenty years, our conversations were familiar and comfortable, often filled with gossip or reminiscences. Our commute took us on Interstate-95, the easternmost north-south run of the grid of interstates that define long-distance automobile travel in the United States.

In retrospect, I-95 was a pretty good place to have a twice-a-week conversation on the everyday, it being such an everyday condition itself; a wide asphalt line on the ground for the transport of people and goods. Over the years of our shared commute, the nameless food and fuel stops became McDonald's and Mobil stations—a transformation to name-brandness apparently sanctioned by some turnpike authority. Similarly, the exclusive suburban residential developments just off the highway grew evermore extravagant as the ready dollars of the 1980s purchased houses that were absurd amalgams of aspirational imagery and bombastic size. Our ongoing observation seemed to find that the banal landscape, the fuel for our conversation on (and subsequent teaching of) the everyday, was each day becoming less anonymous and certainly less banal.

We realized that the replacement of the ordinary by the brand-nameable was not an innocent transformation of the everyday, but rather the usurpation of the everyday by advertising. To confuse ubiquitous logos with generic identity was to mistake successful marketing for "popular" culture. Indeed, today even the idea of popular culture bears an ambiguous relationship to the everyday. So often it seems to be merely the way the everyday appears on high culture's radar screen.

Of course, every aspect of reality is mediated in some way. But the everyday may still be the place that is least mediated by the forces that seek to limit or absorb its vitality. This is the promise it holds. For architects this is a cautionary tale and a genuine opportunity. We are invited to enter into the real and the good aspects of everyday life, but we must do so without destroying it.

In the opening paragraphs of her 1964 essay "Notes on Camp," Susan Sontag writes: "It's embarrassing to be solemn and treatise-like about Camp. One runs the risk of having, oneself, produced a very inferior piece of Camp." I feel that the same could be said of trying to make or write about an architecture of the everyday. The difference between an "architecture of the everyday" and everyday buildings lies precisely in the consciousness of the act of making architecture. This is precisely where the strategy I am proposing is most susceptible to criticism, a fact of which I am well aware. An architect cannot pretend to be naive. Architecture is not innocent. Likewise, the making of architecture is a highly conscious, indeed a self-conscious, act. But the everyday is also not naive. To assume so would be to confuse it with a sugary and debased notion of the vernacular—with nostalgia for some state of original purity or innocence. The everyday flirts, dangerously at times, with mass culture. But the everyday remains that which has not yet been co-opted.

JAMES CASEBERE

WINTERHOUSE, **1984**

CONTRIBUTORS

MARK BENNETT is an artist who lives in Los Angeles and is a postal worker in Beverly Hills by day. His work has been exhibited nationally and published in the book *TV Sets: Fantasy Blueprints of Classic TV Homes.*

DEBORAH BERKE is a practicing architect in New York City and an associate professor at the Yale University School of Architecture. Her built work at both the residential and small institutional scale is part of an ongoing investigation in the use of ordinary materials and the straightforward expression of program.

SHEILA LEVRANT DE BRETTEVILLE is director of graduate studies in graphic design at the Yale University School of Art, and a graphic artist who has designed numerous publications, posters, and fine press editions. She currently works in the public sphere to create permanent, site specific works that involve local communities in the expression of their history.

JAMES CASEBERE is an artist who lives and works in New York City. His work has been widely published and exhibited, and appears in numerous public and private collections, including the Museum of Modern Art, the Solomon R. Guggenheim Museum, and the Whitney Museum of American Art.

GREGORY CREWDSON, an artist who lives and works in New York City, teaches in the Graduate Photography program at Yale University. He has had numerous one-person exhibitions in the United States and abroad, and his work appears in the collections of the Metropolitan Museum of Art, the Museum of Modern Art, and the Whitney Museum of American Art, among many others.

PEGGY DEAMER is a practicing architect in New York City and director of advanced studies at the Yale University School of Architecture. Her articles have appeared in various journals including *Assemblage*, and in the anthologies *Drawing/Building/Text*, *Hejduk's Chronotope*, and *Thinking the Present* (Princeton Architectural Press, 1991, 1996, and 1990, respectively).

DEBORAH FAUSCH teaches architectural theory and history at the Parsons School of Design, and has practiced architecture in New York and Minnesota. She is an editor of *Architecture: In Fashion* (Princeton Architectural Press, 1994), and her essays have been published in journals and anthologies including *Architese*, *ANY*, and *Architecture and Feminism* (Princeton Architectural Press, 1997).

BENJAMIN GIANNI is director of the School of Architecture at Carleton University. His architectural projects and writings have been extensively published, and he is co-author of the book *Dice Thrown* (Princeton Architectural Press, 1989).

PETER HALLEY is publisher of *index* magazine and a painter whose work has been widely exhibited. His writings have previously been published in the anthology *Peter Halley: Collected Essays 1981–87.*

STEVEN HARRIS is a practicing architect in New York City and an associate professor at the Yale University School of Architecture. His work explores commonplace, familiar buildings and their relationships to each other and their surroundings. His projects have been featured on the covers of *A+U*, *Casa Vogue*, *Deutsche Bauzeitschrift*, *Hauser*, *Progressive Architecture*, and the *New York Times Magazine*.

HENRI LEFEBVRE (1901–91) was a leader of the French left for much of the twentieth century and the author of more than sixty books. Charismatic in both person and print, his integration of history, Marxism, philosophy, politics, sociology, and urbanism has influenced generations of thinkers.

MARY McLEOD is an associate professor of architecture at Columbia University, where she teaches architectural history and design studio. She is co-editor of *Architecture, Criticism, and Ideology*, and *Architectu-re-production* (Princeton Architectural Press, 1985 and 1988, respectively). Her articles have appeared in numerous journals and anthologies, most recently *Architecture and Feminism* (Princeton Architectural Press, 1997).

PAT MORTON is an architect, historian, and theorist who teaches at the University of California, Riverside and SCI-Arc. Her research and writing focus on issues of race, gender, marginality, and the politics of form in modern architecture and urbanism. She is currently writing a book on the 1931 Colonial Exposition in Paris.

JOAN OCKMAN is director of the Buell Center for the Study of American Architecture at Columbia University, where she also teaches history and theory of architecture. She is the editor of *Architecture Culture: 1943–1968: A Documentary Anthology* in collaboration with Edward Eigen, and her own writings have been published in numerous journals, including *Assemblage*, *Casabella*, *Oppositions*, and *Werk Bauen + Wohnen*.

ERNEST PASCUCCI died in June 1997 at the age of twenty-nine. A senior editor of *ANY* and a regular contributor to *Artforum*, he was pursuing a doctorate in the program of History, Theory and Criticism of Architecture at the Massachusetts Institute of Technology.

MARY-ANN RAY is an architect and partner, with Robert Mangurian, in the Los Angeles firm Studio Works. Their projects include furniture, buildings, publications, and urban design. She teaches graduate architectural design at SCI Arc, and is the author of *Pamphlet Architecture 20: Seven Partly Underground Rooms and Buildings for Water, Ice, and Midgets* (Princeton Architectural Press, 1997).

MARK ROBBINS is an assistant professor at the Knowlton School of Architecture at Ohio State University and the curator of architecture at the Wexner Center for the Arts. His architectural installations and constructions explore the use of design as a medium for social critique. His work has appeared in many publications, including the monograph *Angles of Incidence* (Princeton Architectural Press, 1992).

MARGIE RUDDICK is a landscape architect practicing in Philadelphia and New York City who teaches landscape architecture at the University of Pennsylvania. Her projects include a water-cleansing riverfront park in Sichuan, and a family compound for a Caribbean country singer on eastern Long Island. Her current work focuses on the use and conservation of water and water systems.

ROBERT SCHULTZ grew up in suburban New Jersey and is an architect practicing in Bombay. With partner Vrinda Khana, his recent projects include villas for Bollywood—India's answer to Hollywood—movie stars and Indian industrialists.

PETER TOLKIN is a practicing architect and photographer in Los Angeles. His work has appeared in journals including *Nowtime*, *Offramp*, and *Sites*. He is currently working on a photographic book of religious buildings.

MABEL O. WILSON is an assistant professor of architectural design at the University of Kentucky, and a partner in the design collective Architecture et al. Her writings on racism and architectural discourse have appeared in *ANY*, *Assemblage*, and *Practices*.